FIELDS OF THE TZOTZIL

THE TEXAS PAN AMERICAN SERIES

Fields of the Tzotzil

THE ECOLOGICAL BASES OF

TRADITION IN HIGHLAND CHIAPAS

GEORGE A. COLLIER

UNIVERSITY OF TEXAS PRESS

AUSTIN

*The Texas Pan American Series is published
with the assistance of a revolving publication
fund established by the Pan American Sulphur
Company.*

Library of Congress Cataloging in Publication Data

Collier, George Allen, 1942–
　　Fields of the Tzotzil.

　　(Texas Pan American series)
　　Bibliography: p.
　　Includes index.
　　1. Tzotzil Indians—Agriculture. 2. Tzotzil
Indians—Social life and customs. 3. Human ecology—
Mexico—Chiapas. 4. Indians of Mexico—Agriculture.
I. Title.
F1221.T9C64　　301.29′72′7　　75-12840
ISBN 978-0-292-73999-4

First paperback printing, 2012

TO DAVID, LUCY, & JANE

CONTENTS

Preface   *xiii*

1. Introduction   3

2. Forms of Land Utilization   *19*

3. Land and the Family   *49*

4. Land Inheritance in *Apas*   *79*

5. Soil Erosion in Chamula   *109*

6. Marginality   *125*

7. Ethnicity   *137*

8. The Refuge-Region Hypothesis   *183*

9. National Indianism and Indian Nationalism   *191*

10. Conclusion   205

Appendix: Methodology   *213*

Bibliography   225

Index   *241*

ILLUSTRATIONS

PLATES

1. Settlement Pattern in Ladino San Cristóbal *11*
2. *Navencauk* *22*
3. Central Highland Topography *24*
4. The Pan American Highway *24*
5. Highland Forest *26–27*
6. Pitch Pine Tree *44*
7. *Apas*, a Hamlet of Zinacantán *70*
8. Chamula Center *71*
9. Amatenango Center *74–75*
10. Small Clusters of Homes in *Apas* *82–83*
11. Todos Santos Rites *92*
12. Regrowth Patterns *112–113*
13. Incipient Grassland *114*
14. A Stage of Erosion *116*
15. More Advanced Erosion *117*
16. Severe Erosion *117*
17. An Early Postclassic Site *118*
18. A Lowland Farm Camp *127*
19. Boundary Marker *143*
20. Zinacantán Center *152–153*
21. An Ejido Colony *162–163*
22. Aguacatenango Center *164–165*
23. A Small Ejido Colony *166*
24. San Cristóbal *168–169*
25. Chamula Instruments *170*
26. Amatenango Pots *171*
27. Bootleg Liquor *172*
28. Periodic Market Site *178–179*
29. Rural School *188*
30. National Indian Institute Regional Headquarters *189*

MAPS

1. Chiapas in the Mexican Nation *4*
2. The Roads of Chiapas *5*

3. Tzotzil and Tzeltal Speakers in Chiapas *10*
4. Relief Map of Chiapas *21*
5. *Apas* Farmland *29*
6. The Location of Firewood near the *Apas* Settlement *45*
7. Six Mayan Communities *63*
8. Hamlet Settlements of Zinacantán *80*
9. *Sna* Aggregates in the *Apas* Settlement *85*
10. Settlement Property of Romin Heronimo in *Apas* *104*
11. Zones for Zinacanteco Lowland Rental Farming in 1966 *131*
12. Ejido Lands in Zinacantán *140*

FIGURES

1. The Swidden Farming Cycle *31*
2. *Apas* Farmland Acreage in Cultivation *36*
3. *Apas* Farmland Production and Population Growth *37*
4. Key to Figure 5 *41*
5. Fallow Patterns in *Apas* Farmlands *42*
6. Conflict Model *51*
7. Solidarity Model *51*
8. A Synthesis *51*
9. Unilineal Descent *54*
10. Nonunilineal Descent *55*
11. Agnation and Population Density in New Guinea *57*
12. The Fit of the Maya Examples to the Curvilinear Model *77*
13. The Distribution of Nicknames in an *Apas* Lineage *87*
14. Genealogical Distance *94*
15. Labor and Capital Inputs to Farming *129*
16. Population Pyramid for Tzotzil and Tzeltal Townships *159*
17. Craft Marketing *180*

TABLES

1. Behavioral Measures   *66*
2. Typical Forms of Family Organization   *67*
3. Overall Assessment of Patrilineal Emphasis and Land Availability   *76*
4. *Apas* Domestic Groups in 1963   *84*
5. Lineages Ranked by Segment Size   *93*
6. Nickname Sharing in Sets of Brothers   *95*
7. Patrilocality and Name-Group Size   *96*
8. Property Transfer Modes through Time   *98*
9. Landholdings and Name-Group Size   *99*
10. Land Purchase and Name-Group Size   *101*
11. Transfer of Settlement Parcels through Women   *102*
12. Quality of Settlement Parcel and Sex of Heir   *103*
13. Farming Budgets   *128*
14. Lowland Farming Scale   *130*
15. Lowland Profits   *132*
16. Lowland Farming Costs   *132*
17. Returns   *132*
18. Transportation   *133*
19. Partially Adjusted Returns   *134*
20. Rent   *134*
21. Fully Adjusted Returns   *134*
22. A Condensed Chronology   *141–142*
23. Population Trends   *158*
24. Early-Marriage and Birth Rates   *159–160*
25. Status of Fields   *220*
26. Use of Fields   *221*
27. Fields of Rapid Regrowth   *222*

PREFACE

THE research leading to this book began in 1966 as a study of land use and tenure in Zinacantán within the paradigm of local adaptation predominant in cultural ecology. I had been fortunate enough to participate in Harvard University's longitudinal study of that and adjacent *municipios*, or townships, of Tzotzil-speaking Indians in central highland Chiapas, Mexico. Many specific topics had been explored by other project members,[1] but land use and tenure had not been studied thoroughly. Moreover, the Harvard Chiapas Project had just acquired excellent aerial photographs of central Chiapas enabling extremely detailed description of land-use patterns through photo interpretation. The topic appeared suitable for dissertation research. But, as I delved into the study, I became increasingly aware of an apparent paradox. Indeed, local land was central to Zinacanteco life as a source for subsistence, as property whose inheritance shaped social organization, and as a token in factional fights within Zinacantán and in Zinacanteco dealings with the outside world. On the other hand, Zinacanteco land tenure could not be understood as local adaptation. Distant lowland rental farming arrangements competed with highland farming for subsistence. A variety of economic alternatives to farming conditioned land's value for inheritance. And politicking over land was just one kind of activity in a region-wide system of intertribal and interclass ethnic relations. The study of land led outward inevitably to conditions and influences distant in space and sometimes in time although nonetheless immediate in their impact on Zinacanteco life. Understanding the paradox required modification of the cultural ecological paradigm to stress the immediate rather than the local in human adaptation.

This realization grew on me gradually as I began to combine my writing with my teaching. I became aware of a school of biological ecology exemplified by the Australian biologist H. G. Andrewartha (1961), which placed emphasis on variables with direct impact on an organism and which condition its survival—that is, the variables that

1. By 1966 Cancian had published on the Zinacanteco ritual *cargo* system (1965); Vogt on Zinacanteco settlement pattern (1961) and ritual organization (1964, 1966); and Colby and Van Den Berghe (1961) on ethnic relations. Many student colleagues had progressed far in their study of Zinacanteco marriage, law (J. Collier 1968, 1973), humor (Bricker 1973), language (Laughlin n.d.), and a dozen other topics.

constitute the organism's niche as opposed to its habitat or the place in which it lives. I also became intrigued with general systems theory (Ashby 1960) because of its notion of a hierarchy of conditions that shape adaptation at one level of system but are themselves variables in a higher, encompassing level of system. Correspondingly, I began to develop a clearer sense that the variables shaping Zinacanteco land use need not be local but may be part of the very evident hierarchy of social relations leading upward from family to hamlet, township, intertribal, and interethnic relations embedded in a context of state and national processes.

As this clearer conception of ecological explanation took hold, I found myself increasingly capable of understanding those features that are truly distinctive in Tzotzil life: the apparent stress on tradition in tribal ethnic behavior. Tzotzil tradition could be viewed as a dynamic adaptive response that these groups make to their special placement in a larger, encompassing system. Correspondingly, the book that I have written lays bare what I perceive to be the bases of Tzotzil tradition through an ecological analysis of the factors bearing on Tzotzil land use.

Many friends and colleagues contributed to my understanding of Tzotzil life through their comments on and criticisms of early drafts of the book. Vicki Bricker, Frank Cancian, Bill Carver, Jane Collier, Paul Diener, Nancy Donham, Munro S. Edmonson, Charles Frake, Michelle Rosaldo, G. William Skinner, and Aram Yengoyan are among those who, I hope, will accept credit for improvements. Others who contributed their companionship, knowledge, or insight include Franzi Cancian, Nick and Lore Colby, Gary Gossen, John and Leslie Haviland, Robert and Mimi Laughlin, Duane Metzger, Ronald Nigh, Ben and Lois Paul, and Francesco Pellizzi.

I owe a special debt of gratitude to Evon Z. Vogt, director of the Harvard Chiapas Project, and Nan Vogt. Since 1960 their inspiration, guidance, support, and friendship have been constant and strong, and I cannot say enough to express my deep appreciation to them.

The Harvard Chiapas Project sponsored my research in Zinacantán from 1960 to 1968 partially through National Institute of Health Grant no. MH–02100 and National Science Foundation grants nos. GS–262, GS–976, and GS–1524. I am grateful for the support of a National Science Foundation Predoctoral Fellowship and a Public Health Service Predoctoral Fellowship. Study of ethnohistoric materials at Tulane bearing on Chiapas was enabled by Public Health Service Postdoctoral Fellowship no. MH–32,736.

Among the many who helped me in the field, José Hernández Pérez was closest to my work and contributed to it immeasurably. I would also like to thank Gertrudis Duby de Blom, Manuel Castellanos, Leopoldo Velasco, Prudencio Moscoso, and Armando Aguirre for their contributions to my research in San Cristóbal de las Casas, Chiapas, Mexico.

Most of the diagrams of the book are the work of Kip Nigh. Aerial oblique photos are courtesy of the Harvard Chiapas Project and the Cía. Mexicana de Aerofotos, S.A. Frank Cancian deserves credit for the photographs in chapter 7. Solveig Stone, Pam Snodgrass, Terri David, and Mary Ann Orndorff helped in production of the manuscript.

Portions of chapters 3 and 4 appeared in *Estudios de Cultura Maya* (G. Collier 1966) and in the *American Anthropologist* (G. Collier and Bricker 1970) and have been revised for incorporation into the book. I am grateful for permission to present these materials in their present form.

Finally, I wish to thank my wife and children for their patience and their understanding help to my writing. The book is dedicated to them.

NOTE: In many of the maps, and in some portions of the text, place names and other Tzotzil words have been used, written in an italicized phonemic script to distinguish them from English and Spanish words. Tzotzil phonemes include c, x, and z, pronounced "ch," "sh," and "ts." The consonants c, k, p, t, and z contrast with the glottalized consonants c^*, k^*, p^*, t^*, and z^*. Tzotzil also has the glottal stop, $?$, in its inventory of phonemes.

Fields of the Tzotzil

CHAPTER ONE

INTRODUCTION

THIS is a book about a region in the highlands of southeastern Mexico populated by descendants of the Maya, Indian tribes of distinctive ethnic character that live according to traditional life ways. Its purpose is to characterize the causes of traditional behavior and the reasons for its persistence. Anthropologists are coming to view the tradition of ethnic groups as responsive to the circumstances of their lives and of those surrounding them, and this book is intended to further this view. Rather than attributing the tradition of Tzotzil tribes to their isolation, we attribute it to their environment. We see these remote groups as engaged in a web of relations extending far beyond their geographic locale and including a range of influences and conditioning factors whose impact is strong even though their source is spatially or temporally far away. No setting is truly isolated from such influences, and in the late twentieth century their impact is increasing. So even the remotest groups have to be seen as parts within larger wholes that can be understood completely only by a perspective of the many levels of their engagement.

This book develops what might be called an "ecological" approach to such a perspective, one that relates the internal features of a system to its environment, comprehensively viewed. Kinship, social organization, and ethnic-group relations are semiautonomous traditional systems that can be studied in this way. These systems have regular, recurrent, or relatively stable features of internal organization that are conditioned by external factors. The conditioning factors are the "environment" of the system: they may be the local physiographic features that we ordinarily attribute to the environment; they may be the less tangible, though equally important, impacts of, for example, distant markets or national political ideology.

THE PROBLEM OF THE ENVIRONMENT

The central mountainous region of Chiapas, Mexico's southernmost state, sustains sizeable Indian populations. The Indians speak Tzotzil or Tzeltal, Maya dialects. Their tribes are organized as townships—each township generally arrayed as a ceremonial center surrounded

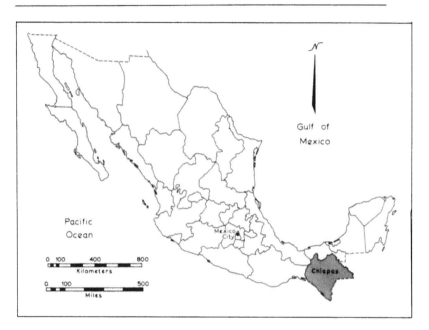

Map 1. Chiapas in the Mexican Nation

by scattered hamlets—and are oriented toward socially and culturally distinctive traditional life ways. The Indian townships of Chiapas surround the colonial administrative seat, San Cristóbal de las Casas, a Ladino (mestizo) city whose social and cultural orientation is toward the nation. Taken as a whole, the central highlands are an island of tradition in a backwater area that has always been linked only tenuously to the Mexican nation.

But are highland Chiapas groups set apart and detached from one another and from Mexican life? The environmentalist or social economist might trace the flow of resources and the pattern of production to answer this question. He would find groups in Chiapas partially self-sufficient, using local resources in a region where the volume of trade is low and communications with the distant outside world are difficult. But, by focusing on concrete, local features, he might fail to perceive intangible social, economic, and political facts that also bear directly on production. He might, that is, analyze the adaptations that groups make to their locality rather than those they make to their environment.

This book examines four contexts in which external factors condition the livelihood of highland Chiapas natives: (1) a highland township whose subsistence farming is supplemented and stabilized by lowland farm rental; (2) another highland township in which de-

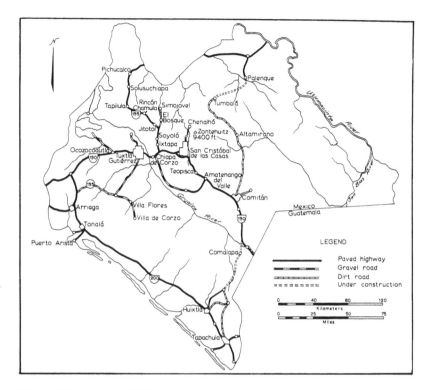

Map 2. The Roads of Chiapas

structive overpopulation is spurred by distant wage-labor markets;
(3) a system of ethnic differentiation derived from the marginal relation of a "refuge region" to a broader economy; and (4) a nativistic
colonization effort that is spurred by nationalist agrarian ideology. In
each case external factors are intangible parts of the environment
linking local systems to larger systems.

An examination of the local adaptations of these highland communities would include much to support the idea of the autonomy—
and hence the isolation—of these communities. Zinacantecos, a tribe
of Tzotzil corn farmers, value their farmland both for agriculture
(see chap. 2) and as inheritance affecting family organization (see
chap. 4). In this respect Zinacantecos are like other contemporary
Mayas discussed in chapter 3: those that have adequate land assets
have more coherent patrilineal kin groups, whereas those for whom
land is not a relevant asset run weakly or not at all to patriliny. The
interaction of kinship and local resources might well seem to justify
treatment of this man-land unit as autonomous and isolable.

Yet, in this example of man-land interaction, the highland farms provide only 20 percent of Zinacanteco income. The remainder is from rental farming in the adjacent lowlands (chap. 5), which has risen in importance as the township's population growth outstripped its highland subsistence base. Lowland farming sustains the value of highland farmland by preventing its ruin from overuse. It thus stabilizes the native kinship-property relationship, lending to the local man-land system an appearance of autonomy actually dependent on an external influence.

External factors condition land use in Chamula (another Tzotzil township) in quite a different way (see chap. 6). The Chamulas have severely abused their lands, and heavy erosion has required special cropping techniques and the search for nonagricultural sources of income. Chamula lands are less productive because of their high altitude, but their inadequacy is increased by the area's rapidly burgeoning population. Distant wage-labor markets thus appear to encourage Chamula's high fertility. And, thus, once again the local man-land system must be explained in terms of external conditioning factors.

Like many regions of ethnic character worldwide, highland Chiapas is an island of tradition on the fringe of a larger system. Gonzalo Aguirre Beltrán (1967) has characterized such areas as "refuge regions" and has argued that their ethnicity is an adaptation to marginality. In chapter 8 the castelike character of the regional social organization—in which a Ladino elite dominates differentiated Indian tribes—is analyzed as an adaptation that the central highlands made in response to their marginal relation to the colonial, later national, economy. Once again, an external relation conditions the internal state of a man-land system.

Finally, there is land reform. As a nationalist ideology and an economic policy, land reform has reached down to the remotest corners of the nation and into the consciousness of the natives. And the leaders of these natives have drawn upon land reform to better the land base of their constituencies. Their awareness of land-reform ideology inspires native groups to take action at the local level to better their resource base (one such colonization effort is described in chap. 9). Land reform, a nationally based program, cannot be ignored as an element in the environment of local land use.

Lowland rental farming, distant wage labor, the castelike character of the refuge region, and land reform have obvious bearing on the man-land adaptations made by the Chiapas natives. Is it too much to call these features part of the environment, shaping native systems of livelihood? Given this broader conception of the Tzotzil environment, we cannot help but see these groups as interconnected rather than isolated from one another, from the region, and ultimately from the nation.

THE PROBLEM OF DISTINCTIVENESS

The study of Mesoamerican townships dates from the definitive article by Sol Tax (1937) identifying the *municipio*, or Spanish township, as a fundamental unit in western Guatemala. And the township has been the primary unit of study in highland Chiapas for many ethnographers[1] since—and for good reasons: as in Guatemala, the natives identify themselves with townships; the township has administrative functions in a system of government of Spanish origin; and the social and ritual organization of the tribes is coextensive with that of the townships. The township thus stands out as the obvious unit of study.

But is it the right unit? This book demonstrates that different problems are appropriately studied with different units; local-descent group, hamlet, township, and region may each prove to be appropriate, as shown by the following examples: (1) a relation between kinship and land tenure explained best in terms of the local-descent group; (2) a pattern of local organization typical of the hamlet; (3) occupational specialties associated with townships; and (4) ethnic distinctions between Indians and Ladinos of the "refuge region." In each case, selection of the "right" unit depends on the problem studied.

Comparison of kinship and land tenure in several Maya communities (taken up in chap. 3) reveals a pattern in which patrilineal kinship has a curvilinear relation to land shortage. In extreme situations, either where land is abundant and a free good or where land is inadequate as a basis for subsistence, Maya family organization lacks a descent principle. But, where land is valued and available, family organization is patrilineal. This pattern is explained best through analysis of landholding units, as in chapter 4 where land is found to affect the organization of the local-descent group through the inheritance mechanism.

Tzotzil settlement is primarily in hamlets within the "vacant-town" framework. In contrast to the Ladinos, who live in compact towns, each Indian tribe inhabits loosely aggregated scattered hamlets within a township whose center, although an administrative and

---

1. Such as Cancian, Guiteras Holmes, Hill, Holland, Nash, Pozas, Siverts, and Vogt.

ceremonial focus for the tribe, rarely has more permanent population than a large hamlet. Local organization within a hamlet exhibits a mix of social groups of varying size. The simplest and smallest such group is the household of parents and children. Because married sons generally live near their father's home, several households may form a larger group, which is localized and descent based. Other kinsmen, and even unrelated individuals, may be part of the neighborhood surrounding a local-descent group, and such a neighborhood is often identified as the *sna*, or home, of its leading member. Neighborhoods cluster around springs or wells, and these water-hole groups function in ritual for water and rain. Finally, the hamlet itself is a territorial and political unit with ritual functions. Households, local-descent groups, neighborhoods, water-hole groups, and hamlets are thus units of increasing size, each made up of one or more units of smaller size. But the mix of constituent units within a given type of unit is variable. Within this mix some local aggregates have little influence on local affairs, while others stand out, providing leadership for the entire hamlet. In chapter 4, this mix is explained as the natural result of the distribution of property between local-descent groups in a hamlet. And because the hamlet is a relatively closed system as far as kinship and property are concerned, the constant redistribution of property through inheritance, marriage, or sale results in a fairly stable mix of significant and insignificant local groupings within the hamlet. This pattern is understandable when the hamlet is the unit selected for study.

Occupational specialties are an example fruitfully studied in relation to the township. Several Indian townships have long-standing reputations for the distinctiveness of their crafts or the specialization of their labor. It might be supposed that these distinctions reflect differentiations in the resources available to the townships. But, when townships' products and resources are compared, the specialties prove to be more a matter of reputation than a reflection of reality. Occupational specialization thus is like other ethnic differences between townships that are more apparent than real. Such findings bear on our understanding of why ethnic and tribal identities coincide at the level of the township.

Although townships are a convenient unit for the study of intertribal differences, all Indians have a similar subordinate relation to Ladinos. This relation is region wide and is best studied in relation to the region as a whole, as in the examination of the refuge-region hypothesis in chapter 8.

Human systems operate at many levels simultaneously, as these examples illustrate. In this book, the scope of the problems increases progressively from kin group to hamlet, tribe, and caste system. Each is a subsystem with a degree of analytic autonomy that justifies its selection for the study of particular problems. An ecological orientation that sees the encompassing aspects of the larger unit as the environment of its subsystems encourages the analysis of a region like highland Chiapas at several different levels. Thus, this book seeks to avoid the limited perspective that selects for study just the obvious unit—the distinctive Indian township.

TRADITION: SOME ORIENTATION

Other writers have described Tzotzil traditions in some detail. Although the thrust of this book is explanation that goes beyond ethnographic description, certain ethnographic assumptions and orientations must be taken up at the outset. Two aspects of the region's ethnic behavior are also important as orientation to the later chapters. The first is the dual division between Indian and Ladino life ways. The second is the pluralism of Indian tribal differences.

Ladinos and Indians

Ladinos are the mestizo population concentrated in San Cristóbal de las Casas, the major highland commercial center (plate 1). Indians are the tribal populations of San Cristóbal's rural hinterland. Ladinos are of Mexican national culture; Indians are of Maya culture. Intermarriage between the groups is infrequent, and a caste relationship is evident. Biologically and institutionally distinct, the castes are in an explicit hierarchical relation, with the Indian subordinate to the Ladino. The intercaste boundary is a dual division of society into groups that contrast in almost every way.

The systematic contrasts between Indian and Ladino are more striking in the highlands of Chiapas than in any other region of Mexico. The contrasts exist at many levels—in the behavior identifying individuals' group affiliation, in economic and settlement patterns, in social institutions, and in world view and ideology.

Language and clothing clearly delimit caste membership. Despite four centuries of Spanish domination, Tzotzil or Tzeltal are the only languages of some 113,000 highland Indians and the first language for perhaps half again as many who have learned rudimentary Spanish in schools or through commerce. Ladinos, by contrast, are Spanish

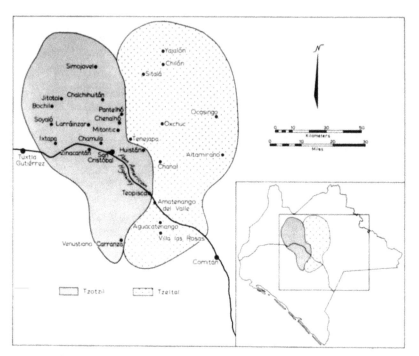

Map 3. Tzotzil and Tzeltal Speakers in Chiapas

speaking from earliest childhood. Clothing also identifies status. Ladinos wear the sex-typed clothing of developing Western nations—pants and shirts, skirts and blouses, either factory woven or factory made. Indian costumes vary from township to township, but the colorful, handwoven or embroidered garb or the ribbon-festooned hats of traditional use are impossible to confuse with their Ladino counterparts.

The sixteenth-century conquistador believed civilization to be tantamount to village or city life and determined to reorganize dispersed aboriginal settlements around town centers. In the Chiapas highlands this policy defined administrative units that have survived in modern Indian townships, but by and large the effort to reorganize Indian settlement was not successful. Typically, a Tzotzil or Tzeltal township has a ceremonial and political center housing public civil and religious officials who have left their normal life in the hamlets to serve their community for a year. The center may have a permanent population as well, but generally the bulk of the township citizenry lives in widely scattered, loosely clustered hamlet aggregates. Ladino settlement differs in adhering to fundamental Spanish concepts of the

1. Settlement Pattern in Ladino San Cristóbal. (Photo courtesy of Harvard Chiapas Project and Cía. Mexicana de Aerofotos, S.A.)

nature of social life. Rural settlement is ranch style. Yet Ladinos prefer truly "civilized" settlement, necessarily urban. Their cities and towns are nucleated and compact, with streets in a rectilinear grid centered on the town hall, central square, market, and principal church.

Indian family life is usually confined to the local-descent group and rarely extends outside the hamlet of birth. As children of a couple mature, the sons marry and move out into houses built adjacent to the father's, whereas the daughters, once married, move away to the homes of their suitors. The resulting aggregates of patrilineally related male-centered houses may continue to produce and consume as a unit and to function as a bloc in hamlet organization. Ladino kinship is ideally bilateral, with an overlay of Spanish patriarchality and the sexual double standard. But many families, particularly among the Ladino poor, are the mother-child households typical of urban Latin America, where a core of women, mothers and their daughters, are the mainstay of a domestic unit supported in part by males whose enterprises may carry them far afield, to other regions and even other states.

The typical Indian family subsists on highland swidden (slash-and-burn) corn farming. Where population pressure is greatest, Indians either intensify land use by substituting horticulture for fallowing, supplement their farmlands by lowland field rental, or seek income from other sources, such as wage labor for Ladinos and other Indians or household craft production. While some Ladinos farm for subsistence, most town dwellers are commercialists, dealing in goods that can be marketed through stores or by traders to Indians. Candles, sandals, sisal rope, fireworks, tools, bread, bricks and tiles, and beef are some products of Ladino manufacture for which Indians exchange corn, beans, firewood and charcoal, fruits, eggs, vegetables, and other basic commodities. Most Ladino enterprise is of cottage-industry scale, but a few integrated industries, such as that of sugar grown in the lowlands and refined into molasses, white sugar, and distilled rum for regional and national distribution, have been developed by the wealthiest Ladino families. Viewed as a whole, the relative position of the Indian and the Ladino in the productive system is clear-cut: Indians extract primary products, food and manpower, for consumption; Ladinos convert these into secondary products for redistribution in commerce or trade.

The pervasive dual division between Indian and Ladino extends into the realm of ideas. From schooling, Ladinos are aware of their relation to the state, the nation, and other nations. Indian world view has retained most components of age-old Maya cosmology. The earth is a rectangular plane upheld by spirits at its corners. Several separated underworld planes lie parallel to the earth. Between each layer pass the ribbons of heaven, which are paths for the sun, moon, and other celestial spirits. Deities residing in the earth give rain for agriculture, wind, lightning, and the agents of evil that cause illness and death through soul loss. Man lives in essential fear of the cosmological order and designs his life so as to maintain a precarious harmony with it. Thus, while Indians are nominally Catholic, their religion has syncretized Catholicism with fundamental Maya cosmology, which Ladinos recognize as different from their own but rarely understand.

The Indian and the Ladino ways of life, then, are separable in their basic axioms and in their principles of organization; linkage between the two systems is primarily in the sphere of economics and production, and it is from there that Indian subordination extends to other spheres. The dual system is castelike in that change from one way of life to the other is difficult. Group membership is as though determined by birth and is reified into essentially racial contrasts by participants in the system.

Indian Pluralism

Contrasting with the dual division between Ladino and Indian is the pluralism of the latter caste, taking the form of tribal ethnicity in ritual organization, territoriality, and, to a lesser degree, economic specialization.

Indian ritual organization is of the *cargo*-system type found widely in Mesoamerica. The township center is a ceremonial precinct typical of Maya settlement, in which, in Indian eyes, ritual functions far outweigh the public civil functions required by law. Characteristically, *cargo* ritual is limited to men of the township who take positions associated with the care of Catholic saints. The positions are ranked into levels, service in all but the first level presupposing earlier service at the level below. Every mature male is expected to provide ritual service for the community at some point in his life by occupying a ritual position at the lowest level. During his year of service, the man will leave his hamlet to live in the township center to perform ritual at great personal expense. The heavy cost of this ritual requires years of careful savings of the meager excess of farm production above subsistence needs. Yet the spiritual and social rewards of service are such that many seek subsequent service at additional heavy cost in positions at higher levels of the hierarchy later in life. Indeed, those men who succeed in performing at all of the hierarchy's levels have proved themselves worthy of the greatest respect.

Ritual *cargo* systems are so widespread in Mesoamerica that their presence demands explanation. Many scholars have emphasized the importance of the institution for integrating Indian society in several ways: (1) social homogeneity is promoted through the shared values that participation in the system implies; (2) participation defines the boundaries of community membership; (3) *cargo* ritual was a format within which aboriginal ritual could be syncretized adaptively to Spanish Catholicism; and (4) the institution has a leveling effect on wealth differences that would otherwise accumulate. A more recent analysis (Cancian 1965) points out that these systems function to convert the wealth of participants into prestige, particularly where positions within the hierarchical levels differ in their costs. Since wealthy men in the system studied chose the more expensive, prestigious *cargo* positions, the system seemed to validate existing stratification within the community more than it promoted economic homogeneity. Both of these interpretations support the generalization that the ritual institution reifies the importance of township membership for the Mesoamerican Indian.

Township territoriality is another important component of Indian pluralism. Beginning in the sixteenth century, township boundaries were set by land titles granted to communities by the Spanish crown. Throughout the colonial period, Indian communities fought vigorously to defend themselves from continual encroachment by colonists by careful revalidation of their land titles. After independence, for instance, natives carefully revalidated their holdings under new state and national guidelines. When nineteenth-century policies converted Indian communal tracts into individually owned parcels, township territoriality was temporarily undermined, but land-reform laws from the Mexican Revolution restored the alienated lands to community title. In general, native tenure conforms to the fundamental principle that land is ultimately invested in the community despite de facto private ownership. Thus, legitimate land tenure implies an individual's allegiance to the political and religious institutions of his township.

Although both the religious *cargo* system and territoriality contribute in these ways to Indian township integrity, each also contributes to differences between communities. *Cargo* participation is always limited to township members. Outsiders may only observe a township's major fiestas, unless they form part of the visitation teams that townships exchange for major rituals. Similarly, sale or exchange of land is an exclusive prerogative of township members intended to keep out members of other townships.

Language and clothing are additional mechanisms for township differentiation. Linguists have confirmed the native belief that dialect differences permit the hearer to identify the speaker's township of origin, differences found not only at the level of phonology and morphology but also in the systematic stylization of ordinary discourse, such as the reciprocal greetings used when Indians meet along a trail. Tribal costume, too, is distinctive and indicative of community membership.

Finally, although the majority of highland Indians are swidden agriculturalists, some occupational specializations have the reputation of being indicative of tribe affiliation. Zinacantecos, for instance, are known in the region as salt merchants and muleteers even though only a few Zinacantecos make a living from these activities. Amatenango, which produces the distinctive pottery marketed throughout the region, is thought of by distant natives as a town of potters. Chamulas manufacture crude furniture, musical instruments, wool, and a variety of other specialties.

THE PROBLEM OF TRADITION

Indian life ways include many features of obviously non-Western origin and, at the same time, many elements that clearly are Spanish. Yet native Mesoamerican culture is more than just a system in which distinctive cultural complexes have syncretised and survived. This book conceives of Tzotzil tradition as not vestigial or residual but as constituting a dynamic, active response that Indians make to their peripheral position in a larger, changing system. Such an approach can account for the integrity with which Tzotzil tradition responds to its contacts with the non-Indian world.

What accounts for the integrity of Tzotzil tradition? Is Tzotzil culture a well-articulated and persistent combination of Mesoamerican life ways that have withstood the test of time? If so, slow communications could protect the isolated region from outside forces for change. Cultural differences within the region could serve as barriers to internal change through borrowing. Local adaptations might encourage further differentiation of each local system from its neighbors. In this view, cultural differences, either among Indians or between them and Ladinos, would persist if cultural features were compatible with one another and as long as local boundaries served as effective barriers to communication.

This book assembles evidence that compels us to reject such an explanation of the persistence of tradition. The evidence is of three kinds, showing that tradition persists in spite of (1) the substantial information and forces for change that penetrate the Tzotzil community from afar; (2) the migration intermixing Tzotzil peoples of different traditions; and (3) the apparent lack of tradition's basis in local economic adaptation.

Colonial and national land policies are forces for change of which Indians have been acutely aware since the Spanish Conquest. Chapter 7 reviews ethnohistoric proof that natives repeatedly responded to change in public policy so as to reinforce their control of township lands. Astute native leadership continues today to work Mexican land reform to the advantage of tribal territoriality. In this example, natives' knowledge of and responsiveness to the outside world actually reinforces township integrity and distinctiveness.

Gradual but continual migration within the central highlands has repeatedly relocated Indians of one tribe within the territories of other tribes in a manner violating township rules of territorial exclusiveness. Yet this intermixture (also discussed in chap. 7), does not reduce tribal differences. Rather, newcomers adopt the dress and customs of their neighbors and eventually deny their true origins. Traditional systems are not ordinarily thought to be able to withstand such mobility.

Occupational specialties associated with township differences do not appear to be the basis or actual cause of tribal differentiation. As shown in chapter 7, production in the highlands is much less specialized than native accounts might lead us to believe. Instead, crafts are a metaphor for tribal differences that are more apparent than real. Townships' reputations for specialization are the product, rather than the underlying cause, of differentiation.

These examples compel a view of Tzotzil tradition as vital and dynamic, an ongoing process of differentiation that is responsive to external influences and information and unimpeded by internal mobility. In the view of this book, Tzotzil tradition is an ethnic phenomenon that is fundamentally social, rather than cultural, and that has an ecological basis.

Fredrik Barth (1969, pp. 10–11) has characterized ethnic groups as populations that (1) are "largely biologically self-perpetuating"; (2) share "fundamental cultural values realized in overt unity of cultural forms"; (3) make "up a field of communication and interaction"; and (4) have "a membership which identifies itself and is identified by others as constituting a category distinguishable from other categories of the same order."

In highland Chiapas the third and fourth attributes underlie the first two. The region is a social field in which Indians and Ladinos constitute two orders of social category, one a dual order and the other a plural order. Moreover, as shown in chapter 8, these social categories interact so as to maintain the appearance of biological self-perpetuity and cultural autonomy. Stability of the social field is the fundamental reason that biological and cultural "distinctiveness" can coexist with mobility and outside forces for change.

Ecological factors underlie the stability of the social system. Highland Chiapas is a peripheral area that is marginal to a larger economic system. Caste duality was an adaptation to marginality developed in the colonial era. Tribal pluralism further enabled the subordinate caste to live with extremely limited resources. In the manner recognized by Aguirre Beltrán's refuge-region model, Indians and Ladinos have developed institutions that preserve the configuration of their statuses in the social system. A special example of this is the manner in which Indians manipulate nationalist policies for essentially nativist ends in their quest for colonization lands under land-reform policies (chap.

9). Indians occupy and defend a special niche in a regional system whose structure comes from a marginal relation to a larger, national system. Marginality is the environment of ethnic groupings and the ecological basis of Tzotzil tradition. Ethnic behavior is the vital, dynamic response that these groups make to peripheral placement in a larger system.

What, then, is our assessment of the ethnic peoples of highland Chiapas? They are groups that are remote but not isolated from an encompassing national system. Their distinctiveness is self-applied and must not be mistaken for idiosyncracy or uniqueness. For these groups share a structural position of subordination in a larger social field. They are groups whose ethnicity is not a form of cultural survival, but an active, adaptive response to placement in a system. They are groups whose identities are consonant with the nativist thrust of modern nationalism. In these respects, Tzotzil Indians are like ethnic groups everywhere, in the subarctic environments of Scandinavia, in marginal Appalachia, or in the ghettos of our cities.

CHAPTER TWO

FORMS OF LAND UTILIZATION

THE widespread practice of swidden corn agriculture in central highland Chiapas bears scrutiny in the microcosm of a typical agrarian village in which local issues reflect problems general to the region. This chapter treats of the technical facets of farming in *Apas*, a hamlet in the township of Zinacantán, both depicting commonly used farming practices and delineating the general problem that rising population poses for a region whose resources are declining.

The highland Tzotzil region and its lowland surroundings have a complex physiography differentiated primarily by altitude into distinctive biotic zones. Even a small village like *Apas* has land in more than one zone and activities taking advantage of the region's diversity. The chapter first sketches the principal variations of central Chiapas physiography. Then attention is placed on *Apas* through a general description of its farmlands and agricultural cycle. The techniques of highland and lowland farming are similar, and climate permits Zinacantecos to dovetail and combine mountain farming with lowland rental farming operations.

The detailed study of *Apas* farming practices through aerial photographs (see Appendix) allowed reconstruction of village land use parcel by parcel since 1940. These data lend themselves to quantitative analysis of fallowing patterns through a model that reveals trends in the intensity of land exploitation. Although population in the hamlet has grown continuously, exploitation of the zone first grew to a level that would feed the average family in the 1950s but since has declined. A discussion of the fallow cycle, the factors affecting regrowth, and analysis of use histories in three categories of land of different regrowth potential shows that the recent decline in highland farming is confined to the higher altitude zones with slower regrowth rates. The lower (and more temperate) farming zones are still in intensive exploitation.

Although the zone has uses in addition to farming, its resources are in general decline, steadily outstripped by growing population. Obviously farmers have come to rely on alternative sources of income, particularly in distant lowland rental farming. Is the *Apas* farming zone, then, a microcosm that can be understood in its own terms? The findings of this chapter suggest that optimal portions of the zone continue to be farmed with a self-contained traditional swidden cycle in which use and regrowth are roughly balanced; but the integrity of this process depends on the harvests Zinacantecos obtain from rental farming elsewhere.

PHYSIOGRAPHY OF HIGHLAND CHIAPAS

Despite the common image we have of Mexico as a parched desert filled with cactus or a lowland area of tropical forest, Chiapas, like almost all Mexico and Central America, is of mountainous form, an extension of our Rockies to the South American Andes as the volcanic ridges providing the physiographic backbone of the Western Hemisphere. An examination of the topographic map of the state reveals several major zones (map 4). The state is bounded by lowland areas on three sides, a narrow Pacific coastal plain, the Isthmus of Tehúantepec, and the broader Gulf coastal plain of Tabasco. To the southeast lies the Guatemalan lowland Petén region where the Maya Classic civilization reached its peak. To the south, Guatemala contains the extensions of the two principal mountainous formations.

The first of these formations is the Sierra Madre de Chiapas, rising up from the Pacific coastal plain; the western slope of this formation is known as the Soconusco, famed for its aboriginal cacao production and, today, its coffee plantations. Of direct interest to us is the central highland formation, rising to the southwest in a steep escarpment from the Grijalva River valley and from the north and east more gradually from the Gulf coast plain and the Petén. Basically a limestone uplift, this central plateau is broken through by extrusive volcanic formations that provide the peaks of altitude in the extinct volcanos Huítepec and Zontehuitz. Actually, the plateau is quite broken, extremely rugged, characterized by small-to-medium-sized valleys drained internally not by river systems but by limestone sinks and underground channels (plates 2, 3, and 4). The largest of these highland valleys is the site of the colonial capital, San Cristóbal de las Casas, and it is the region immediately surrounding this valley with which we are concerned.

A major adjunct to the central highland region is the adjacent depression through which the Grijalva River flows from its source in the Cuchumatán Mountains in Guatemala and into the chasm leading it to drainage in the Tabasco coastal plain. This broad lowland valley

Map 4. Relief Map of Chiapas

system is the locus of cattle ranching and corn farming that provides much of the state's income.

The annual cycle of climate in Chiapas is not so much one of temperature as of rainfall. Rains begin in late May or early June and continue through late October, earlier and more prolonged in the highlands than the lowlands. Sometimes torrential in volume (see fig. 1), they reach a peak in late June and September, slacking off slightly in intervening July and August. From November through May, however, rains are an anomaly, sometimes brought in the form of wind-driven mist storms that blow from the continental United States over the Gulf of Mexico, battering themselves out on the northern slopes of the central plateau. While the annual cycle of rainfall is regular and predictable, the character of weather during the rainy season exhibits dynamic interaction with topography. Once the rains have begun, they may be generated locally across the hundreds of

2. *Navencauk.* The limestone sink draining the valley hamlet of *Navencauk* is not equal in capacity to the flooding of summer rains. (Photo courtesy of Harvard Chiapas Project and Cía. Mexicana de Aerofotos, S.A.)

3. Central Highland Topography. View from the central highland summit of Zontehuitz. (Photo by author)

4. The Pan American Highway. The Pan American Highway climbs from the lowlands passing several hamlets of Zinacantán. (Photo courtesy of Harvard Chiapas Project and Cía. Mexicana de Aerofotos, S.A.)

valley systems, each with characteristic convection and evaporation patterns. As the region heats up by day, clouds form within topographic pockets and gradually rise up to form towering thunderstorms that precipitate locally with great violence.

Monthly mean temperatures at any given place show only a moderate range of variation against the backdrop of the striking contrast between wet and dry, but they vary dramatically according to altitude. Thus, a frost line restricts agriculture above 6,000 feet, while the lowlands may never experience temperatures below fifty degrees Fahrenheit.

Given these regularities of climate and systematic variations of topography, natural vegetation of the Chiapas region will proceed through a well-ordered but lengthy succession culminating in one or another type of forest cover (plate 5). An ecologist would be quick to note that the type of climax forest achieved is in large part determined by altitude. In the cooler highlands, above 8,000 feet, the climax growth is cloud forest characterized by a thick broad-leafed evergreen canopy with a dense understory of ferns and vines. Mosses and epiphytes, such as bromeliads, cling to the trees there, preserved by the misty cloud cover that tends to shroud the higher peaks. Lower, from 3,000 to 8,000 feet, absence of the continual cloud shroud causes the drought of winter to impinge; climax forest species that adapt to the drought by leaf loss abound, but the understory is still as dense as in the cloud forest, and epiphytes are still common. Only to the east of the highlands, below 3,000 feet, where the seasonal contrasts of wet and dry are less clear-cut, is the climax type of tropical rain forest found.

Today, such stands of climax forest are located only where topography makes agriculture impossible. Elsewhere, the land is everywhere either in cultivation or in fallow, thus exhibiting characteristics of the successive stages before climax forest is attained. Once again, the nature of this succession is closely related to altitude. In the hot lowlands, the metabolism of life is so rapid that dense, thorny scrub quickly overruns the cornfield abandoned from the previous year. Somewhat higher, scrub regenerates more slowly, particularly if soil fertility has been drained by overuse. In the highlands, fallowed land may be taken over by grasses if particularly exhausted, giving way, gradually, to pine forest and, finally, to a range of species more characteristic of the climax. More fertile abandoned cornfields revert directly to gradual scrub growth. In general, then, the highland succession is much more protracted than that of the lowlands, exhibiting more apparent stages of succession.

5. Highland Forest. Nondeciduous oaks and pines form dense forest on the higher mountain slopes, as in the foreground here. (Photo courtesy of Harvard Chiapas Project and Cía. Mexicana de Aerofotos, S.A.)

Swidden farming takes advantage of the process of succession. Tracts that have approached a stable climax are felled, in effect pushed back to an earlier successional stage in which harvests are nourished by the humus of the climax. Fallowing allows the succession toward climax to rebuild soil nutrients. Felling and fallowing can be balanced to fit the needs of a stable population. But, in highland Chiapas, as we shall begin to see in the study of *Apas* farmlands, population has outstripped the capacity of farming within a stable swidden system.

FORMS OF LAND UTILIZATION IN *APAS*

People of Zinacantán often contrast "fenced" land of their hamlet settlements with the "forest" or mountain scrub that they own for farming. This chapter describes the technology with which the second class of land is exploited and assesses the relative proportion of overall income supplied by highland farming to Zinacantecos of *Apas* in recent decades.[1]

The *Apas* settlement, a hamlet of Zinacantán, lies on a narrow shelf near the crest of the central highland southern escarpment. On the other side of the crest, like fan segments, radiate a series of erosion-cut valleys sloping down with south and southwestern exposure toward the Grijalva Valley. The land is a patchwork of field plots in various stages of regrowth except for rare, untouched cloud-forest stands on nearly inaccessibly steep ridge faces between the valleys. A network of major trails follows these ridges from the settlement downward to take Zinacanteco farmers and their beasts of burden to their lowland farming. Smaller trails link valley to valley. This is the *Apas* farming area, bound on the west by the deep gorge leading around the crest into the settlement, on the south by the rocky badland pine forests of the Grijalva Valley edges, and on the east by an important highland to lowland trail (see map 5).

Within this area are three zones of differing tenure history. The westernmost segment is a portion of former "communal" lands, owned in part by men of other hamlets and thought of as ancestral private property. The wedge-shaped middle section is owned by descendants of men who purchased the tract from Mestizos about one hundred years ago; the current owners live now in several hamlets. The remainder of the land is ejido expropriated from mestizo ranches after

1. The reader interested in the field methods and data analysis employed in the study of *Apas* land use and tenure should consult the Appendix at this juncture.

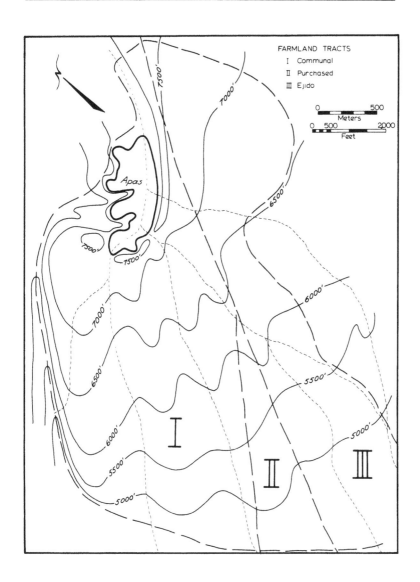

Map 5. *Apas* Farmland. (Adapted from Harvard Chiapas Project RC-9 photograph 1732–961)

1934 and turned over to *Apas* men by the land-reform program. In all three zones the principal exploitation is corn farming.

THE AGRICULTURAL CYCLE

The agricultural cycle in the *Apas* land is closely tied to the yearly alternating wet and dry seasons. As is true of most of Mexico, the Chiapas highlands' rainy season is one of increased warmth. It begins in May and continues into October. followed by six months of relative drought and cold. The swidden agricultural system used almost universally is linked to the advent and disappearance of rain. Regrowth is felled early enough in the dry season so that it will burn well and leave the ground free for seeding. Crops are seeded when rain is sure to produce germination before pests take their toll. Figure 1 shows how each of the corn-farming activities is coordinated with the others and with the basic seasonal cycle. But a description of each step taken in the agricultural endeavor will clarify how land is used.

Preparing the Land for Seed

Techniques for preparing the land for seed depend upon its state following the previous farming season. Fields used the immediately preceding year are easiest to prepare, requiring only felling and burning of dried corn, bean, and weed growth left by domestic animals allowed to forage freely after the harvest. Fields long unused are more difficult to prepare. Ax, billhook, and machete serve to fell several years' forest and brush growth that is left to dry for several weeks before burning, and this process takes from ten to twenty man-days per hectare (hereafter abbreviated as mdph). depending upon the density of the growth to be felled. In the higher areas where forest will not grow back, fallow land must be chopped up with pickax or hoe, requiring twenty to thirty mdph.

The land is burned prior to seeding to destroy roots and seeds of undesirable weeds and render it easily accessible to the worker. While Zinacantecos recognize vegetal ash as a fertilizer. there is no idea that the heat of the fire "brings out the juice of the soil" (Reina 1967, p. 5) or affects fertility in any way. First. a firebreak is cleared to enclose completely the area to be burned and prevent spread of the fire. If the area to be burned were a clockface tilted with the twelve-o'clock position at the highest point and with the circumference the firebreak, the fire setters would begin their work at the twelve-o'clock position and

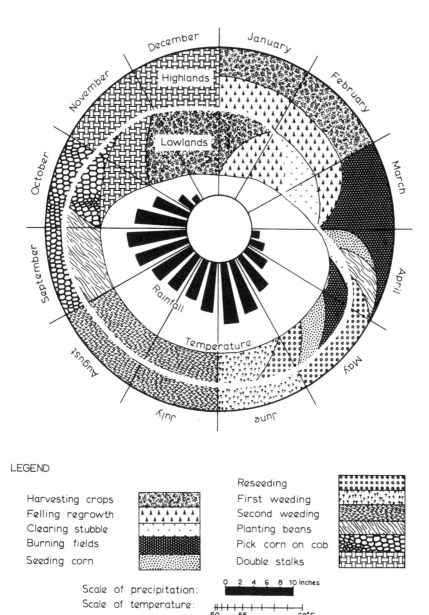

LEGEND

Harvesting crops	Reseeding
Felling regrowth	First weeding
Clearing stubble	Second weeding
Burning fields	Planting beans
Seeding corn	Pick corn on cob
	Double stalks

Scale of precipitation:
Scale of temperature:

0   2   4   6   8   10 Inches

50   55   60°F

Fig. 1. The Swidden Farming Cycle. Annual cycle of temperature,
rainfall, and associated corn-farming activities.

work their way in opposite directions around the edge of the face to meet at the six-o'clock position, causing the fire line to burn down the slope. This technique contains the fire. Were workers to set the fire from the bottom edge of the plot, the fire line might burn up the slope quickly enough to jump the firebreak before they could intercept it. After the burning, unburned branches and stumps are left, possibly to be used as firewood by the women. Often, owners of adjacent parcels will cooperate in burning their fields, effectively reducing the total length of firebreak needed to enclose the area. While actual burning of almost any size of farm plot requires only a day, constructing the firebreak and piling up the brush and waste to be burned may take two or three mdph.

Seeding

Seeding begins at least several days after the fields have been burned and in anticipation of onset of the rains. Since showers begin in the higher portions of the area earlier, these are seeded first. Custom requires that there be a moon, however partial, during the portion of the month selected for seeding. Workers should avoid seeding on Sundays to prevent infection of their crop by smut.

Several varieties of corn and beans are seeded in the land area owned by *Apas*. The seed is planted in rows that follow the edge of the land parcel and run up and down its slope to make later weeding easier. The seeder carries a net bag full of the selected seed in one hand and an iron-tipped digging stick in the other. Beginning at one corner of the parcel, he thrusts the stick into the ground before him and pulls it to one side to open up a cavity for five or six corn and two bean seeds. After these are dropped in, the stick is moved back and forth and then removed. The worker then takes a half-stride forward and thrusts the stick through an arc into the next seed location, using the length of the digging stick to regulate the approximate one-meter distance between seed holes.

Initially, only five or six corn kernels are planted, for, were more to sprout at one mound, none would yield properly mature ears. If heavy rains follow the initial planting, the seeds will sprout well. But periods of misty drizzle cause the seed to rot or remain in a dormant state vulnerable to birds and rodents. Should this happen, reseeding when the milpa has grown to about five centimeters will replace the missing sprouts. Again, the digging stick is used to insert three to five new kernels into mounds where less than three of the original seeds sprouted. Altogether, seeding and reseeding will have required four to six mdph.

Weeding

Other grasses that compete with young corn for water and light must be destroyed, usually twice, before the corn matures enough so that its shade depresses its competitors' growth. Weeding begins in mid-June when the cornstalks are thirty-five to sixty-five centimeters high. Since weeds grow more rapidly than the corn, threatening to choke it, and because of the large scale of farming in lowland fields, the farmer will hire help to hasten the time-consuming first weeding (14 mdph). The second weeding, usually not required of fields that have long been fallow, follows the first by about four weeks, or less if rains followed the first weeding and sped up weed growth.

Zinacantecos use the narrow hoe to weed out the *Apas* cornfields, even in the rockiest soils. Starting at either lower field corner, they hoe in adjacent rows up the slope and parallel to the plot boundary, following the rows as they were seeded and leaving the cleared weeds piled up between rows. While initial weeding may begin at either lower corner, the second weeding must follow the path of the first, for weeds will have grown highest where the first weeding was begun.

Field Ritual

The purpose of milpa ritual, usually performed after the second weeding when the corn tassels appear, is to avoid damage from Wind. Wind, while it physically destroys the corn by flattening it, is harmful because it steals the soul of the corn as it passes by. But when Lightning, which lives in the earth and hills, rises from the earth, Wind must pass high above the cornfields and cannot damage them. Milpa ritual appeals to Lightning to protect the corn from Wind. The ritual requires the attention of a shaman, who prays while candles, incense, liquor, and a meal are consumed in the field and home of the farmer.

The Harvest

The fruits of farming labor are first appreciated when fresh corn comes in from areas near the community seeded with fast-growing corn. Fresh corn is selected from those stalks that have only one ear by feeling to assure that the ear is firm and full. The ear is removed and the stalk either bent over to show it has been harvested or cut off about a foot below the ear to feed to horses and mules. After the fresh-corn season, hard corn should be doubled over to prevent dripping rain from penetrating the ear and causing it to rot.

At the height of the dry season when leaves, stalk, and husk are dry, the corn and beans are harvested. Beans are harvested before the corn, stripped from the vines while the dew is on, for later in the day the dried-out pods would burst, scattering the beans around. In the case of corn, a deer horn, heavy piece of wire, or stick of special hardwood rips open the husk so that the ear can be removed. The rest of the plant is flattened to the ground. The ears are then sorted into three groups—partially rotted ones for domestic animal fodder, the longest and fattest for seed, and the remainder for consumption or sale. Ears of seed corn should have not even one rotten kernel and should have cob ends with small kernels removed. Otherwise, they are left intact. Other corn is beaten from the cob at the field or stored at home to be shelled as needed. By the end of February highland harvests must be complete, for animals are let loose to forage the harvested fields in March. But most men find no difficulty (at 4 mdph) in completing the harvest before that time. By then the cycle has begun to repeat itself.

The sequence of farming operations in the annual cycle is much the same as that used in the lowlands. But there the intense heat and later advent of rain permit a growing season that is shorter, compressing seeding to harvest to the span from May to December. Many Zinacantecos take advantage of the different schedules to farm in the highlands and on rented lowland tracts simultaneously, traveling back and forth between zones to care for their fields. This alternative to highland farming, which is explored in chapter 6 as a facet of Indians' placement in a regional economy, has become of greater importance in recent years (Cancian 1972) as the intensity of highland farming has declined.

RECENT TRENDS IN FARMING INTENSITY

Aggregate Trends

The oldest informants remember that *Apas*, at the turn of the century, had only ten or fifteen households. Men farmed only the land they owned in the sector of former communal lands. Many other families had been residents of *Apas*, but by the turn of the century they worked as indentured laborers for lowland ranches. The land was much more heavily wooded than it is today. Indeed, ancestors are thought to have laid claim to their holdings by felling the primeval forest.

When indentured laborers were freed in 1918, many returned to *Apas* and borrowed dwellings from their wealthier compatriots. Slowly, they purchased land from them, too. Then the ejido movement gave seventy-one men additional lands in 1940, expanding the community's land base.

Today *Apas* has 147 married men. Of these, 57 own no farmland at all, but 30 of this group, mostly under age 40, can expect to inherit from their fathers. Altogether, only 27 landless men can expect no inheritance at all. Today, therefore, over 80 percent of the men have rights over highland property. On the other hand, use of this farmland accounts for only about one-fifth of current net corn production, for the bulk of farming utilizes rented lowland fields.

That the community land contributed more to family income in the past is indicated by approximate figures for average highland corn yields per family during several time periods back to 1940. These figures derive from yearly estimates of the area under cultivation and from a projection of community size back through time, as will be shown below.

Older informants provided data on plot use as far back as 1940, which can be converted into yearly estimates of the area under cultivation. The line graph in figure 2 shows that the percentage of plots in use each year varies considerably. Plots were weighted by size, and their use was averaged over periods of years so as to reduce variability for the earlier years. The bar graph in the same chart makes it clear that after 1940, when the ejido land was received, land cultivation became more and more intense, but that it has tailed off considerably since 1960.

Figure 3 brings in variation in community size. The line graph shows estimates of the number of married men in *Apas*, starting from the current number (147) and interpolating back through time on the basis of official census estimates of Zinacanteco population (Cancian 1965, pp. 162–166). The bar graph assumes that corn was harvested at the current rate of about 44 net units to each unit of seed in the highlands, resulting in a yield of about 3.66 fanegas per almud of seed planted. (A fanega equals 180 metric liters; an almud is 15 metric liters.) It incorporates percentage of area under cultivation during each period (from fig. 2) to estimate the number of fanegas of corn produced per family on *Apas* land. Finally, the broken line shows

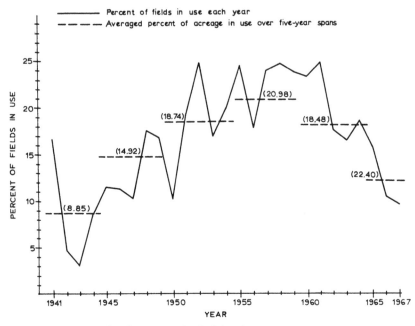

Fig. 2. *Apas* Farmland Acreage in Cultivation

the amount of corn that the average family eats yearly, assumed to be constant.

Interpretation of this figure should bear in mind that the current net production per family from highland and lowland farming combined is about 13 fanegas. The figure shows that, during the periods of most intense land use, the area may have provided over twice the current contribution to family support, but it never provided the average family with more than food, about 5 fanegas per year. It is obvious that *Apas* has had to rely on lowland farming to supplement production from its own land since 1940. While the land may have yielded a significant proportion of family income from 1945 to 1960, more recent farming has turned markedly to rental of lowland fields, and the land area is dwindling in its economic significance (see chap. 6).

Fallowing

An examination of the use and fallowing patterns of several hundred plots will demonstrate that the decline in aggregate exploitation is not

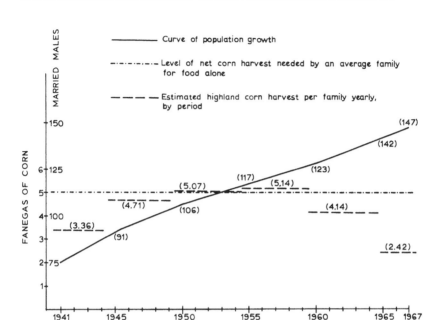

Fig. 3. *Apas* Farmland Production and Population Growth

general to all categories of land but tends to be confined to the zones of higher altitude and slower regrowth. Regrowth rates (and consequently fallowing patterns) vary considerably within the study area, especially by altitude, as an examination of the factors affecting regrowth will show. But, even when regrowth potential is controlled for, actual use can be shown to have declined in all but the zone of most rapid regrowth.

Apas farmers do not fallow according to the simple rule, six years' rest after one year's use, which governs regrowth in a nearby settlement. Richard Price has made an excellent study (1968) of Zinacanteco farming in *Muk*ta hok*, a community of thirty-nine households endowed with ejido lands amounting to more than twice the land area controlled by *Apas*. *Muk*ta hok* men are able to reap 75 to 95 percent of their annual harvest from their ejido following a system in which they generally leave fields fallow for six years after each year's use. Occasionally men who happen to have few six-year fallow fields at the beginning of a season must select from their five-year fallow fields for land to fell, but such variation is definitely an exception to the explicit fallow rule.

Apas farmland is not exploited according to any similar simple fal-lowing mechanism. The region includes some fields that may recover forest growth in four or five years and others that require fifteen years of fallowing before they can be recultivated. *Apas* men consider that they cannot determine the necessary fallow period by a simple rule, and owners of adjacent plots often differ in their judgment as to when their fields have "enough" regrowth to be farmed again.

Altitude is the principal component of variation in the rate of re-growth. A walk down one of the steep ridge trails takes one from the chilly slopes 7,600 feet high, where scrubby grass and brush may persist for a generation after a field is used before giving way to pine cover, down to temperate frost-free zones where bananas, coffee, and mangos grow in spring-moistened groves and where a dense broad-leaf regrowth can overtake a fallow field within a few years of aban-donment.

Two kinds of grass are prevalent in the *Apas* land. One, confined to fields above 6,000 feet, is the thatch used in roof construction. It grows in fields not likely to be taken over quickly by denser brush. The second is a runner grass that drastically reduces field fertility. This grass has invaded half the farmland below 6,000 feet in the past thirteen years. Zinacantecos, noting the early prevalence of the grass along trails, believe its seed has spread in the manure of transport mules and horses returning from the lowlands, but it is more likely that its invasion is both a product and a·symptom of overuse of the land. The grass is not found in fields long unused, but it quickly in-vades a field plot after a year of corn farming. It forms a dense root network that strangles the corn in the second year of planting. Furthermore, it slows down regrowth in the fields it has invaded and requires that fields to be reused have particularly dense scrub or forest to ensure that firing the land will destroy the grass roots and seed.

Only one factor predicts field regrowth independently of altitude. Stoniness favors more rapid regrowth throughout the farming area with the exception of flat areas, where past generations have cleared the stones away. Although the stonier fields tend to be those with steepest slope, the relation between stoniness and regrowth holds inde-pendently of slope. Zinacantecos recognize that stony fields will most quickly recover from use. Their explanation is that stony land retains topsoil and humus better than otherwise similar fields.

Field slope, while correlated with stoniness, has no independent effect on the rate of field regrowth. Zinacantecos, however, highly value the scarce flat parcels at valley bottoms, which collect topsoil

and moisture and which can be farmed year after year without intervening fallow periods.

One other idiosyncratic factor of land fertility is accidental burning.
During the dry season, accidental fires are frequent. Set by travelers
of the highland-to-lowland trail to heat mealtime coffee, or for the
perverse pleasure of watching a grass fire, the blazes sweep through
unprotected fields, retarding but not destroying brush growth and
encouraging the invasion of grass. Since these fields may be burned
repeatedly by trailside fires, they are rendered almost useless for
swidden corn farming.

An astute Zinacanteco, aware of these influences on field fertility,
would have no difficulty in choosing at will the land he would own
for corn farming. He would favor land of the lower altitude zones in
a region where invading grass was not a threat, and he would select
first the flat valley bottoms and then rocky parcels of whatever slope,
providing that these were not near trails lest passersby set them afire.

Natives' understanding of the variations in field regrowth potential
makes it clear that the description of the fallow cycle for *Apas* land
requires a model of greater flexibility than does that for *Muk*ta hok*
land. An appropriate model, often used in actuarial statistics, specifies
the probability of an outcome when certain factors can be taken as
given. These conditional probabilities can be determined empirically
from recorded past events and can be tested for stability through time.
In the case of the *Apas* fallow cycle, the conditional probability of
choosing to cultivate a parcel can be examined for parcels of similar
regrowth capabilities and similar fallow status, when these factors are
taken as givens.

For analysis, the *Apas* land parcels were divided into three categories on the basis of informants' estimates of their inherent regrowth
capabilities. First are those fields that they judged could obtain
enough regrowth for cultivation after seven or fewer years of fallow,
and these fields are referred to as having "rapid" regrowth. Second are
fields of "gradual" regrowth requiring from eight to twelve years of
fallow. Fields with "retarded" regrowth require thirteen or more years
of fallow. Because of the very high correlation between regrowth rate
and altitude, these land categories can also be thought of as land zones,
the area of retarded regrowth being closest to *Apas* and the area of
rapid regrowth being farthest away.

Within each land category, fields were classified by their state in
the fallow cycle. Fields used for one, two, and three or more years
were grouped into three corresponding "in use" categories. Other
fields were classified as having been fallow for one or two, three or

four, . . . , nine or ten, and eleven or more years only when the length
of the fallow period was clearly defined by prior use.

Natives had provided data on the use of each of several plots, in
some cases back to 1940. Thus, each field could be defined in terms of
the above factors for each year in which there was adequate information. For the purpose of simplified analysis, the choice of whether or
not to cultivate a field was considered an annual one resulting in as
many outcomes per field as there were years in which there was
enough information to specify the factors. Finally, so as to highlight
the recent changes in intensity of land exploitation, these outcomes
were grouped by years. Outcomes for the years 1963 to 1967 were
grouped because the most dramatic decline in recent use took place
during that period (see fig. 2). Those of 1957 to 1962 were grouped
as representing the period of most intense recent use. Outcomes from
1953 to 1956 were considered the earliest reliable ones.

Figure 5 (for which fig. 4 is an indispensable key) shows graphical-
ly the swidden status of fields classified by land category, length of
fallow, and historical period of observation. (Quantitative data for the
graphs are in the Appendix.)

The size of the three leftmost columns in each subtype represents
the proportion of fields in use. Clearly, the recent decline of *Apas* land
use has involved land of 'gradual' and 'retarded' regrowth primarily,
while land of 'rapid' regrowth is being farmed in about the same
proportion as in earlier periods. Further, the proportions of land of
'gradual' or 'retarded' regrowth, which have been fallow longest and
thus are readiest for use in the 1963–1967 period, equal or surpass the
corresponding proportions during the preceding period of more intense
use. The current decline, therefore, is not the result of a temporary
scarcity of fields fallow for a long time.

The proportion of each column that drops below the baseline represents the proportion of fields in each fallow status actually cultivated.
Clearly, Zinacantecos do not follow a fixed fallow rule. As would be
expected, though, the probability of cultivating a field tends to increase
with the length of its fallow, at least up to a certain point. Moreover,
of fields actually in use, many are cultivated for more than one year
running.

The graphs illustrate trends in highland farming and help pinpoint
the nature of the recent decline in highland farming. In the case of
the first group of fields—those in which regrowth is 'rapid'—the likelihood of use of fields fallow for whatever length of time is shown to be
unchanging throughout the study periods. During the period of most
intense use, however, there was an increase in the proportion of fields

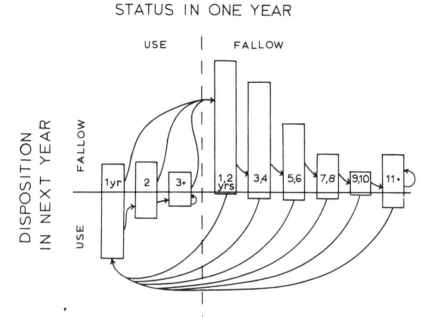

Fig. 4. Key to Figure 5. The diagram is a flow chart of fields through use and fallow status. Each column represents a field status. The leftmost column represents fields that are in their first year of use. The third column represents fields in their third or subsequent year of successive use. Columns to the right of the vertical division represent fields in fallow. Field statuses are grouped by pairs of years for simplicity, and fields fallow eleven or more years are grouped together.

The size of each column represents the proportion of fields in a given status. In the example, more fields were one or two years fallow than in any other status.

The proportion of each column below the horizontal base line represents the probability that a field in that status would be farmed in the following year. Arrows indicate the change of status for fields that, once fallow, are farmed or, once farmed, are let fallow.

Figure 5 displays a diagram similar to that of figure 4 for each of nine categories of field cross-classified by time period and regrowth rate. Quantitative data for the diagram are in the Appendix.

REGROWTH CATEGORY

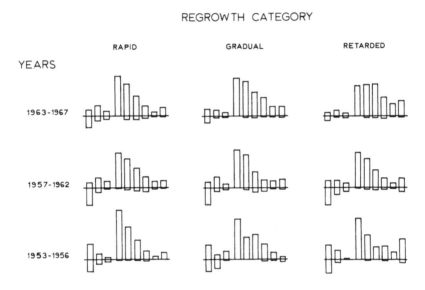

Fig. 5. Fallow Patterns in *Apas* Farmlands

given a second consecutive year of use, but a decrease in the proportion of fields given four or more years of consecutive use. In the most recent period of diminished highland farming, these fields of rapid regrowth seem to have received the same kind of use characteristic of the whole study period.

Fields in the middle category of regrowth rate reveal a slightly different pattern. Here again, the period of most intense use brought an increase in the proportion of fields given a second consecutive year of use. But fields entering their third year of use tended to be left fallow. Meanwhile, fields that had been fallow five to eight years were used quite frequently. Recent diminished use takes the form of a low rate of felling of long-fallow fields that are abandoned after a year's use.

Those fields that have the slowest regrowth also show a higher proportion of second- and third-year use in the period of greatest farming intensity, accompanied by a sharply increased rate of use of fields fallow eleven or more years. The subsequent decline has brought the greatest curtailment of use to this category of fields.

The general pattern that emerges from this breakdown is one in which farming has declined in intensity in all the highland tracts except those of most rapid regrowth. Areas of recent decline appear to have undergone heavy exploitation during the period 1957–1962, apparently at a level that has reduced their suitability for continued intense use. In some portions erosion has set in, a characteristic sign of Tzotzil land abuse that is most visible in Chamula (see chap. 5). In the more recent period, *Apas* farmers have compensated for the highland decline by expanding their lowland rental farming. In the highland zones of most rapid growth, however, farming operations give a return to labor and capital investment that competes with the returns provided by lowland rental farming (see chap. 6) and explains the sustained level of use.

OTHER TYPES OF LAND EXPLOITATION

Apas land is put to several other uses. These are of much smaller economic significance to the average household than corn farming but are nevertheless important aspects of the community's relation to the land.

The chief land-oriented activity of women is wood gathering (plate 6). Every morning, groups of women equipped with tumpline, billhook, and ax set out to bring back wood for the cookfires. In contrast to the situation in other hamlets like *Navencauk*, where women must seek firewood on their own or their husband's land, *Apas* landowners cannot refuse any woman the right to fell their trees for firewood. Once felled, the tree becomes the property of the woman who felled it, and she can return at her leisure to pack its sectioned branches and split trunk into bundles to carry back to store under the eaves of her home. Were another woman to be caught stealing wood from a tree she had not felled, she could be forced to replace the stolen wood.

Wood gathering, while a year-round activity, is most intense in the months of spring when the trails are dry and the days long enough for women to make up to three trips a day for wood. In other seasons, rain and slippery trails make more than one trip per day unpalatable, and other household activities are given greater attention.

The wood types available for cooking vary in the amount of heat they produce. Slow, hot-burning woods are preferred because they can be used for any kind of cooking. Cooler-burning woods, for instance, could not be used to cook ritual corn gruel. While the wood types used to be distributed much more evenly in the area near the community, the current distribution (see map 6) shows that women have exhausted the nearby supplies of the best wood types and have begun to use closer but less efficient substitutes.

In the lower portions of the land area untouched by frost, coffee

6. Pitch Pine Tree. Pitch pine for lighting fires is slashed from the fork of this tree. (Photo by author)

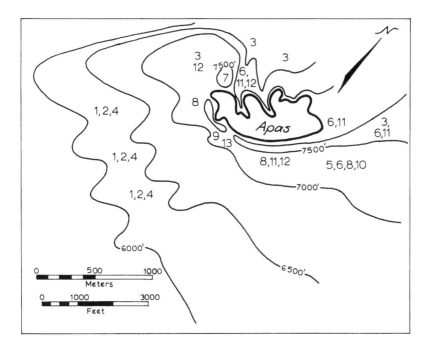

Map 6. The Location of Firewood near the *Apas* Settlement. Numbers
indicate the firewood types as follows. The best firewood: (1) *sap yok*
(*Quercus candicans*), (2) *baz*i te?* (*Quercus crassifolia, Q. polymorpha,
Q. mexicana*), (3) *cikinib* (*Quercus acatanangensis*), and (4) *tulan*
(*Quercus rugosa, Q. peduncularis*); less efficient firewood: (5) *pomos*
(*Holodiscus argentus, Ceanothus coeruleus*), (6) *toh* (*Pinus ocarpa,
P. montezumae, P. michoacana, P. oaxacana*), (7) *nukul pat*
(*Cupressus lusitanica*), (8) *xaxib* (*Acacia angustissima*), (9) *mes te?*
(*Baccharis vaccinioides*), (10) *k*an ic* (*Coreopsis mutica, Verbesina
neriifolia, V. perymenioides*), and (11) *?on te?* (*Arbutus xalapensis*);
least efficient firewood: (12) *nok* (*Alnus ferruginea*) and (13) *hom
?ak*an* (unidentified).

grows around springs that provide moisture throughout most of the dry season. Men of *Apas* harvest their coffee, usually the produce of three to five bushes, for household consumption and occasional sale. When ejido lands were first distributed, the existing coffee lands were reserved for those who had organized the movement or served on its committee in the earlier years. It was as a later political ploy of *Apas*'s recently deceased political boss, Romin Heronimo, that the inequity of coffee tenure was brought to the attention of regional ejido officials, resulting in equal distribution of the premium coffee parcels to all ejidatarios.

Yet another use of the land is the grazing of domestic animals. Many women keep sheep at night in small corrals near the home to be taken during the day to feed on grass wherever it can be found. While tending sheep is woman's work, one man owns a flock of sheep that he takes to the lower farmlands to graze on his trail-side parcel, which has come to bear heavy grass because of frequent accidental burning. It has been mentioned that horses, mules, and other domestic animals are allowed to forage freely over the farmlands, beginning in March and lasting until seeding begins. After that time, domestic animals must be tied or fenced to avoid damage to others' crops.

The land area serves a large number of additional purposes, too many to recount in detail. Hunters shoot deer, squirrel, and a variety of other game, which is becoming ever more scarce. Men and women gather wild berries, mushrooms, and other delicacies that provide seasonal variation in diet. While some herbs are cultivated near the home, other plants of medicinal and ritual value can be found only in the wild. The best examples of these are the pine bough and needles used in every ritual setting. Nearby mountains used to provide all the timber and materials needed for house construction. But today, house timbers must be hauled from several miles away, while commercial substitutes for other materials are becoming more common. The oldest informants can remember the time when timber was plentiful enough to fire lime kilns to supply the hamlet with lime for cooking the corn. Thus, many of these additional uses are becoming memories as the land area is exhausted of its resources by overuse.

CONCLUSION

In the land use of *Apas* we have explored one facet of a system of traditional highland life that is, as subsequent chapters show, semi-autonomous, exhibiting internal organization with characteristic features that are conditioned by an environment extending from the local to beyond the regional. The farmland is identified with the hamlet and integrated with it as a source for cooking fuel, fodder, hunting grounds, and other resources essential for a partly self-sufficient, isolated hamlet life. Farming is in the traditional swidden pattern with a fairly regular cycle of land-use practices that would feed the hamlet were its population smaller and stable. But it is not. Increasingly so, rising human needs require that local harvests be supplemented by lowland rental farming. It is because the lowlands provide four-fifths of hamlet income that the highland farms retain their value in Zinacanteco eyes. The lowlands are a safety valve that buffer the demands that growing population would otherwise place on local resources. Although highland resources are dwindling, their value is still appreciable. Thus, expandable rental operations in the lowlands are the external condition that permits population to rise, while highland patrimony is farmed through traditional swidden patterns.

The highland farm zone is the locale of the Zinacanteco life way. We will explore further the degree to which such a locale can be considered part of the environment of that life way. We shall see that farmland is a socially valued commodity whose distribution strongly shapes Zinacanteco family processes. To this extent the farm zone is part of the environment of Zinacanteco tradition—but only a part; for, as subsequent chapters show, Zinacanteco life ways are as profoundly shaped by regional and national attributes and processes.

CHAPTER THREE

LAND AND THE FAMILY

I N thinking about their highland fields, Zinacantecos do not divorce technical facets from the social facts of their use. Fields are farmed by families, adjacent fields commonly have been divided between brothers, and the subdivision of larger tracts often mirrors the complicated ancestry of many related families. To understand land use, we must explore family life.

Kinship commonly patterns social relationships of many kinds so as to give societies a characteristic appearance in which certain kinds of social groups predominate. When many activities in a system are kin based, stable family patterns maintain the traditional configuration of social groups. What, then, are the factors that give shape to family life? Land tenure is one factor. To understand family life, we must explore how land is used.

Thus, family life and land use affect one another, and through the analysis of their interaction one can hope to uncover the processes that underlie a society's traditional patterns of social organization. Indeed, existing theory and the perspective of comparative studies in many parts of the world strongly support this assertion. This chapter will review studies of the mechanisms by which land tenure can affect kinship by developing a model in which scarcity of land and emphasis on descent-based kinship are causally related. Then, a comparison of kinship and land-tenure variants in several Maya communities will set the background for the detailed analysis in the chapter to follow of how the dynamic interaction of property and kinship structures social life in *Apas*.

THEORETICAL CONSIDERATIONS

How may kinship and land tenure be related? By way of introducing theoretical and substantive answers to this question, let us contrast two explanatory elements. The first stresses the conflict between those who compete for rights in land. The second emphasizes the solidarity of those who hold land jointly. The conflict or solidarity of land users is the link between their land tenure and kinship.

Competing claimants necessarily invoke principles to legitimize their interests. Clear-cut principles that all accept point to unequivocal resolution of conflicting claims. Kinship often limits the succession of rights in property from one individual to another by linking succession to descent, and though kinship facts are sometimes a matter of dispute, descent principles usually are not. A small colony of settlers will apportion abundant land without conflict, but as its population grows and land becomes scarce, conflicting claims should enhance descent-based principles, clearly defining the lines of legitimate succession. Correspondingly, the significance of descent-based social groups should be greater where land is scarce (see fig. 6).

By contrast, the solidarity of groups whose interests are in shared resources should decrease if the resources cease to have value. Solidarity comes from sharing and certainly is reinforced by the unity with which members confront poachers. Kin groupings will be solidary if united in use and defense of valuable property. But if membership grows to the point where a share is too small to be of much value, the significance of such groups will decline (see fig. 7).

That land pressure should undermine the solidarity of the very kin groupings it creates through conflict is a paradox that can be understood by considering the severity of resource scarcity. It is for groups settled in abundant lands that pressure on resources requires rules of succession like those based on descent principles. Only severer land shortages undermine the solidarity of descent-based groupings. The two explanatory elements combine into one curvilinear[1] model relating the importance of kin-based social groups to the entire range from abundance to shortage of land (see fig. 8).

Existing land-tenure studies do lend qualified support to the model combining the conflict and solidarity principles. The support appears to be of two kinds. First, there is theory, such as Meyer Fortes's discussion of unilineal descent groups, which explains why descent-based kinship is so useful a device for succession to land and for lending coherence to political, economic, and ritual organization. Second are the instances in which the model obtains support from comparative studies within delimited geographical areas. M. J. Meggitt's survey of New Guinea materials demonstrates that principles of agnation (patrilineal descent) are stressed in areas where land is scarce. Ward H. Goodenough's findings in Polynesia that nonunilineal descent groups are enhanced by land pressure do not, as it might first

---

1. The model is curvilinear because in it the dependent variable (stress on descent) first rises and then falls. The model is depicted as two straight lines because theory does not tell us what shape the curve should have.

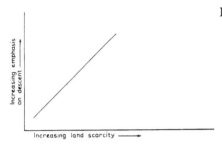

Fig. 6. Conflict Model. Conflict over scarce resources is resolved by descent principles.

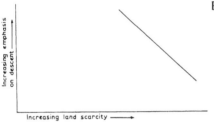

Fig. 7. Solidarity Model. Solidarity of descent-based kin groups breaks down as their land resources become inadequate.

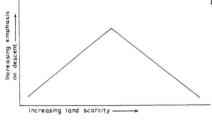

Fig. 8. A Synthesis. A curvilinear model combines the conflict and the solidarity principles.

appear, invalidate Meggitt's results but rather with them lends support to the curvilinear model relating descent systems to land pressure.

But there are several serious qualifications that limit the generality of the model. For one, there are the agricultural societies that lack descent-group organization altogether, notably peasant systems as described by George M. Foster. These show that land pressure and descent-based kinship have no necessary relation to each other. For another, as Meggitt has pointed out, cross-cultural validation requires formulation of any model in terms general enough to permit application to a wide variety of societies and yet precise enough to cope with the special characteristics of different geographical regions. To date, the model is still best couched in terms appropriate to controlled comparison within geographical regions. Thus, a meaningful cross-cultural test awaits formulation. Finally, there are logical difficulties that beset the test of a hypothesis as powerful as the simple curvilinear model we have developed.

The genealogical diagram in figure 9 helps illustrate Fortes's (1953) explanation of the functions of unilineal descent systems. With unilineal descent, shared ancestry traced through only one sex of parent defines group membership. The lineal descendants of some individual (say A) form a group that is discrete from any other group of lineal descendants from another individual not in his line (say B). By contrast, in a cognatic or bilateral system (fig. 10), where ancestry is traced through either sex parent, the descendants of any given individual may well form a group that overlaps with another's group of descent. It is easy to see that unilineal descent maps out discrete groups in which membership may come to mean more than merely shared genealogy.

Political, ritual, and economic features are frequently linked to unilineal descent and fused into a descent group's corporate organization. Further, if a property owner's lineal heirs customarily coreside on his lands, the descent group will form a distinct and stable residential unit. In such a situation, assets may be treated as though owned corporately by a group that outlasts the lifetime of member individuals, potentially in perpetuity.

Within and between such groups, genealogy may also provide a metaphor for status and ranking. Branches within a descent group may be recognized as internal segments with founders who share lineal ancestry. Ranking of segments can be in terms of genealogical closeness of the segment founder to the group founder. "Brother" segments may be deemed equals or be ranked by relative age. Nested subdivisions within segments may be of subordinate status as "children" to the "parent" group. The hierarchy implicit in unilineal genealogical structure may be carried over into other domains, giving meaning to political relations and significance to the morphology of local groups. Thus, it is not surprising that, in societies with corporate unilineal descent groups, genealogical charters are often of great importance, frequently being juggled to maintain a good fit with the perception of existing hierarchical group relations.

The utility of unilineal descent for sustaining corporate organization is obvious. In relation to land, a unilineal descent principle could reduce conflict by defining rights to land unambiguously. Fortes has pointed out that unilineal descent groups are "most in evidence in the middle range of relatively homogenous, precapitalistic economies in which there is some degree of technological sophistication and value is attached to rights in durable goods" (1953, p. 24). Unilineal descent groups are not ordinarily found in societies where people live in small groups, depend on rudimentary technology, and have little durable property. And they tend to break down in societies that develop a modern economic framework with occupational differentiation, productive capital, and a money-based medium of exchange. Thus, unilineal descent organization appears to be a viable alternative to a statelike structure with many functions, including that of regulating access to property. In principle, then, existing theory (as well as many excellent West African examples, such as Fortes 1945, 1949; Evans-Pritchard 1940; Bohannon 1953, and many others) support the idea that descent-based kinship can be a useful vehicle for regulating land tenure.

Substantive examples in the literature support the hypothesis of a relation between land pressure and stressing of descent principles. Meggitt's analysis of New Guinea cases explicitly relates stress on agnation (patrilineal descent) to population pressures. Goodenough's survey of Malayo-Polynesian examples reaches the conclusion that nonunilineal descent groups are elicited by land pressure, while unilineality may characterize more sparsely populated societies. Although the conclusions of Meggitt and Goodenough appear contradictory, the differences between them can be resolved through the model developed here.

Meggitt's analysis begins with residence variations in clan parishes of the closely related Mae-, Laipu-, and Taro-Enga groups (1965, pp. 10–11). In a sample of six parishes, the three having lowest population density have higher-than-average proportions of nonagnatic resident kinsmen; by contrast, of three parishes with denser population, two have lower-than-average proportions of nonagnatic resident kins-

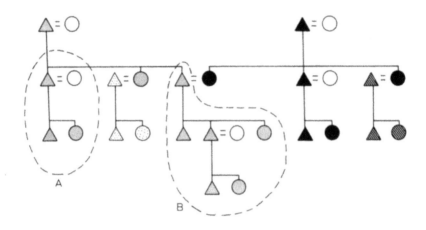

Fig. 9. Unilineal Descent. The genealogy is drawn with lines of descent through males only. The principle of patrilineal descent assigns each individual to one and only one descent tree, resulting in descent groups that do not overlap. Within the largest descent group, two subdivisions, potential segments of the group, are formed by descendants of the individuals labeled A and B.

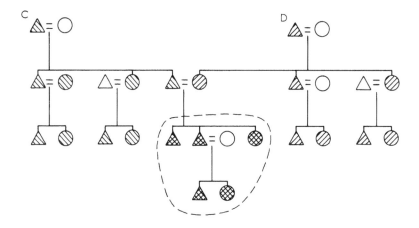

Fig. 10. Nonunilineal Descent. The genealogy contains individuals
related exactly in the same manner biologically as in figure 9, but
descent lines are drawn to indicate that individuals can trace ancestry
through parents of either sex. Hatching indicates the descent groups
of individuals C and D. Individuals within the broken circle are in
both descent groups, illustrating the fact that nonunilineal descent
groups have overlapping membership. Any individual potentially
belongs to as many nonunilineal descent groups as he has ancestors.

men. This skimpy but suggestive evidence is buttressed by an analysis of Mae-Enga local group dynamics. Local-descent groups are in constant competition for scarce land, conveniently defined by agnatic ideology as ancestral territorial domains. Larger (and denser) descent groups are better equipped to meet the expectations of their role in local organization, particularly in defending their own territorial integrity and in seizing the territory of other groups. And they readily redefine their genealogical charters so as to allow agnatic ideology to best conform to their true situation. These groups tend to exclude non-agnatic kinsmen from scarce lands even as they export their own members, who seek land rights for their offspring by taking up non-agnatic residence in the less densely populated territories of other descent groups.

In his conclusion, Meggitt extends his general argument by controlled comparison to include other New Guinea societies. Ranking fourteen cases according to population density and agnation, he finds the relation illustrated in figure 11 a strong positive association of emphasis on patrilineality with pressure on land resources (1965, p. 279).

Meggitt's examples fit well with the conflict explanation of the link of descent groups to land. New Guinea swidden farmers have laid claim to all virgin territories and are beginning to exhaust lands in the most densely populated areas. Conflicts over land range from threatened to actual seizure. Claims are couched in terms of agnatic descent whose principles are crucial both for defining the groups that should hold lands jointly and for excluding would-be poachers from ancestral lands. Here descent-based kin groups are buttressed by the growing land shortage.

Goodenough (1955, 1956) deals with Malayo-Polynesian societies and their presumed evolution from a common prototype, which, according to G. P. Murdock's reconstruction (1948, 1949), had bilocal extended families, bilateral kindreds, and the absence of unilinear kin groups. Goodenough adds that individual rights to land depended on membership in two kinds of kin group. One was an unrestricted descent group including all the descendants of an ancestral landowner. The other was a descent group with membership restricted to the landowner's descendants whose parents remained resident on the tract after marriage. In both cases, descent through both sexes of parent was recognized, descent therefore being nonunilineal.

Yet many modern-day Malayo-Polynesian societies have been described as patrilineal or matrilineal. Goodenough argues that a group of prototypic organization moving into an area of abundant land could

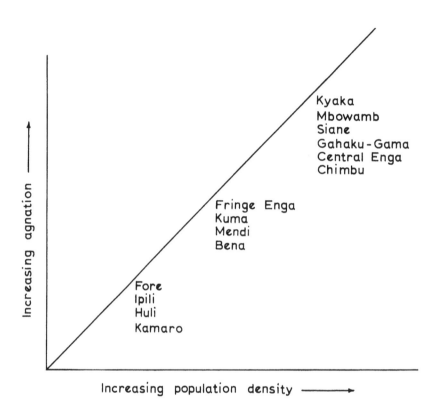

Fig. 11. Agnation and Population Density in New Guinea. (Adapted from Meggitt 1965, p. 279)

change from bilocal to unilocal residence; and over time the composition of local groups would thereby appear the result of unilineal descent, patrilineal in some cases, matrilineal in others, according to the residence preference.

While unilineal systems could develop in the context of ample land, strict adherence to unilineal principles would result in inequities in land distribution. For, through random variation, some unilineal groups would grow in numbers while others would shrink. Such inequities would lead to conflict unless other mechanisms developed to redistribute people or access to land. Use rights might be transferred outside the landowning group. Or adoption might transfer land-poor individuals to richer groups. Or unilinear groups could become non-unilinear and bilocal once again, allowing individuals to choose residence with and membership in the better-endowed of their parents' descent groups. Goodenough gives examples of these and other solutions. In every case, land pressure results in the breakdown of unilineality.

At first glance, Goodenough's conclusions appear to contradict those to be drawn from New Guinea, for he suggests that land pressure leads to the breakdown or modification of unilineal descent. But the different conclusions can be reconciled.

For one, Goodenough's observation that unilineal principles will result in conflict over land because of inequities in distribution fits New Guinea materials well. Indeed, Mae-Enga descent groups are in constant competition for each other's lands. When one group seizes lands of another, population is redistributed. and the groups' genealogical charters are altered to fit new realities. Thus, agnatic ideology may be enhanced by the very conflict that nonunilineal systems avoid.

For another, Goodenough's conclusion that unilineal descent groups faced with extreme land pressure may give way to nonunilineal groups fits the idea that land pressure can undermine the solidarity of descent-based groups. Thus, the land pressure that Goodenough is concerned with may be beyond the point tolerated by New Guinea groups organized on principles of unilineal descent but well within the range in which unilineal descent would disappear.

Thus, the contradictions between Meggitt's and Goodenough's conclusions are resolved by the model combining conflict and solidarity as the links between land pressure and kinship. Both studies give substantive support to the model, suggesting that it has cross-cultural relevance. But several qualifications make it difficult to accept that conclusion so easily.

Despite theory emphasizing the utility of unilineal organization for middle-range agricultural societies. the example of many peasant societies seems to rule out any necessary relation of such organization to land tenure. Most peasant societies lack unilineal descent groups; individual rights to land are better explained by residence in domestic groups than by membership in kin groups that are shallow and ephemeral. Peasant villages are often corporate (Wolf 1955, 1957), excluding outsiders from access to land. Thus, locality is the usual basis for peasant organization rather than descent-group membership. Yet, as Foster (1961) has pointed out, peasant societies are comparable in size, technological level, and subsistence patterns to those Fortes associates with unilineal descent; they differ in their external relations, being semiautonomous in relation to a state that structures political, economic, and ritual organization. Foster suggests that ego-centered networks of dyadic contracts of reciprocal exchange at the local level complement the organizing functions of the state. Casual organization, therefore, can fulfill the same functions as unilineal descent. In short, there are demonstrable alternatives to organization of middle-range agricultural societies on the basis of descent.

The difficulties of typology and definition inherent in cross-cultural validation further qualify the generality of our model. As the example of peasant societies suggests, there are types of society in which land rights are not distributed through kinship but by sale, rental, or other mechanisms. Yet to exclude examples on typological grounds is to risk oversimplification. Definitional problems further complicate the picture. The test variables of land pressure and descent-based kinship must be defined generally enough to apply cross-culturally and yet sensitively enough to avoid misinterpretation of specific examples. Land pressure, for instance, cannot be defined in terms of per capita acreage alone, for soil fertility, technological level, alternatives to farming, and perception of subsistence needs all vary among societies and across geographic zones. Nor can stress on descent be measured easily without distinguishing between local organization and apparent ideology (which may not be coordinate). Typological and definitional problems are interrelated, definition being most difficult when divergent examples are not excluded on typological grounds. The method of controlled comparison reduces both problems by confining study to an area of geographic or cultural uniformity in which societies are likely to be of the same type and variables are easier to define. But controlled comparison limits the generality of one's conclusions. As Meggitt has pointed out, the test variables we are concerned with have not been defined well enough to apply cross-culturally, and generalization of the conclusions suggested by controlled comparison must await theoretical refinements.

A final qualification is that the hypothesis of a curvilinear relation between land pressure and descent-based kinship (fig. 8) is difficult to test because of its power. In so far as the test variables are difficult to define or measure precisely, examples in their middle ranges will be difficult to evaluate. Depending on whether they are deemed to have land pressure lesser or greater than the threshold at which descent principles break down, they may be interpreted as confirming or disproving the hypothesis. In the preceding discussion, for instance, interpretation of Meggitt's and Goodenough's materials could be questioned on these grounds, and a definitive evaluation of their materials is beyond the scope of this book. The curvilinear model, therefore, has dangers in its elegance.

FAMILY AND LAND IN THE MAYA AREA

A general comparative perspective points to succession of rights in land as the human problem through whose solution land scarcity shapes kinship. Now a more selective comparative perspective will underscore the features of solutions characteristic of Tzotzil and other Maya societies.

Controlled comparison (Eggan 1954) of variations among societies that share cultural history and geographical setting distinguishes the unique from the general features of a process. We will develop a controlled comparison of man-land relations in six Maya communities both to test and illustrate the man-land model we have developed and to highlight the features we should uncover among the Tzotzil. In four of them (Chichicastenango, Santiago Chimaltenango, *Apas*, and Chan Kom), swidden agriculture dominates the economy. In two (Chamula and Amatenango), farming is eclipsed by wage labor and craft specialties. That family organization in the first four should reflect the principle of patrilineal descent, while in the latter two kinship is bilateral, reflects a functional connection between kinship and land use. The substance of this connection appears linked to Maya inheritance customs and beliefs about the obligations between parents and children. This key relation is viewed in comparative perspective among the Maya here, and in the microscopic details of *Apas* social organization in the chapter following.

The human life forms that are found in the Chiapas highlands exhibit a number of patterns that are characteristic of a much larger area, that which Mesoamericanists have designated the Maya culture area. Peoples of the area speak languages that historical linguistics have demonstrated as descendant from a common language stock. In blood type, stature, and other physical features they exhibit similarities suggestive of a common genetic stock. Virtually all are subsistence corn farmers who utilize the slash-and-burn or "swidden" system of agriculture. Furthermore, they share many features of social organization: a settlement pattern of loosely aggregated hamlets focused on an administrative and ritual center, a tendency toward local social groupings based on patrilineal kinship, a ritual organization incorporating complementary functions of organized priesthood on the one hand and shamans on the other, and a complex cosmological ideology emphasizing divination on the basis of calendrics. Finally, archeologists have demonstrated that these patterns are deeply rooted in the area's prehistory.[2] Because of the coherence of these patterns not only today but also in the past, scholars have seen fit to treat life forms of the area as belonging to a spatial and temporal unit much akin to the ecologist's biome, implying not only that external factors have affected it uniformly but also that functional relationships found between patterns in one portion of the unit are of significance in other portions as well.

This discussion assumes that the Maya area is indeed such a unit, comprehending the Maya language speakers of Guatemala and Mexico, and it explores the relationship found within the unit between subsistence systems, on the one hand, and family forms, on the other. Thus, it relates to one another two characterizations often made of the unit as a whole. The first, largely accepted by Mayan scholars, is that the subsistence system was and is based on the cultivation of corn and beans in a swidden type agricultural system. The second, not so widely accepted by scholars, is that Mayan social structure was and is characterized by patrilocal extended families, patrilineages, and, in some cases, fully developed patriclans.

Everywhere in the Maya area corn and beans are the staple diet, the staff of life. Yet there are important variations to be found in Maya subsistence patterns. There is no doubt that swidden farming in the highlands differs from that in the lowlands, for instance, requiring differential adaptation to the rates with which regrowth will restore an abandoned field's fertility. Additionally, there are variations in farming technology ranging from fluid, shifting swidden exploitation to intensive horticulture of fixed property parcels. Variations in population density render some areas so well endowed with land that anyone can farm it and other areas so poorly endowed that significant proportions of the population must engage in wage labor or other enterprises to generate income with which to purchase food. It is this variation in land availability that is one of the two variables in our general model.

The near universality of patronymic naming system among Maya speakers is the most general evidence we have for the implicit importance of patrilineal descent to the Maya. Yet there is significant variation in the way in which family patterns are structured into patrilineal kinship. In some areas economic, residential, and social groupings evolve around a core of men related to one another in the

2. In taking this position, I follow the general argument behind Vogt and Ruz's *Desarrollo cultural de los Maya.*

male line so coherently that they can be treated as corporate entities with respect to the transmission of property in inheritance and the exchange of women in marriage. At the other extreme are the areas in which no significant economic, residential, or social groups are structured on the descent line emphasized by patronymics; rather, groupings are bilateral, taking equal cognizance of descent traced through either sex, or nonlateral, having no relation to descent at all. We will focus on the manner in which variations between these extremes of Maya social organization may be related to land availability.

The materials that follow are derived from ethnographic studies of six Maya communities: three located in the Chiapas highlands, two in the Guatemalan highlands, and one in Yucatán. These studies have been selected because they provide excellent information on property transmission as well as on the domestic cycle in each case—crucial evidence because it suggests a plausible mechanism by which family forms could be related to and perhaps derived from land-tenure systems. The design of the study will be macroscopic, characterizing each community by way of its typical, normative, or most frequently exemplified family and property tenure patterns. As such, the relationship between land tenure and family form that will emerge will take little account of variations within the communities, although the following chapter will demonstrate by microscopic study that such internal variations are subject to explanation by means of the same principles that emerge from the macroscopic study.

Chichicastenango

Chichicastenango is a large township of Quiché speakers located in the western highlands of Guatemala (see map 7), a community that was studied by Ruth Bunzel (1952) during the early 1930s. It consists of a ceremonial center famous for its weekly markets and of a vast number of outlying hamlets in which intensive agriculture is the principal economic activity. The land is rich, producing cash crops of wheat and vegetables in addition to corn and beans for both subsistence and export.

From Bunzel's evidence, it appears that farm property is at the root of Quiché social structure. Land tenure is intimately related to the domestic cycle and to Quiché patrilineal ideology. Landownership is a symbolic requisite of mature male identity and of status within the community. In native theory, paternal ancestors own the land, and their descendants, the current users, must pay them "rent" in the

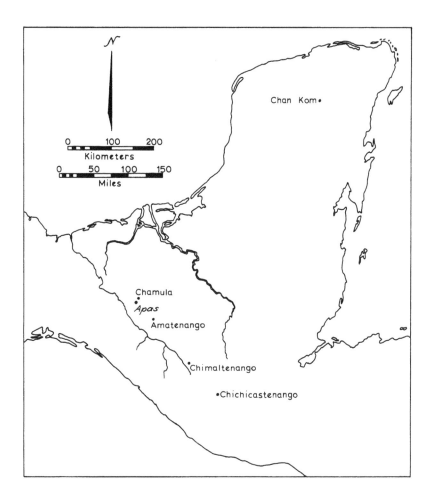

Map 7. Six Mayan Communities

forms of candles and incense consumed in the frequent agricultural rituals. Land should not be alienated from the male line of descent, for instance by sale, except through elaborate ritual propitiation of the ancestors. In many respects, then, land is a sacred symbolic component of Quiché concepts of descent. But, for our purposes, it is instructive to see how transmission of land property from living owners in one generation to those of the next actually takes place.

In the domestic cycle, the unmarried son works jointly with his father and brothers, all living together under one roof. When a son reaches puberty, his parents initiate his courtship, selecting his bride and beginning the payment of a substantial bride price to her family in the form of luxury produce delivered to them on ritual occasions over a number of years. When the payment is complete, the young couple are married, and they take up patrilocal residence within the house of the groom's father. These early married years are a period of trial for the young couple. The groom continues to farm in strict subordination to his father and elder brothers; the young bride is tested by her female in-laws, who burden her with the most strenuous household chores. Even the birth of two or three children to the young couple brings them no independence until the domestic group disperses in a crisis precipitated by a son who will not tolerate subordination any longer.

The crisis unfolds dramatically when one of the sons suppliantly petitions his father for permission to leave the home. The father meets the request with rage, accusing the son of disobedience and disrespect. Brothers mutually accuse one another of self-interested manipulation of family resources, resurrecting long-standing rivalries and hostilities. The father calls in witnesses—elder paternal relatives—to hear the formally traded accusations. He ritually flogs the disobedient son who would depart from the home, and then he forecloses the crisis by deciding with the witnesses how best to divide up all his farm property.

The property distribution is primarily to his sons, who should inherit land equally. The usual pattern is for the eldest son to retain the father's home; other sons will receive house plots, and all brothers cooperate in the construction of new houses. When construction is completed, the extended family breaks up, each son moving into his own house. From this time on, each son acts as the head of an economically independent household. The eldest son assumes the responsibility in the parental home, supplanting the elderly father in his position of leadership. Indeed, Bunzel interprets the domestic group dispersal as one in which the sons have relegated their father to the status of an ancestor, for while they visit him periodically with ritual gifts, they actually cooperate with him now in very few ways.

Bunzel's description of Quiché domestic-group dispersal is of particular value because it focuses on the psychodrama that links property and inheritance to interpersonal relations within the Quiché family. Especially salient are the patterns of authority and control, and the complementary attitudes of obedience and respect, which attain between the core males of the family reflecting the importance attached to descent. Unfortunately, ethnographic descriptions of the other communities to be examined do not depict interpersonal attitudes with comparable insight, requiring their inference from typical interpersonal behavior for comparison between communities. To assess these attitudes of intergenerational control and respect between males, we shall examine each community with respect to four questions, summarized in table 1. First, is it the pubescent son or his father who makes the selection of a young man's bride and initiates his courtship? (In Chichicastenango it is the father.) Second, is the newly married son economically dependent upon his father in the years following marriage? (The Quiché pattern is of marked dependence.) Third, do fathers manipulate land inheritance so as to elicit obedience and punish their sons' disrespect? (Bunzel implies Quiché adherence to the principle of equal distribution of property to sons despite their attitudes.) Finally, is the period of postmarital residence in the paternal home for a young couple lengthy? (While the pattern in most Maya communities is for at least a short period of such residence to follow upon marriage, the typical Quiché groom can look forward to several years of such residence.) It is clear that, for Chichicastenango, these measures adequately reflect the importance of authority and respect, control and obedience as critical attitudes in the operation of the domestic cycle.

Despite the strength of Bunzel's treatment of Quiché interpersonal attitudes, her monograph supports only inference of the statistically most frequent forms of family organization summarized in table 1. The Quiché ideal is for a son who has left the home to establish residence patrilocally, and apparently most sons do live close to their parental home on inherited plots. Although Bunzel gives no data on the distribution of Quiché family types, her descriptive treatment indicates that extended households are common, often housing several married sons living together with their father. Because these fracture totally with the crisis of dispersal, however, residential clusters of patrilineally related kinsmen do not appear to have corporate character either socially or economically.

TABLE 1. *Behavioral Measures*

	Chichicas-tenango	Chimal-tenango	Apas	Chamula	Amatenango	Chan Kom
Individual who selects a young man's bride	Father	Father	Son	Son	Parents	Parents
Is a son dependent economically on father after marriage?	Yes	Yes	Yes	No	Occasionally	No
Do fathers manipulate inheritance to elicit obedience and respect?	No	Yes	Yes	No	No	No
Typical period of residence in groom's paternal home following marriage	Several years	Several years	2–3 years	None	Sometimes 1–2 years	None

Note: Behaviors reflect descent-based attitudes of control, authority, obedience, and respect.

TABLE 2. *Typical Forms of Family Organization*

	Chichicas-tenango	Chimal-tenango	Apas	Chamula	Amatenango	Chan Kom
Ideal pattern of post-marital residence	Patrilocal	Patrilocal	Patrilocal	Patrilocal	Where economic advantage is greatest	Patrilocal
Typical pattern of actual post-marital residence	Patrilocal	Patrilocal	Patrilocal	Patrilocal	Random	Neolocal
Existence of joint households of father with married son	Common	Common	Common	Rare	Occasional	Rare
Existence of joint households of father and several married sons	Common	Occasional	Occasional	Rare	Rare	Rare
Salience of descent-based social aggregates beyond the domestic group	Little	Little	Great	Little	None	Little
Salience of descent-based economic aggregates beyond the domestic group	Little	Great	Great	None	None	None

Santiago Chimaltenango

Located in the Cuchumatán Mountain range to the west of Chichicastenango and just east of the Mexican-Guatemalan border is Santiago Chimaltenango, a township of Mam speakers with most of its
population concentrated in its ceremonial center. Although land there
is somewhat poorer than in Chichicastenango, not permitting the cultivation of cash crops, it is fairly abundant and constitutes the basis
for the principal economic activity, corn farming. In poorer families,
farming is supplemented by wage labor on distant haciendas or
plantations.

The distinctive feature of Chimaltenango's social organization is the
large, localized family groups found there, groups whose members
share patrilineally inherited surnames and who are related to one
another primarily in the male line. Such a group will encompass the
households of a group of brothers, male paternal cousins, sons, and
grandsons—together with their wives and unmarried daughters—all
living contiguously. But these groups rarely function as corporate
units. Rather, Charles Wagley, who studied Chimaltenango in the
1940s, saw them as a statistical outcome of the operation of the domestic cycle within individual households.

This is how Wagley's explanation runs. As in Chichicastenango,
sons farm with their father during and after puberty, marry a bride
selected by him, and continue to live with him for an extended period following marriage. But, in contrast to the Quiché pattern, a son's
request to leave the parental household does not precipitate division
of the father's property. While the father gives his son a nearby plot
for house construction, he does not relinquish his farmland. Instead,
he loans farmland to his sons on a year-by-year basis, retaining title
and control over the property until his advanced age or death. Thus,
even long-married sons depend entirely on their father for land to
farm, and they vie with one another to curry their father's favor, both
in annual distribution of land for use and for its ultimate distribution
as inheritance. As he advances in age, the patriarch will indicate how
his estate is to be divided, often bestowing exceptionally large shares
upon particularly favored heirs; these expressed wishes are binding on
the actual inheritance distribution.

As a result of this practice, there are many mature family heads in
Chimaltenango—some with married sons—who have no farmland to
claim as their own; they are dependent upon an aging patriarch whose
wish is effectively their command. They dare not quarrel with their
brothers lest they incur the patriarch's displeasure. Nor can they leave

the community as full-time wage laborers without jeopardizing their inheritance. Such a state of affairs is enough to explain the dominant pattern of large, localized family groups strongly related in the male line (see table 2) and to reflect why the community ranks high on measures of intergenerational control and respect (table 1), as we would expect in any situation where the sons' economic future is dependent on their father's good graces.

Apas

A third example in our survey of Maya land tenure, inheritance, and family organization patterns is from within the Tzotzil-speaking township of Zinacantán, in highland Chiapas. It is the variations within one of the township's constituent hamlets, *Apas* (plate 7), which are subjected to microscopic analysis in the following two chapters; generalizations that can be drawn from treatment there, however, typify patterns of the township at large.

Apas exhibits features of family organization and inheritance that are most similar to those found in Chimaltenango. Although native theory calls for equal distribution to sons of a man's farm property, favoritism is the word that best characterizes the actual interplay of land inheritance and the domestic cycle. After puberty, boys marry girls of their own choosing and live temporarily in the paternal household, moving out as younger brothers marry, but continuing to cooperate with their father and brothers in farm work. As each son leaves the household, the father may distribute piecemeal plots for house construction and farming to them, but only if he deems them worthy and loyal. Ultimately, a son's inheritance of property is conditional on a final symbolic token of his respect and obedience, the sharing of the father's funeral expenses.

The differential treatment of sons in the distribution of living sites results in a diversity of residence in *Apas*, but the overall tendency is for dispersing domestic groups to settle down in a pattern of clusters of houses owned by men related patrilineally, usually brothers living on house sites near the parental home. Within such a group, households may be economically independent in farming, symbolized by separate storage of corn for each household; but the group members may cooperate in farming, as they most certainly will in ritual, especially the *cargo* ritual of the father or other group members. We describe these groups as patrilineal-patrilocal extended family groups, as larger local-descent groups, and occasionally as localized patrilineages in *Apas* and other Zinacanteco hamlets (see table 2); and we know, as well,

7. *Apas*, a Hamlet of Zinacantán. (Photo by author)

that within such groups the fundamental attitudes between patrilineal kinsmen of authority and respect, control and obedience are salient in day-to-day family life as well as in ritual (see table 1).

San Juan Chamula

Adjacent to Zinacantán is the Tzotzil township of Chamula (plate 8), which was studied by Ricardo Pozas Arciniega in the 1940s and early 1950s (cf. Pozas 1959). Chamula stands out among the highland Chiapas native communities as having the largest and most densely distributed population and the most heavily eroded land, a feature that will be studied in chapter 7. Chamula's farmlands are so depleted that the typical family cannot rely upon farming alone for subsistence. Economic specialization in small household industries to produce trade goods (including pottery cookware, woolen fabric, cheap pine furniture, crudely distilled cane liquor, musical instruments, and many other items) and wage labor on lowland farms and plantations are mainstays of family income. What viable farmlands remain among

8. Chamula Center. The vacant-type ceremonial center of Chamula houses only current civil and ritual officials. (Photo courtesy of Harvard Chiapas Project and Cía. Mexicana de Aerofotos, S.A.)

the continually eroding hills are highly fragmented by an inheritance system in which all offspring of a couple, regardless of sex, inherit equal portions of each parent's estate.

Pozas reports that it is the son who usually initiates mate selection, whereupon the arrangements for courtship and marriage are settled upon through the use of a go-between. After marriage, the groom works for his father-in-law for a short period and then moves to live near the home of his youth in a house constructed immediately after marriage. Although this home is located patrilocally, it is economically independent from the start; as a result, localized family groups are shallow and unintegrated. There seem to be very few mechanisms by which a Chamula father can retain control over his sons after they marry, for they can readily resort to wage labor or economic specialization for their support. Thus, in almost every respect, Chamula patterns of family organization and typical Chamula intergenerational attitudes of control and respect contrast with those assessed in tables 1 and 2 for the other communities we have examined.

Amatenango del Valle

Yet another highland Chiapas township is Amatenango del Valle (plates 9 and 28), a Tzeltal township in which pottery making is the renowned economic activity, supplemented by wage labor and some farming of very scarce land (Nash 1970).

In the domestic cycle, the young married couple may choose whether to live for a period of about two years in the home of the groom's parents or that of the bride's, selecting the household that is economically better off. Later, they will move into a house built adjacent to either of the parental households. Inheritance of scarce farmland and village property is bilateral, the ideal being to provide each child with at least a parcel for house construction; when their village holdings are too limited to permit endowment of each child, parents will favor unmarried daughters over sons in land distribution, as males are thought better equipped to earn cash to purchase land through wage labor. Many young couples must live where purchased land can be found, while the more fortunate are equally likely to live near either parental home. As a result, Amatenango has no unilateral residence groupings at all. Thus, as in Chamula, ownership and use of lands is not an effective mechanism by which parents can control the younger generation, and patrilineal descent has expression in little other than patronymic naming.

Chan Kom

Finally, we can turn to the Yucatec community of Chan Kom, which was studied by Robert Redfield and A. Villa Rojas (1934) in the earlier part of this century.

Chan Kom was founded in the 1880s by a small group of people who splintered off from nearby Ebtún and settled themselves in long-fallow, untitled national lands. Initially, the unused lands were cleared and farmed by anyone for the short period of years that the lowland environment permits, then abandoned to fallow. But, once labor had been invested in clearing the best virgin land, use rights became effective property rights for the first users. Nevertheless, Redfield's study found marginal lands still available for farming by whoever wished to clear and thus claim them.

The nuclear family household, consisting of a couple and their immature children, was the predominant social and economic unit to be found in Chan Kom. Of thirty households, only two were extended families in which a father and his married sons lived and worked together as a unit. In the other twenty-eight cases, young couples had set up independent households immediately after marriage, and only a minority chose to live patrilocally in the communally owned village settlement. Despite the looseness of residential and affiliation patterns associated with the communal nature and easy availability of living and farm sites, however, Chan Kom exhibited a tendency to emphasize kin relations in the male line, especially in the case of two larger family groups—which the ethnographers called "great families"— which functioned in opposition to each other in local-level politics.

Significantly, these "great families" traced their descent back to the town's original settlers, whose early takeover of the best nearby farmlands gave their descendants every reason to claim inheritance of their use rights when good land became scarce at a later date.

The six ethnographic sketches above provide a reasonable sample of variations in family organization and the domestic cycle in the Maya area. Tables 1 and 2 summarize measures of the strength of expression of patrilineal descent in each community as seen in interpersonal attitudes and overt social groups. The overall importance of patrilineal descent for these attitudes and overt behavioral patterns is summarized in the first two lines of table 3. Meanwhile, we must review the ethnographic evidence showing the relative importance of land for farming income (as opposed to other sources of income) in each community, abstracted in the third row of table 3.

In four of the six communities, there is objective evidence that land is available for agriculture in amounts adequate for support of the typical family and that farming clearly outweighs other endeavors as a source of family income. Just the reverse is true of the remaining two communities of the sample. Bunzel notes that one Quiché household with less extensive farm property than most families held an equivalent of 238,000 square feet of land; the figures for average holdings in Chimaltenango, *Apas,* and Chan Kom, in thousands of square feet owned per household, are 490, 97, and 248. By contrast, the comparable figure for Amatenango private holdings is 14.5, plus a roughly equal additional amount derived from Mexican land reform. Figures are unavailable for Chamula, but the high density of its population and the heavy erosion of its land justifies its being classed with Amatenango as having typically small farming estates. The relative importance of household industry for family income in these two communities, however, is great, while none of the other four communities have any significant trade-good economic specialization. Finally, the relative importance of wage labor for income is great only in Cha-

9. Amatenango Center. The ceremonial center of Amatenango contains most of the township's population. (Photo courtesy of Harvard Chiapas Project and Cía. Mexicana de Aerofotos, S.A.)

TABLE 3. *Overall Assessment of Patrilineal Emphasis and Land Availability*

	Chichicas-tenango	Chimal-tenango	*Apas*	Cha-mula	Amate-nango	Chan Kom
Kin groups beyond the domestic group organized on the male descent line are predominant?	No, but there are large patriarchal families	Yes	Yes	No	No	Some
Intergenerational attitudes of control and respect, authority and obedience are strongest in the male descent line?	Yes	Yes	Yes	No	No	No
The community is substantially supported by adequate farmland?	Yes	Yes	Yes	No	No	Yes

mula. Some wage labor is reported for Chimaltenango, *Apas*, and Amatenango, but little or none for Chan Kom and Chichicastenango. An overall economic assessment clearly singles out Amatenango and Chamula as the two communities almost totally dependent upon household industry and wage labor, while the remaining four appear to have adequate lands to support community members.

Between the summary variables in table 3, a certain relationship seems to hold. Family organization into units deeply extended in the male line, reflected in local residential clustering or otherwise, and interpersonal attitudes of authority, respect, control, and obedience between patrilineally related kinsmen are confined to communities with substantial farmland, while the two communities almost devoid of patrilineal emphasis have almost no land at all. This leads to the hypothesis that, in the Maya culture area, patrilineal emphasis in social organization is strong where land is highly valued as a resource and is available in amounts great enough so that it can serve as a mechanism, through inheritance, for binding together the affairs of a man and his heirs. Only Chan Kom fails to fit the hypothesis perfectly, and, there, the lack of emphasis on patrilineal kinship relations can

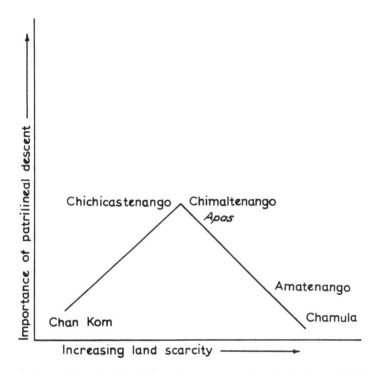

Fig. 12. The Fit of the Maya Examples to the Curvilinear Model

be attributed to the superabundance of its land. Thus, the six communities can be arranged between the variables of descent and land in a manner that supports the general curvilinear model (see fig. 12).

Assuming that this model validly accounts for macroscopic variations in family systems viewed across communities within the Maya culture area, will it serve to explain microvariations in these patterns within a community as well? This question, which is broached in the later analysis of patterns in *Apas*, is methodologically important. For the sample of communities we have examined here has not been controlled for size, history, or any number of factors both internal and external to each community that might account for the variations. Yet the hypothesis postulates that it is the inheritance mechanism and domestic-group process that combine to account for the variations found. This connection must be found valid at the microscopic level as well if the influence of other uncontrolled variables is to be discounted.

Finally, we must recognize in our general model a second example of how a stable process depends upon external conditions. Family life retains traditional forms in which resources of social value and roles in domestic units are in stable relation to one another despite the constant flow of maturing individuals through domestic statuses. A fixed level of population density giving resources a stable social value is a condition permitting kinship principles, domestic processes, and the resultant configuraton of social groups to endure. Of course, human populations tend to grow. to compete with surrounding populations for resources. Thus. external conditions influence the balance that a population achieves with its resources and. through them, the stable forms that the social system will assume. In the Maya area, we have seen examples in which external conditions limiting access to resources have shifted the equilibrium of kinship from patrilineal to bilateral in populations that are expanding.

CHAPTER FOUR

LAND INHERITANCE IN *APAS*

Wᴇ have seen that Zinacantán may be classed with other Maya communities exhibiting lineage-based local organization apparently derived from agricultural land tenure. The hypothesis has been developed that land ceases to be a free good when brought under swidden cultivation and becomes scarce, and hence valued, as the exploiting population becomes dense; it suggests that patrilineality will be emphasized wherever land is valued for agriculture and can serve as a mechanism, through inheritance, for binding together the affairs of a man and his heirs. This idea reflects the perspective from land-tenure studies elsewhere, in which property and unilineal kinship organization are functionally related through the domestic cycle. Microscopic analysis of family organization and land tenure in *Apas* will demonstrate that land tenure does indeed promote emphasis of patrilineal descent through the mechanisms of inheritance. But the analysis will go further to elucidate two mechanisms, inheritance by women and land sale, which counterbalance the emphasis of patrilineal descent. The social structure of the community, then, will be seen as reflecting a kind of equilibrium between two countervaling tendencies. Finally, the impact of a variety of other factors capable of displacing the point of equilibrium between the opposing trends will be introduced to suggest how the community's social structure is likely to change.

THE MORPHOLOGY OF SOCIAL GROUPS IN *APAS*

As a hamlet, *Apas* holds a position within the Zinacantán township essentially similar to that of other hamlets. Hamlets are administrative units directly subordinate to the township center; each has men who fill distinct roles of tax collector, land committeeman, school representative, and so forth for the community and who represent the hamlet in the ceremonial center. Further, each hamlet has recognized elders to whom disputes that cannot be settled in the family are sent for mediation before the disputants turn to township officials for arbitration. Ritually, each hamlet has sacred shrines visited by shamans for curing and agricultural rites. In addition to these formal attributes,

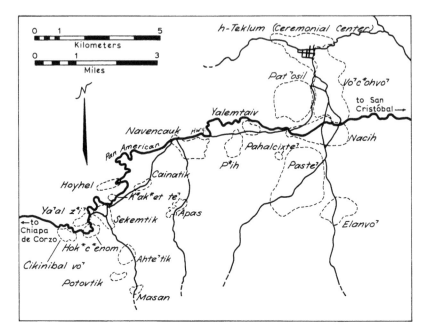

Map 8. Hamlet Settlements of Zinacantán. (After Vogt 1969, p.156)

hamlets, being spacially circumscribed, are the outer bounds for
activities limited to near neighbors. Marriage, for instance, usually
takes place within the hamlet, and in marriages between hamlets, it
is the bride who usually leaves home. These patterns cause virtually
all kin relationships, especially those based on patrilineal descent, to
be confined to the hamlet. Ordinarily, then, the hamlet is the lower
limit of township-wide organization and the outer bound of most
kinship activity.

Internal organization of the Zinacanteco hamlets has been described
best by Vogt (1969) as assemblages of people "into three basic social
units of ascending size, the domestic group living in one or more
houses in a compound, the *sna*, consisting of two or more domestic
groups, and the waterhole group, composed of two or more *snas*."
Superimposed on these groups is the characteristically Maya pattern
of patronymic naming.

The Domestic Group in Apas

A domestic group is a collection of family members who produce and
consume as a unit. The unit is formed when a married man sets

up his own household, and it will come to include all women joined
to them by marriage and the children they bear. Ordinarily, individuals leave the domestic group if, as is customary for women, they
marry into other groups, or when men married for a few years
formally set up their own household. Members of the domestic
group always live within one compound, and they usually live under
one roof. Their economic activities are directed by the senior male
toward production of the common corn supply for food and for
market exchange for other consumption goods (plate 10).

In 1963, *Apas*'s population of 644 lived in 142 domestic groups, each
of them separate households of composition ranging as shown in
table 4. Clearly, the two-generational elementary family was the
most characteristic type, and others can be seen as having derived
from it through the domestic cycle.

The Sna *in* Apas

Although the smallest functioning unit within the hamlet is the
domestic group, economic cooperation and close kin ties often extend
outside it to unify a cluster of patrilineally related domestic groups.
Such clusters form as young married men, following a preference for
patrilocal residence, set up households of their own on sites provided
from their fathers' estates. In most Zinacanteco hamlets, the entire
neighborhoods surrounding such dispersing clusters are referred to as
the *sna*, or "home," of that cluster's lineage. In most hamlets, members
of each *sna* join together twice yearly in ritual demarcation of their
territory. When this happens, nearby domestic groups that may be
linked to the *sna*'s dominant cluster by marriage become ritually
merged to it.

In *Apas* some, but by no means all, neighborhoods are designated
as *sna*s, taking on a name designating the neighborhood's dominant
family cluster, as shown in map 9. Indeed, only about half the village
households are included in such groups. Furthermore, *sna*s in *Apas*
differ from their counterparts in other Zinacanteco hamlets in having
no corporate ritual functions. It is important, however, not to under-
rate the groupings in *Apas* that are termed *sna*s. In a community
where a man's high aspirations are to head a line of descendants who
will honor and respect him, the designation of a neighborhood as his in
kinship and leadership is worthwhile recognition. Of all the local
groups found in *Apas*, the *sna*s are the best organized and most tightly
knit; they are also the basis of grassroots political organization, serving
as the nuclei of local factional groupings.

10. Small Clusters of Homes in *Apas*. (Photo by author)

TABLE 4. Apas *Domestic Groups in 1963*

Type of Household Composition	Number
One-generational	
Man and wife	8
Unmarried siblings	3
Women living together	5
Divorced or unmarried woman, alone	15
Man, divorced, alone	2
Two-generational	
Elementary, in formation	60
Elementary, in dispersion	21
"Extended," with one or more married children	5
With father dead, mother alive	5
Other	4
Three-generational	
With both paternal grandparents	3
With paternal grandmother only	9
Other	2
Total	142

Water-hole Groups in Apas

Most hamlets have several named water sources, limestone sinks or springs that are operative seasonally or continually. They support drinking, washing, and watering of animals by the households of the nearby *snas*. Twice yearly, these water-hole groups unite in ritual for the source, and their solidarity is reflected in application of the water-hole name to the entire immediate territory of its users.

In *Apas*, however, water-hole ritual does not partition the social universe. Although each neighborhood makes day-to-day use of the most convenient water source, the entire hamlet joins in ritual for all its water holes. In this regard, then, *Apas* differs from other hamlets in which water-hole groups have been discussed by Vogt (1969) as quasi-kinship aggregates possibly serving to unify several related lineages into hypothetical clans.

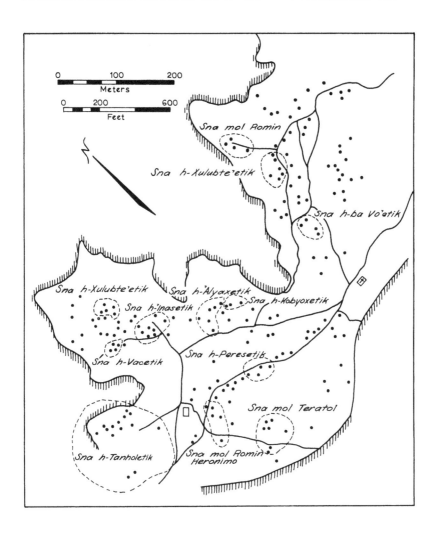

Map 9. *Sna* Aggregates in the *Apas* Settlement

Patronymics and Nicknames in Apas

Zinacantecos use a system of patronymic naming to trace patrilineal descent in the manner found generally in the Maya area. At baptism the infant assumes (a) one of a set of Spanish-loaned first names and takes on for life (b) the Spanish and (c) the Tzotzil surnames of his father. Women do not change their name at marriage, nor are their surnames passed to their offspring. Thus, for example, if a man, *Marian Peres Tanhol* ($a<1> + b<1> + c<1>$), and a woman, *María Lopis Ciku* ($a<2> + b<2> + c<2>$), marry, their offspring will bear for life an indeterminate first name and the surname pair *Peres Tanhol* ($a<i> + b<1> + c <1>$). Since the Tzotzil surnames ($c<k>$) form mutually exclusive sets, each set linked with only one Spanish surname ($b<j>$), and since Zinacanteco marriage is exogamous with respect to Tzotzil surname, any Zinacanteco's patrilineal kin are confined to others who share his linked surnames, although this group may include individuals with whom no genealogical link can be remembered.

In *Apas*, the bulk of the population is included in fifteen patrilineages, groups of people who share linked Spanish and Tzotzil surnames and who can trace common descent from a known ancestor. The genealogy of a group of married men who make up the core of a representative lineage is shown in figure 13 and it illustrates, as well, features of a system of nicknaming used in *Apas* as an alternative to reference by means of patronymics. Apparently, nicknames are humorous appellations acquired by a man and passed on to his descendants unless these in turn acquire nicknames of their own. The genealogies show that, when descent is traced back through one or more generations from a group of individuals sharing a nickname to a common progenitor, only intervening relatives who also shared the nickname will be encountered. As such, nicknames can be thought of as defining subsets within the patrilineage that are segmented from one another by descent; hereafter, we shall refer to them as nickname groups and as lineage segments interchangeably, and subsequent sections will make use of a measure of lineage cohesiveness or solidarity based on the degree to which it is segmented by nicknaming.

In a general way, then, the morphology of social groups in *Apas* is similar to that found elsewhere in Zinacantán and bears a close resemblance to that of social groups found in many Maya communities. The pattern is one of local aggregates based on lineal descent. In their simplest form, these aggregates may correspond to the elementary family domestic group; increasingly broad aggregates are focused on

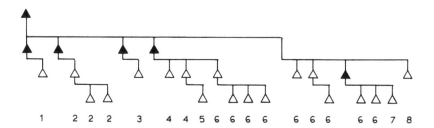

Fig. 13. The Distribution of Nicknames in an *Apas* Lineage. Nineteen living married men of the lineage make up eight nickname groups. Dead men are shaded. Nicknames are indicated by arbitrary number.

increasingly comprehensive lineal segments: the local-descent group, the localized lineage, and, in some cases, the clan. That such groups are bound together through control of land resources is a hypothesis that the following case study of *Apas* will support.

A DESCRIPTIVE MODEL OF INHERITANCE IN *APAS*

Inheritance in Zinacantán usually involves two stages. After heirs marry and as they set up independent households, they should receive a share of those goods essential for a livelihood, land on which to live, minimal housewares and clothing, corn and beans to last until the first harvest, and, when available, land to farm and a mule or horse for transportation. At a later date, when parents die, transmission of goods to the heirs is completed when they divide up the remainder of their parents' property.

Ordinarily, one's heirs are one's children, who are expected to hold respect for and to uphold certain obligations to their benefactor. Children must recognize the burden of their upbringing. Sons should prove worthy of inheritance by working unstintingly at family farming before and after marriage, by obedience, and by circumspect and proper behavior toward their parents. Both sexes should share in the expenses of an aging parent's illness, death, and burial, and they must honor his soul after death.

These qualities of an heir are not fortuitous but reflect the delicate balance of resources that is sought as the domestic group begins to disperse. Up to the time of marriage, when a son brings his wife home to work under his mother's direction, he represents a drain on family resources for food, clothing, treatment of illness, and a portion of the bride price paid during a two-year courtship—outlays only partly returned by his help in farming after puberty. When he asks to leave home, his father faces not only loss of two workers who more than earn their way but also a decrease in his assets and working capital if he is to provide the couple with living essentials. By helping his sons in this way, he jeopardizes his own economic security and his ability to pay for illness in old age and death. To protect himself, he extracts a pledge of his heirs' loyalty and support as a condition for inheritance and distributes a portion of his property to bind the pledge. He rewards heirs with goods in proportion to their demonstrated fidelity while retaining enough property to support himself and to provide additional inheritance at death. He seeks out respected witnesses to whatever distribution of goods takes place. And he emphasizes that the heirs must not quarrel over shares thus given fairly. In all these ways, he attempts to strike a balance that maximizes the solidarity of family members to whom he must turn for support after dispersal has taken place.

It is adherence to these principles that underlies the exceptions to the rule that one's heirs are one's children. An adopted child will share in the patrimony on an equal footing with stepsiblings if he is willing to assume the obligations of an heir, and it is common for an elderly person without children to pledge his property to a young couple who promise to care for him in old age as actual children would. On the other hand, a child whose parents separated could not expect to inherit from a father who had not raised him without reaching a special accord and relation with him, agreeing to share in his burial expenses. Finally, a child who scorned his parents' authority could lose his inheritance privileges completely.

Of the inheritance goods, land is the most valuable. First, there is the settlement area, called the "fenced" land, formed by the houses and their nearby gardens and set apart between a canyon on one side and a mountain ridge on the other. Second is mountain farmland granted the township under nineteenth-century land law and thus termed "communal" despite its division into privately owned parcels. Finally, "ejido" land was expropriated from nearby ranches under recent land reform and granted in hectare plots to cooperating villagers who refer to it as "stolen" land. The inheritance of each land category varies according to its use and to law. Since even a domestic group headed by a female must own a house site, both sexes have rights to inherit land of the settlement. A man who distributes residential parcels he and his wife own will designate small parcels for his daughters, especially the unmarried ones and those whose husbands cannot provide a house site. Upon his death, his daughters (or their husbands) should receive shares of the remaining land in proportion to their contribution to burial expenses, but the bulk of residential land usually goes to male heirs. Exploitation of private farmland, however, is by men, and women receive it as inheritance only when there are no male heirs. Ordinarily, it is distributed to a man's sons in portions reflecting the esteem he holds for them, or, after his death, in proportion to their share of burial expenses. Ejido farm parcels would be distributed as private land if law did not require that they be transmitted intact from owner to one heir.

It is usually the request of a married son to leave the home that triggers off the process of land distribution. Sometimes urged on by a wife dissatisfied with working for her in-laws or aggravated by tensions with his brothers, he faces taking the full responsibility of farming independently. Recognizing the strains for the parents of losing their labor, the young couple plan carefully the best opportunity for making the ritual request. The moment arrives, and they kneel crying before the seated parents, offering a gift of the strongest liquor to lend force to their plea to see if they can bear their poverty, their misery, alone. (In Zinacantán, every request is accompanied by a gift of liquor and by self-debasement of the suppliant.) The dismayed father tries to ferret out the angry words or unjust deeds that provoked the request, but the couple deny provocation, claiming initiative and responsibility for the idea. Once the parents accept the liquor and the request, they must decide what goods can be spared for the departing couple. Together they agree on witnesses to the division of goods, which should include a house site, a share of the last harvest, and cookware. If there is an empty house in the compound, the young couple borrow it until they can build for themselves. Otherwise, the two families will live under one roof, using separate cookfires, housewares, and food until the new house is completed.

At the departure of the first son, the father may choose to make a general distribution to his heirs. Otherwise, he gives to each son as he leaves the home, unless the sons as a group agree to risk seeming insolent in asking for property. Wherever the initiative comes, distribution follows the pattern of division of goods for one son. Each son buys liquor to present at the request, at which time the father extracts oaths of loyalty and pledges of support in his old age. Respected elder kinsmen or community officials are selected as witnesses and honored with the father at a meal financed by the sons. The party then sets out to divide land parcels as the father prescribes, using the measuring rope that has been handed down from the original ejido division by each hamlet ejido representative to his successor to assist in parcel division. By taking a measurement and doubling the equivalent rope length into equal segments, points are established that divide opposite borders of an affected parcel into equal line lengths. The points are then connected together by boundary lines cleared at once by the recipient of each portion and marked with small piles of rock. As the party moves from one location to another, the heirs ply father and witnesses with drink and vie with words to demonstrate their worthiness and respect. The father gives each heir his portion and specifies which property he will retain until death. Often, he will reserve the share of the youngest son, who will live with his parents after marriage and take over their household property at their death. When the distribution is complete, the group returns to the father's home where he and the witnesses are feasted once again by the heirs.

The partial distribution of a man's estate is completed after his death. But at that time the first order of business is the funeral. Grief-stricken, the family members pool their cash and borrow additional funds, choosing one among them to purchase a coffin, five or ten gallons of liquor, several cartons of cigarettes, and a large supply of candles. They hire musicians to help keep the wake and prepare fifteen or more chickens and an enormous supply of tortillas to feed mourners of the hamlet. After the body is placed in the coffin, it is carried to the graveyard and buried with grave goods needed by the soul in afterlife.

While the substantial burden of funeral expenses may be offset by savings of the deceased, the remainder is borne by the heirs. A typical funeral costs nine hundred pesos, not much less than an average farmer would net in a year. Females, whose work is in the home, supply the chickens and whatever cash they can spare. Males, however, supply the bulk of cash, which they take from their savings or borrow, using their inheritance as collateral. If they cannot raise enough money, they must sell the father's estate to supply it. At the time of the funeral they contribute as they can, keeping careful record of cash amounts. Later, they divide up the cost among them.

The death of a family head necessitates reorganization of his domestic group. Usually his wife survives him and continues to raise his immature offspring, retaining his estate until her death. She, too, must be buried by her husband's heirs, who then are free to divide up their father's estate. They do so in proportion to their contribution to the cost of the two funerals. Heirs who will not share the funeral costs fairly can be taken to court, where they face loss of their inheritance.

In addition, heirs who are not children establish definitive right to their portions by sharing in the funeral costs.

After the parents' death, ritual obligations of the heirs continue. Upon expiration, the soul of the deceased leaves his body and retraces the routes of its journey through life for three days, while heirs light candles at the head of the grave. For thirteen years thereafter the soul rests in the grave by day, leaving it at dusk to labor for God's forgiveness and returning with the dawn. Sundays and saints' days are days of repose when women come to the graveyard to light candles, the soul's food, and decorate the graves with flowers. Each year at the Feast of All Saints the souls of the dead revisit their homes, and the living deck household altars with luxury food whose essence is consumed by the wandering souls. In the graveyard, graves are adorned with flowers and laden with fruit, and children of the dead gather in groups to relax and drink together. Year after year, each group of heirs is brought together in this remembrance of the dead, which inevitably reaffirms the solidarity of the living (plate 11).

LAND AND THE SOLIDARITY OF LINEAGES

The foregoing description of Zinacanteco inheritance patterns shows land tenure is related to a complex web of beliefs and expectations. The hypothesis that transmission of land through inheritance promotes descent-group solidarity seems congruent with this web of ideology. But it is possible to demonstrate that more than a qualitative system of belief links landholding to lineage solidarity: by considering the lineage as the unit of analysis, an ordinal measure of lineage solidarity will be shown correlated to a similar measure of lineage property holdings.

Nickname groups, or lineage segments, will provide a measure of solidarity within the lineage. One lineage will be defined as more solidary than another if its segments' average size is larger than that of the other lineage. Consider, for instance, the genealogy of household heads shown in figure 13. The 19 living married men are segmented by nickname into eight groups; the average size of segment is thus 2.38 individuals. When a comparable figure is computed for the fourteen remaining *Apas* lineages containing at least two descent groups, the lineages can be ranked ordinally by segment size from least to greatest, as shown in table 5. Since two lineages tie for fourth and fifth position in the ordinal rank, the rank assigned to them is 4.5; by the

11. Todos Santos Rites. A descent group at the grave of their benefactor. The fruits and liquor are to feed his soul at the Feast of All Saints. (Photo by author)

TABLE 5. *Lineages Ranked by Segment Size*

Lineage Number	Rank Order of Segment Size
1	1.0
2	2.0
3	3.0
4 ⎫	
⎬	4.5
5 ⎭	
6	6.0
7	7.0
8 ⎫	
⎬	8.5
9 ⎭	
10	10.0
11 ⎫	
12 ⎪	
⎬	12.5
13 ⎪	
14 ⎭	
15	15.0

Note: The lineage with the largest average segment is no. 1; that with the smallest average segment is no. 15.

same token, two lineages tie for position 8.5 and four for position 12.5. Thus, the rank-order variable of segment size is a crude one at best, but it will serve our purposes.

The selection of average segment size as a measure of lineage solidarity may seem somewhat arbitrary. But other criteria help validate its use.

First, a finer measure of closeness of genealogical relation will establish that nicknaming segments incorporate individuals whose lineal relationship is close. Figure 14 illustrates how the genealogical distance between two lineal kinsmen may be computed as the number of steps connecting them via a common ancestor, where each step is an ascending link from a son to his father. The unit of analysis in the accompanying matrix is every possible pairing of two married household heads within each of the fifteen lineages. The matrix characterizes each such pair of individuals by the lineal distance between them and by the fact that they do or do not share a nickname. Clearly, the large deviation from expected values according to the matrix margins

(a)

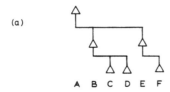

A   B   C   D   E   F

(b)

	A	B	C	D	E
B	1				
C	2	1			
D	2	1	2		
E	1	2	3	3	
F	2	3	4	4	1

(c)

Genealogical "Distance" between Dyad Members

	1	2	3	4	5	6	7	
Dyad members are of same name group	29 (+16)	54 (+27)	23 (+5)	21 (-18)	41 (-20)	51 (-8)	4 (-2)	223
Dyad members are of different name group	3 (-16)	12 (-27)	21 (-5)	76 (+18)	112 (+20)	97 (+8)	10 (+2)	331
Totals	32	66	44	97	153	148	14	554

Fig. 14. Genealogical Distance. (*a*) Hypothetical genealogical tree including six men labeled A, B, C, D, E, and F; (*b*) Matrix showing the genealogical "distance" between A, B, C, D, E, and F; (*c*) Matrix showing the genealogical "distance" between all dyads of within-lineage relationships in *Apas*. (Deviations from expected values according to marginal distributions are in parentheses. Goodman and Kruskal's G = 0.471)

indicates a strong degree of relationship between nicknaming and genealogical distance. Another way of expressing this relationship is to note that kinsmen who share a nickname are separated by an average genealogical distance of 3.72 steps, while those differing in nicknames are, on the average, 4.85 steps apart. Furthermore, this relation is not an artifact of the distribution in just one or two large lineages; it reflects the pattern observable in almost all the lineages when tabulated separately. Thus, nickname groupings prove to correspond well to this more sensitive measure of formal genealogical connection.

Second, name-group membership can be shown related to divorce, which fosters fission within the lineage because sons who leave the father's home in a separation as immature children have little opportunity later to establish solidary ties with their father and with future brothers. In the fifteen lineages, there are thirty-four sibling sets containing at least two brothers. Table 6 characterizes each such set's offspring of just one, or more than one, marital union. The evidence shows clearly that, when there is divorce in one generation, there is likely to be nickname differentiation in the next.

Finally, the degree of patrilocal residence within a lineage has a relation to nickname-group membership. Patrilocality is the general rule for postmarital residence in *Apas*, but there are occasional exceptions. The proportion of domestic groups that exhibited patrilocal residence was computed for each lineage, and this figure was converted into a rank-order variable reflecting each lineage's relative conformity to the patrilocal residence norm. When this rank variable is compared

TABLE 6. *Nickname Sharing in Sets of Brothers*

	Having One Mother	Having More Than One Mother	Total
Sharing one name group	23 (+3)	4 (−3)	27
Differing in name group	2 (−3)	5 (+3)	7
Total	25	9	34

Note: Deviations from expected values according to margins are shown in parentheses. Goodman and Kruskal's G = 0.87, indicating, in this case, that there is 87% more agreement than disagreement between the rankings of sets of brothers with respect to shared mothers and name group.

with that of lineage segment size (see table 7), the two are found to have a moderate degree of covariation. In other words, where nickname groups of a lineage are large, its domestic groups show more than the ordinary strong preference for patrilocal residence.

To summarize, the use of average size of nickname group as a measure of lineage solidarity is justified in three ways: (1) by the degree of close kinship linking members sharing nickname; (2) by the likelihood that, if there are children of a broken marriage, they will be distinguished in naming from their half-brothers; and (3) by the association between name-group size and patrilocal residence.

To test the hypothesis that landholdings promote lineage solidarity, lineages will be ranked according to the magnitude of per capita landholdings in the area referred to as "communal" land, consisting of private farm plots. There is good reason for excluding tenure of settlement and ejido land as measures of lineage property.

Ejido holdings were obtained by hamlet males under the national

TABLE 7. *Patrilocality and Name-Group Size*

Lineage Number	Size of Name-Group Rank	Proportion of Patrilocal Residence Rank
1	1.0	3.0
2	2.0	4.5
3	3.0	10.0
4	4.5	7.0
5	4.5	1.0
6	6.0	2.0
7	7.0	7.0
8	8.5	14.0
9	8.5	14.0
10	10.0	11.5
11	12.5	7.0
12	12.5	14.0
13	12.5	11.5
14	12.5	4.5
15	15.0	9.0

(Spearman's rank-order correlation = 0.482)

Note: Lineages are ranked by name-group size and by the proportion of patrilocal residence of their members. In the latter case, the greater the conformity to the patrilocal residence norm, the lower the rank.

land-reform program shortly after 1940. Each participant was granted, in theory, four hectare-sized parcels expropriated from mestizo
ranches. Actually, some plots were made larger to compensate for
poor land quality or to fill in the gaps created between rectangular
parcels by the topography. The policy of the program is that each
tenant must select only one heir to receive his ejido holdings at death.
Further, participants who are remiss in contributing the ejido administrative tax can lose their holdings to nonparticipants who agree to
assume the tax obligations. Hamlet members are fully aware of these
principles. Ejido parcels were distributed to seventy-one men. Of these,
thirty-four retain their plots, eight have lost them to others through
default of taxes, and twenty have passed on their holdings intact to
one heir at death, but only nine have divided their holdings among
sons in violation of program policy. Clearly, only the latter twenty-
nine holdings were inherited in any way, and only in the last cases
would their transmission have contributed to the solidarity of the
heirs. Because the principles of ejido transmission are outside the traditional system of tenure and because so few ejido holdings have
passed from one generation to the next, there seems no reason to expect the ejido to have influenced lineage solidarity. On the other hand,
while inheritance of parcels within the settlement area is in accord
with tradition, it is complicated by inheritance by women, whose heirs
are ordinarily of another lineage than they. This problem will be
treated separately later in the chapter.

Consideration of tenure of private farmland involves far fewer
problems. Data on the history of tenure was established by tracing
ownership of each modern parcel back to the limits of memory of several informants. Table 8 is a summary of the forms of transmission
that the private holdings underwent during each decade since 1900.
The table shows that transfer of ownership in all periods except the
most recent was predominantly in the male line, making it a plausible
mechanism for promoting lineage solidarity.

A measure of lineage land property was constructed by considering
the recent history of each private farm plot. If its most recent owner
inherited or purchased it from another member of his lineage, the parcel was deemed to be of his lineage. In a few cases, however, the most
recent owner had inherited or purchased his plot from a person of a
different lineage. In these cases, the parcels were assigned to the lineage that had owned the parcel for the longest time (usually the lineage of the seller), since that lineage should have benefited in solidarity most from its tenure. The areas of each lineage's parcels were

TABLE 8. *Property Transfer Modes through Time*

| | How Parcels Were Transmitted | | | | |
Time Period	Directly from Father to Son(s)	Indirectly from Father to Son(s)	Out of Patriline by Inheritance	Out of Patriline by Sale	Total
1960–1967	3	1	1	10	15
1950–1959	15	15	9	7	46
1940–1949	15	9	4	5	33
1930–1939	13	0	3	5	21
1920–1929	8	3	3	4	18
1910–1919	10	0	6	2	18
1900–1909	8	1	4	5	18
Pre-1900	5	9	4	3	21
Total	77	38	34	41	190

summed and divided by the number of present living household heads to control for lineage size. Finally, the lineages were ranked according to the magnitude of this estimate of per capita lineage holdings.

In table 9 the rank of each lineage's solidarity as measured by name-group membership is compared to the rank of per capita private land-holdings. The rank-order correlation indicates a substantial degree of correspondence between ranks. In other words, lineages that have larger than normal name groups are usually the lineages with more extensive per capita landholdings.

To recapitulate, there is a positive correlation between the mean size of a lineage's name groups and the extent of its landholdings. The relation between name groups, on the one hand. and the close genealogical connection and patrilocal emphasis in residence of their members, together with name-group fission of offspring of divorced parents, on the other hand. suggests that lineages with large name groups have greater patrilineal solidarity. Thus, there is a correlation between lineage solidarity and the extent of its landholdings to the degree that name-group size is a good measure of solidarity. While correlation does not imply cause, the hypothesis that lineage solidarity is promoted by land tenure is supported not only by the correlation but also by the philosophy and principles of *Apas*'s mechanisms of land inheritance. This finding is exactly that predicted by the solidarity element of our general model (see figure 7).

TABLE 9. *Landholdings and Name-Group Size*

Lineage Number	Size of Name-Group Rank	Per Capita Land-holdings Rank
1	1.0	10.5
2	2.0	1.0
3	3.0	7.5
4	4.5	2.0
5	4.5	4.0
6	6.0	5.5
7	7.0	3.0
8	8.5	9.0
9	8.5	5.5
10	10.0	14.0
11	12.5	7.5
12	12.5	14.0
13	12.5	12.0
14	12.5	15.0
15	15.0	10.5

(Spearman's rank-order correlation = 0.624)

Note: Lineages are ranked by name-group size and by the amount of per capita landholdings. In the case of the latter rank, the greater the per capita holdings, the lower the rank.

TENURE BY WOMEN AND SALE

While most land parcels change hands by inheritance in the male line, two other mechanisms, inheritance by women and sale, have the potential of counteracting the solidary influence of land upon the lineage.

In distributing inheritance, most landowners advise their heirs that land should not be sold. But land is sold under certain circumstances. When a married man cannot inherit a house site because his father's estate is too small to divide or because he has quarreled with his father, he will purchase land on which to build a house. With a gift of liquor, he and his wife visit a man known to have extra settlement property, requesting him to sell them a house site. Under these circumstances, it is difficult for a property owner to refuse to sell land, though he may set a high price upon it. Land sale is often the only recourse for landowners when illness or death in the family demand immediate cash outlays beyond the amounts that can be borrowed quickly. In such straits a landowner must give purchase options to the owners of adjacent parcels before offering to sell to another person. Finally, transfer of property rights in a form equivalent to sale results from selling a deceased's estate to provide his funeral expense. Although heirs should bear funeral costs, sudden death of a parent may find them without cash or corn reserves. After ascertaining that no patrilineal relative of the deceased wishes to purchase his land, they may sell it to anyone who can provide cash for the funeral.

These forms of land sale have the potential of transferring ownership of land from one lineage to another whenever adjacent parcel owners, often siblings or patrilineal relatives of the seller (since most parcels are portions of larger tracts that were divided by patrilineal inheritance), forego their option to purchase land put up for sale. On the other hand, this potential is muted by the conditional nature of sale. Long after the transaction is made, the seller or his heirs can attempt to reclaim the land by returning the purchase price to the buyer or his heirs, arguing that the original sale was a temporary loan of cash by the buyer or of land by the seller. Until recently, such claims were supported by township customary law, but now recognition of the purchaser's rights is growing, especially if the seller made out a deed of sale.

When a man sells his land, he undermines his ability to generate the loyalty of his heirs. The purchaser, on the other hand, makes a safe cash investment and enhances his own importance to his heirs. Zinacantecos who have earned farming profits but lack land make an explicit effort to invest in farm and house land for their children. Given the finding that lineages with large segments have the most extensive per capita landholdings, we might hypothesize that lineages holding the least land would be the most active in investing in purchased land.

Data on land purchases by members of lineages having more than one descent group support this hypothesis. The number of men in each lineage who had purchased farm or settlement land since 1930 was divided by the number of living household heads to control for lineage size, allowing lineages to be ranked by their degree of land purchase. These ranks are compared with the ranks of name-group size, in table 10. The rank-order correlation shows that the highly segmented lineages were those whose members most generally pur-

TABLE 10. *Land Purchase and Name-Group Size*

Lineage Number	Size of Name-Group Rank	Degree of Land-Purchase Rank
1	1.0	12.5
2	2.0	15.0
3	3.0	9.0
4	4.5	2.5
5	4.5	9.0
6	6.0	7.0
7	7.0	14.0
8	8.5	12.5
9	8.5	6.0
10	10.0	11.0
11	12.5	2.5
12	12.5	2.5
13	12.5	5.0
14	12.5	2.5
15	15.0	9.0

(Spearman's rank-order correlation $= -0.525$)

Note: Lineages are ranked by name-group size and by the per capita amount of land their members have purchased. In the case of the latter rank, the greater the amount of purchase, the lower the rank.

chased land, presumably in order to consolidate the smaller, newly formed descent groups.

Thus, it seems reasonable to pinpoint land sale as one mechanism whose effect is to promote the solidarity of newly formed lineage segments at the expense of older established descent groups.

Because of lineage exogamy, inheritance of land by women usually results in land being transferred from one lineage to another. Ordinarily, women inherit farmland from their parents only when there are no suitable male heirs. But, recognizing that women should own at least one parcel of settlement land on which to build if they never marry or if their marriage ends in divorce, most parents feel obligated to give their daughters house sites as inheritance. Since a woman's land is divided among her heirs (usually her children, members of her husband's lineage), her inheritance constitutes potential gain of land by her heirs' lineage at the expense of her father's lineage.

A breakdown of ownership of settlement parcels illustrates the significance of tenure by women. In table 11, 264 settlement parcels are classified by sex of current owner and by the way in which ownership was established. Women currently own about 26 percent of the settlement plots (categories D and E), and in about 30 percent of the plots (categories C and D) their tenure has resulted in actual or potential transfer of land from one lineage to another.

A classification of settlement land by topographic criteria reveals that, while in principle women should inherit land for house construction, in practice they receive more than their share of land marginally useful for that purpose. Parcels were deemed marginal for house construction if they bordered on any one of three canyon branches that grow visibly by erosion each year, if they were so steep as to require considerable grading to create a level house site, if they were made up of marshy land surrounding waterholes, or if they were entirely outside the perimeter connecting houses most distant from the core of the community. If a parcel with one or more such defects had a house on it, however, it was classed as suitable for house construction together with flatter parcels forming the community core. One hundred ninety-six parcels inherited by men and women from their parents showed differential suitability for house construction by sex of owner (see table 12). Clearly, men are favored in inheritance, receiving the greater proportion of land suitable for house construction. The long-range effect of this practice is to reduce the rate of transfer through women from one lineage to another of land at the core of the settlement, at the cost of accelerated transfer of land marginal for house

TABLE 11. *Transfer of Settlement Parcels through Women*

Plots Owned by Men	No.
A. Inherited from father	140
B. Purchased	30
C. Inherited from mother or by wife	24
Plots Owned by Women	
D. Inherited from father	56
E. Received from dead husband in trust for children's inheritance	14
Total	264

TABLE 12. *Quality of Settlement Parcel and Sex of Heir*

	Settlement Parcels Inherited from Parents		
	By Women	By Men	Total
Suitable for house construction	26	91	117
	(−7)	(+7)	
Marginal for house construction	30	49	79
	(+7)	(−7)	
Total	56	140	196

Note: Deviations from expected values according to margins are in parentheses. Goodman and Kruskal's G = 0.413.

construction. Nevertheless, both these rates are higher than that at which farm parcels are transferred, because most groups of heirs include at least one male to receive farm property. Thus, inheritance through women foments a gradual redistribution between lineage of settlement property, a mechanism that must facilitate the emergence of new localized descent groups at the expense of older ones.

A concrete example will show how land sale and tenure by women, shown above to be important for the hamlet as a whole and for operationally defined lineages, can redistribute landholdings to the benefit of a man and his heirs. Map 10 shows the settlement parcels once owned by Romin Heronimo. When Romin Heronimo married, he had no land on which to build a home. His sister, however, had married an influential hamlet leader, and Romin prevailed upon him to sell him tract 1. A hard-working man, he accumulated profits for taking one prestigious position after another in the township religious hierarchy. He was also able to loan money to another sister for her husband's funeral, and, when she could not return the loan, she gave him tract 2, a parcel of her husband's land, as payment. Romin had married the daughter of a wealthy landowner who died leaving most of his property to his son and only tract 3 to Romin's wife. Romin took his brother-in-law to court and extracted tract 4 as an addition to his wife's inheritance. Meanwhile, his mother died, leaving him tract 5, and shortly afterward, he purchased tracts 6 and 7 from men of other lineages. By now he was a man of stature in the community, having led a popular movement to distribute prized ejido coffee lands to all ejido participants (see p. 46) and having ousted from the community a political rival who tried to farm one of the hamlet's sacred hills. The

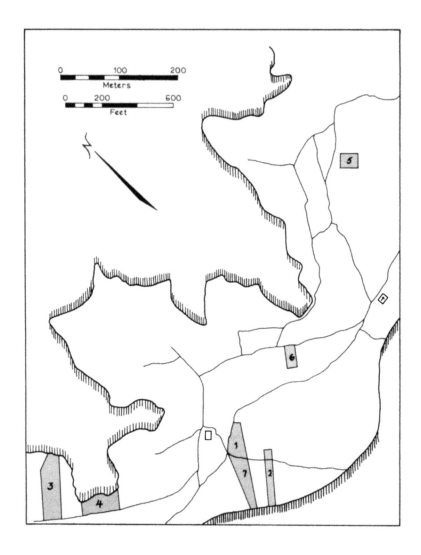

Map 10. Settlement Property of Romin Heronimo in *Apas*. Parcels are numbered according to the order in which Romin Heronimo acquired them, as explained in the text.

area around his home came to be known as *sna mol Romin* in deference to him, and he was frequently sought out to mediate between hamlet disputants. As his sons married, he granted them portions of his property. Finally, in 1963, after having passed the highest position in the ritual hierarchy, he distributed the remainder of his holdings to his children, keeping his house site and his wife's land as inheritance for his immature youngest son. When he died in 1964 his sons were left with property totally acquired through purchase and through women's tenure. Four years later the area around his home still bears his name.

EQUILIBRIUM AND CHANGE IN *APAS*

The foregoing analysis of land-tenure practices in *Apas* has revealed two countervailing tendencies by which property transmission can affect hamlet social aggregates. On the one hand, farm property enhances local-descent–group solidarity, and transmission of property through the male line tends to support group cohesiveness through time. On the other hand, both land sale and inheritance by women can function to transfer land from one lineage to another; the general pattern of the transfer is from lineages with much property and greater solidarity to lineages with little of either. In general, the rate of transfer of property through the male line is far greater than that out of the male line through women or sale. The balance between the two trends is thus in favor of the continued existence of propertied descent groups, at least in the short run. Over extended time, however, transfer through women and sale gradually erode the landed estates of previous generations and permit new local aggregates to form; these, in turn, will endure over the short run, their solidarity promoted by their property. The net effect of the balance between the trends is to give *Apas* the characteristic appearance of local organization based on patrilineal descent at any given point of time—for example, the inclusion of roughly half of hamlet families in neighborhoods conceptualized as *snas*. Through time this appearance is maintained, although the specific local groupings that are most salient gradually change. Within the last twenty years, for instance, the designation of two *Apas* neighborhoods as *snas* has fallen into disuse as more salient local aggregates have emerged (see map 9). Thus, the countervailing trends are in a kind of dynamic equilibrium.

The hypothesis of such a dynamic equilibrium, however, must be qualified by a consideration of other factors that must be held constant for the equilibrium point to remain unchanged. At the root of the model explaining the equilibrium are the reasons that highland property is of value to Zinacantecos. We have seen that inheritance is linked to a complex of Zinacanteco beliefs concerning obligations to parents; were this ideology to change, the mechanisms linking local aggregation to property could become irrelevant. Even without ideological change, the balance of the system could be shifted. A subsequent chapter will show how highland farming is still an attractive alternative to lowland rental farming economically; changes in economic conditions in the Chiapas region, however, are increasing Zinacanteco access to and profits from lowland farming. As highland property decreases in relative economic worth, its importance to local group solidarity should diminish, and local aggregates should break down. Finally, demographic pressures may have the same ultimate effect; as the hamlet's population grows, the relative importance of highland property for personal income will diminish as more individuals seek support from wage labor, lowland farming, or household industry. Both economic changes and demographic trends, then, would support a prediction that local aggregates in *Apas* will become ever more like those of Chamula and Amatenango, no longer structured on the descent principle. Only acquisition of new lands for inclusion in inheritance, as in the manner of the colonization movement described in chapter 9, may buttress the system against such change.

CONCLUSION

This analysis of social organization in *Apas* leads us to draw certain conclusions, to take stock of our place in a chain of argument, and to point out its future direction. First, we have begun to illustrate the value of judicious choice of unit of analysis in the study of Tzotzil tribes. Although the comparative study of man and land in chapter 3 was couched in terms of similarities and differences in townships, we now know that the process underlying the Maya man-land relation is most usefully studied through the local-descent group in a hamlet setting.

The local-descent group has been shown to be more than a segment of long-established lineages associated with neighborhoods. Residential continuity is not what gives the descent group its integrity. (Indeed, air photos reveal that nearly one-fifth of *Apas*'s dwellings were moved in a recent five-year period.) Rather, the descent group is a social unit for the continuing, dynamic transactions in which people and property are gradually but systematically realigned. It is the social unit for which nicknaming is a descriptor, around which clearly and poorly defined residential neighborhoods are defined, and for which ritual and local-level factional politics work.

Yet future discussion will bring other analytic units into focus. Townships themselves deserve study, as in that of Chamula's special position in the chapter to follow. Ethnic relations, however, involve a social field larger than townships, a field regional in extent, which we will find useful to designate as a refuge-region unit.

Second, we have begun the exploration of Tzotzil tradition. Kinship is a traditional behavior that is not a regressive survival from the past but rather a dynamic adaptive response to placement in a setting, a locale with limited potential for human use. Both persistence and change in kinship are facets of traditional behavior that we can explain. Kinship need not be taken as an unexplainable cultural given.

In chapters to follow we will extend our interest in traditional behavior to the entire range of Tzotzil ethnicity, seeking once again the underlying causes of persistence and change of a phenomenon that should not be taken as a cultural given.

Third, and most important, we have spun a web of ecological explanation clarifying the relation between Zinacanteco kinship and land tenure. In doing so, we have taken the study of man and land as far as it is usually taken in ethnographic studies; that is, we have studied fairly exhaustively the dynamics relating a human group and its locale.

Yet we propose to go farther. Have we exhausted the study of the Zinacanteco environment? At least one persistent theme in the materials should indicate that we have not—that is, the repeated allusions to the stabilizing effect of Zinacanteco lowland rental farming. The phenomenon deserves study. In exploring the significance of lowland rental farming to the Zinacanteco, we shall be doing much more than simply trying to evaluate and quantify a major input into a highland social system that otherwise can be studied in its own right. For, by exploring lowland rental farming, we shall be expanding our conception of the Tzotzil environment to ask why Indian tribes like the Zinacantecos are placed in a larger economic system in a special way.

For Tzotzil tribes today are not timeless ahistorical cycling systems; history has had an impact on their development. Their present states and directions of change are rooted in social processes that encompass the Chiapas highlands and link them to a larger social system. The simple fact that Zinacantecos are Indians rather than Ladinos influences the style and strategy of their farming and their access to resources. Ethnic status limits economic opportunities available to Indians and their perception of them as well. Even federal economic programs, such as land reform, affect Zinacanteco economic options. All these factors are part of the environment of Tzotzil life and land use that will receive attention in chapters to come.

CHAPTER FIVE

SOIL EROSION IN CHAMULA

ECAUSE of popular conceptions of "primitives" as mystically more "natural" than "civilized" peoples, anthropological literature is often cited as evidence that human society is capable of a finely attuned, balanced harmony with its environment, comparable to that achieved in a successional climax. Unfortunately, it is all too easy to discover examples of native populations living in obvious disequilibrium with their environments. Chamula is such a community, and this chapter will present evidence that its inhabitants are utilizing their farmlands and forests in such a way as to result in irreversible destruction of their resources.

We have already seen that *Apas* farmlands are overused and in a general decline most visible in the higher zones. Although concentrating on Chamula, the discussion will review land-abuse patterns that can be observed in less extended form in Zinacantán and in many other townships. In this regard, the patterns can be thought of as a characteristic of Tzotzil land use. To emphasize this point, the discussion of man-nature ideology will be couched in terms of beliefs found regionwide.

While land abuse is general to the highlands, there are two reasons for the extreme form of abuse in Chamula. Physiography exacerbates destruction of Chamula lands; they are the highest of the region and cannot generate regrowth at a rate adequate for intense swidden use. Very dense population, beyond that which agriculture alone can support, places extraordinary pressure on Chamula lands. For these reasons, Chamula represents the special case that deserves our greatest attention. But the causes of Chamula's special situation lie outside the township in the economic structure of the region. Chamula's occupational specialties (see chap. 11) bring income to the township from outside. And Chamula's overpopulation may be interpreted as though the township were a breeding ground of wage laborers for lowland ranches and distant coffee fincas. Thus, outside demands for Chamula wage labor and products are the extrinsic conditions within which internal Chamula patterns are worked out.

THE SEQUENCE OF LAND-USE PATTERNS IN CHAMULA

The landscape of Chamula is typical of the Chiapas highland region in many respects, varying according to use from forest to grassy plain and subject to the entire gamut of human exploitation characteristic of the area. In two ways, however, Chamula is distinct in that its lands are generally higher in altitude and more densely populated than are those of neighboring townships. These features have a combined effect on land-use patterns that allows us to discern in the outcomes of short-term exploitation in Chamula the probable long-range effects of such exploitation elsewhere in the highlands. For, in Chamula, dense population is accompanied by more intense land utilization, while the lower metabolic rate of life forms at the higher altitudes hinders recuperation of soil fertility through fallowing, thus hastening the fundamental environmental changes that accompany overuse.

The Chamula landscape consists of physiographically and culturally delimited tracts of land, such as valleys, hilltops, and trail- or fence-bound sectors found in a variety of states that can be thought of as stages in a fairly fixed sequence of land use. Climax forest growth is the first stage of the sequence; infertile, eroded rocky grassland is the last. Although the transition of a tract from the first state to the last may require many generations of human exploitation, the apparent transition of parcels from one state to the next can be discerned in aerial photographs of Chamula taken only a decade apart. This, and the fact that the sequence inferred for Chamula is like that found in similar environments elsewhere, lends credence to the idea that Chamula exhibits an accelerated version of processes general to the Chiapas highlands.

The first stage, that of climax forest, is a hypothetical one, found only as rare and inaccessible cloud-forest stands. The functional equivalents of cloud forest are the more extensive areas of mature regrowth, secondary forest in areas that have not seen agricultural use for many generations. Postclassic archeological sites found in or near these stands, such as those described by Robert M. Adams (1961), are evidence of their probable one-time use for farming. Usually distant from human settlements and at the highest altitudes, being situated on the steeper ridges and hilltops, the forest supplies game to the occasional hunter, wild foods according to season, and timber for house construction and household industry. In Chamula the smaller of these tracts, especially those close to hamlets, are held in private ownership, but the larger, more remote tracts of forest are unclaimed.

The second stage is one of shifting swidden farming. As the forest is opened to agriculture, Chamulas clear and burn the most promising tracts at will, establishing use rights over the land. After a year or more of cultivation, the field may be abandoned. The appearance of such land in aerial photos is of randomly distributed patches carved into the forest canopy at some distance from human settlements and planted in corn or abandoned to regrowth.

In the third stage, farming is intensified over the entire area of former forest. Use rights develop into ownership rights over land, and parcel boundaries become fixed (plate 12). Nevertheless, fields continue to be cleared and burned for use and then fallowed, and the landscape has a distinctive patchwork appearance reflecting variations in parcel regrowth. In contrast to the prior stage, this one is of non-shifting swidden agriculture (also prevalent in *Apas*).

Continued swidden farming of this kind gradually reduces soil fertility and increases the fallow period required to restore it. Farmers have the choice of abandoning their fields or changing their mode of farming from slash and burn to more intensive horticulture. For, as in *Apas*, cornfields inadequately fallowed can be made more fertile by intensive, careful soil preparation. Because population pressure is so high in Chamula and labor in such ready supply, Chamulas willingly choose the intensive farming style. In this stage of incipient horticulture, hamlets will be settled in or near the cornfields to eliminate the daily traveling otherwise required of horticulturalists.

The aerial photos demonstrate that incipient horticulture cannot be practiced indefinitely on Chamula land. As the dependent human settlement grows in size, farming is intensified to include crops other than corn and beans, such as potatoes, fava beans, cabbage, and a variety of other vegetable cash crops. But the least fertile fields cannot withstand intensive horticulture for long, and invading grasses will take over their growth (plate 13). To take advantage of this change, sheep will be introduced, providing wool for clothing and manure for horticulture. To protect their fields from accidental grazing, Chamulas construct fences of sod or thorny brush, giving sharp definition to property boundaries visible in aerial photographs.

Continued intensive horticulture further depletes soil fertility. Gradually, the acreage of grassland increases and sheep herding becomes more prevalent, displacing agriculture as the dominant form of exploitation. The landscape appears relatively barren, with tree growth evident only along hedgerows, and parcel boundaries, no longer maintained as fences, gradually disappearing. By now, farmers have gone elsewhere to seek better lands, and their families may

12. Regrowth Patterns. Nonshifting swidden agriculture with parcels in various stages of regrowth. (Photo courtesy of Harvard Chiapas Project and Cía. Mexicana de Aerofotos, S.A.)

13. Incipient Grassland. Intensive horticulture is giving way to grassland use. (Photo by author)

have moved out, too. The water supply in hamlet water holes becomes variable, the soil having lost its capacity to maintain a high water table through the dry winter season. Heavy summer rains erode the edges of trails that crisscross the grasslands, silting in the natural limestone sinks, which alternately flood and dry as mud flats according to the season.

Continued sheepherding takes its inevitable toll. Because of constant clipping off at the roots, grass gives way to gullies of erosion, which spread out from trails along the hillsides. In a matter of years a hill can erode from grazing land to a heap of rocks devoid of top- and subsoil. The landscape has reached the final stage of total abandonment, probably never to recover its fertility (plates 14, 15, and 16).

The distribution of land-use stages across the Chamula landscape is not random but reflects the systematic way human exploitation spreads from central locations through the countryside in a repeated pattern. The idealized pattern is a set of concentric circles with forest in the outermost band, erosion in the center, and intermediate stages ordered sequentially between them. Actual patterns may not exhibit the later stages of the exploitation sequence, indicating that some areas have been brought into cultivation later than others. Idiosyncratic variations in microgeography, of course, distort the symmetry of the pattern. Nevertheless, it is possible to perceive in the ripplelike pattern a synchronic record of the spread of ruinous Chamula land-use practices through time and space.

The fact that the land-use sequence is more advanced in some regions of the Chamula township than in others suggests that these regions have a longer history of more intense human use. Additional characteristics of these regions permit an educated guess that their exploitation was begun in the Middle and Late Postclassic period before the Spanish Conquest. There is a general relation between the land-use sequence and physiography such that regions that are discrete in terms of land use correspond to valley systems. The larger, more thoroughly exploited regions tend to be the larger highland valley systems, while the smallest valleys are just now being brought into cultivation. Adams's survey (1961) of settlement patterns in highland Chiapas suggests that settlement shifted in location from well-defined headlands and ridges into the larger highland valleys at about the time of the Middle Postclassic (plate 17). Documentary sources from throughout the colonial period indicate that Chamula population is found today where it was at the time of conquest. It seems likely, then, that the scars of overuse that Chamula exhibits are rooted deeply in time and are the outcome of traditional agricultural practices common

14. A Stage of Erosion. Horticulture is giving way to sheep herding and erosion in this sector of Chamula. (Photo courtesy of Harvard Chiapas Project and Cía. Mexicana de Aerofotos, S.A.)

to the aboriginal highland populations. Of course sheep, introduced shortly after the Spanish Conquest, greatly accelerated incipient erosion.

THE TZOTZIL IDEOLOGY OF NATURE AND MAN

The technical facts of Chamula land use are consonant with a native world view prevalent both in Chamula and in neighboring Tzotzil townships, in which man is seen as being in a precarious relation of subjugation to the forces of nature.[1] Natives are unwilling, in many ways, to meddle with the engineering of nature. They have a passive attitude toward resource management, especially in comparison with attitudes and practices of the region's dominant Ladino caste. The connection between Chamula belief and practice in regard to land man-

---

1. For general literature on this topic, see Redfield 1941, 1953; Kluckhohn and Strotdbeck 1959; and Kluckhohn 1958.

15. More Advanced Erosion. Incipient erosion that could still be remedied by terracing. (Photo by author)

16. Severe Erosion. Severe erosion has destroyed this field. (Photo by author)

17. An Early Postclassic Site. An early Postclassic site perches on the ridgeline in the foreground of this view over the San Cristóbal valley. (Photo courtesy of Harvard Chiapas Project and Cía. Mexicana de Aerofotos, S.A.)

agement does not mean that one is the cause of the other but rather that both must be viewed as facets of a traditional system to be understood in terms of broader conditions and causes.

In a detailed study of Chamula oral tradition Gary H. Gossen (1974) has analyzed the native cosmological dimensions of time, distance, temperature, light, sex, and seniority as related to fundamental concepts of Chamula social order. In Chamula world view, the township is at the highest point and center of a rectangular world and thus is closest to the path of the sun, which travels around the earth along a ribbon of sky. At the earth's distant perimeters live foreign and alien creatures associated with chaos and a social disorder of earlier creations. Chamula ancestors came to displace social disorder in this creation through their proximity to the sun and access to its ritual heat, light, and sacred power. Chamulas accumulate heat as they age and maintain social order through ritual involving senior males in a cult of the sun.

Ever present in nature, particularly in the forest, are the forces that would overcome this order and return the world to the chaos of distant space and past time. These include demons living in remoter, wild parts of Chamula that cause eclipses by attacking the moon and sun, threatening the very source of order-giving heat and light; snakes and other transfigurations of the earth lord, whose domain is the wooded mountain that humans should avoid lest he harm their souls; and other dangerous deities. Negative events are associated with the setting of the woods, which "symbolize lowness, coldness, darkness, threat, and behavior that is not rule-governed . . . ; they contain caves, . . . the domain of the earth lords, represented as socially distant Ladinos . . . who have snakes as familiars" (ibid., p. 87).

The deities of the wild threaten individual well-being. Every individual has two animal spirits, one guarded in a corral on Chamula's highest mountain peak, the other tended by the sun deity in a sky corral. "Any misfortune that happens to these souls makes the person with whom they are associated either ill or vulnerable to illness in the near future. . . . Common illnesses involve partial loss of the soul, sale of the soul to the earth god, release of the soul animal from its corral, or beating of the soul animal by another, stronger animal" (ibid., p. 210).

Quite understandably, Chamulas are reluctant to meddle with the dangerous forces of nature that could damage them individually or collectively. This sense of precarious relations with the forces of nature is echoed in the beliefs of other, adjacent Tzotzil townships.

As in Chamula, natives of San Pedro Chenalhó ritually propitiate earth supernaturals who are disturbed by house construction. For the construction materials, on the one hand, having been brought in from the wild forest, are inherently dangerous to humans and must be rendered safe through prayer, while the Holy Earth herself, on the other hand, having been disturbed by the construction activity, must be appeased by a sacrifice of chicken or turkey and by a ceremonial meal (Guiteras-Holmes 1961, p. 26).

In neighboring San Andrés Larraínzar (Holland 1963), natives also believe that each individual is endowed from birth to death with two spirits. One is a wild animal soul, such as an ocelot, coyote, jaguar, or weasel, which lives in the forest. The second is an amorphous essence constituting human consciousness that generally is attached to the body by day but may wander away at night as the owner dreams. Here, too, supernaturals inflict illness by attacking the souls. Thus, gods linked to the wind. rain, sun, moon, sky, and earth itself are the causative agents of illness and chronic disease. The Larrainzeño who ventures forth into the wilderness areas surrounding this hamlet does so with trepidation and ritual precaution, the dangers to him increasing with his physical distance from home.

Finally, there is the example of the widespread importance of agricultural ritual, such as that described for Zinacantán (Vogt 1969, pp. 455–461). Zinacantecos perform rites for the cornfields at the time of planting and later, as the fields mature. The rites are directed to the earth spirits, which send forth clouds, rain, and lightning, all thought to issue forth from caves. Lightning protects the fields from wind; and rain, of course, nurtures the crop. The ritual may take place at several levels, on the small scale of the work group in particular fields, by an entire hamlet for its lands, or by select specialists from the township-wide hierarchy of shamans, who may perform to interdict regional drought. At whatever the level, agricultural ritual emphasizes exhortation of the spirits of nature by prayer and by propitiatory consumption of candles. incense, and other spiritual "foods."

The special character of these beliefs and practices is best brought home by the contrast with our own. The modern homeowner or apartment dweller gives little thought to the manner in which building materials are extracted from natural resources by industrial technology, and he firmly believes that medical research will devise chemical or physical means to cope with illness and disease just as weather satellites, better fertilizers. and new hybrids will revolutionize agriculture. We take for granted man's capacity for mastery over nature, while the Tzotzil native lives in wary fear of disturbing the natural order.

Tzotzil practices contrast with those of the region's dominant Ladino caste as well. Road building and technological improvements in agriculture are examples of recent changes initiated by the national sector. But Ladinos have always approached timbering, ranching, irrigation, horticulture, and orcharding with an attitude toward resources management in which man could dominate the forces of nature. Ladino ritual ideology places no particular constraints on the treatment of nature, which is not deified but approached practically. Tzotzil natives have ignored the techniques of resource management readily visible in Ladino farming.

The distinctive Tzotzil attitude toward nature does not itself explain Tzotzil land-abuse patterns found in and beyond Chamula. In this case, ideology and practice seem to be two sides of the same coin. Native land use is distinctive in contrast to Ladino patterns, and the contrast is related to the pervasive ethnicity with which Indian life distinguishes itself.

CHAMULA'S SPECIAL SITUATION

Chamula shares with other Tzotzil communities its general disregard for land management and its view of man's subordination to nature, but the severity of Chamula's land abuse requires special explanation. Chamula does hold a special relation to the regional economy that distinguishes it from other townships. Chamula wage labor and product specialization both have features that contribute to intense land abuse by encouraging population growth beyond the limits of local resources.

Despite depletion of its resources, Chamula population continues to grow, from 16,010 in 1940 and 22,029 in 1950 to 26,789 in 1960. The most recent census tables available indicate that Chamula women marry at a younger age than in adjacent townships. The higher-than-average proportions of children in the population indicate growth that limited land resources do not restrain. The burgeoning population is heavily dependent upon income from wage labor and household crafts.

Chamula wage labor supplies distant labor markets, ranchers, and even other Indian farmers in the Grijalva River basin and coffee plantations along the Pacific coastal range. Until labor reforms of the 1930s. wage workers were recruited by debt indenturing, a system in which middlemen advanced workers small amounts in return for a binding long-term contract far from the highlands under conditions often horribly abusive. Since the reforms of the Cárdenas government, a labor syndicate oversees coffee plantation contracts from a central office in San Cristóbal de las Casas that includes one of Chamula's political leaders in its staff. A three-month limit to contracts, guarantees for working conditions, and good wages attract the land-poor Indians from many highland townships. but particularly Chamula. Because Chamulas dominate syndicated plantation labor and unregulated wagework in the Grijalva basin as well, wage labor is the most important Chamula occupational specialty.

Wage labor and growing population seem connected in a number of ways. Cash income frees individuals from total dependence on local resources, allowing land-poor families to grow to a size that subsistence farming would not support. Wages encourage earlier marriages by speeding up bride-price payments and reducing the length of courtships. Finally, a demand for wage workers encourages high fertility in families that can sell their manpower. In Chamula, each of these effects is evident to some degree. Thus, Chamula appears to be a breeding ground for distant labor markets.

Yet distant wage labor exacerbates land abuse. Workers' families remain in the highlands to farm whatever lands they have. Workers bring cash, not food, from afar,[2] and food needs are met by supplies as near to home as possible. A heavy local labor supply encourages labor-intensive horticulture, which mines land of its nutrients rapidly, hastening the degeneration of farmlands into grass.

Craft specialization also encourages population growth and strains resources. As we shall see, household industries are found to some degree in all townships but not with the diversity of flourishing craft specialization in Chamula. Pine furniture, string instruments, bootleg liquor, pottery, woolen goods, charcoal, firewood, and other such products of high labor and low-grade technological input are Chamula's wares, giving income to many families. Like wage labor, crafts generate cash, which frees individuals from dependence upon farmland. Unlike wage labor, however, crafts mine local resources for raw material directly. The timbering required by many of these processes—and especially with the extraction of firewood and charcoal for cooking fuel in San Cristóbal de las Casas—contributes directly to land abuse.

Both wage labor and craft production are conditions of special importance to Chamula that appear to contribute directly and indirectly to land overuse. Why should these sources of income involve Chamula more than other townships? In this century Chamula has perpetuated its hold over labor and craft markets through political maneuvering of its astute leadership (cf. chap. 7). Traditional domination of these mechanisms may come from Chamula's location in the center of the highlands, surrounded as it is by other Indian townships, and being among them the only one that has no direct access to the lowlands. Chamulas, especially those living in the center of the township, cannot compete with Zinacantecos, who are better situated for exploitation of the lowlands of the Grijalva basin directly below their homes. Tzeltal townships east of Chamula hinder their efforts to colonize the lowland tropical-forest zone. And outlets to the north are dominated by other Tzotzil, Tzeltal, and Tojolabal townships. Thus, nearby lowland areas are not suitable for Chamula farming. Lowlands relieve popula-

2. Chamulas sometimes receive corn delivered to their homes as wages from Indian employers in the Grijalva basin.

tion pressure in *Apas* through harvests that are readily transported up the highland escarpment. Chamulas reap cash, not crops, from regional craft markets and wage labor farther afield.

Thus, Chamula represents a third example of a local system with characteristic and distinctive internal processes and patterns that must be understood within the context of extrinsic factors. In this case, the local system is township wide, a farming system exhibiting regular and structured patterns of intense overuse. Explanation of these patterns lies in the special position of Chamula in a regional economy for which the township is a breeding ground for labor and a supplier of cheap crafts.

CHAPTER SIX

MARGINALITY

<hr>

ARE marginal farmlands marginal to their farmers? The deterioration of Chamula farmlands and the apparent dependence of Zinacanteco life on lowland rental farming do suggest that the highlands may be marginal to the lowlands for agriculture. Zinacanteco highland and lowland farming may be compared from the standpoint of inputs and yields. The analysis shows lowland rental farming to give the highland-resident Indian a poorer return from his labor and capital investments than highland farming, suggesting that the lowlands, rather than the highlands, are a marginal area for Zinacanteco agriculture. This conclusion runs counter to the unquestioned assumption that the central highlands of Chiapas, Mexico, like other peripheral areas where ethnic populations live, are generally marginal to surrounding lowland areas for agriculture. Consideration of the penalties Zinacantecos pay for lowland farming in transport and rent resolves this paradox. Lowlanders, not incurring these costs, get better returns from inputs than the Zinacanteco farming his highland property. As part of a regional economic system, then, the lowlands are not marginal to the highlands for agriculture—although they may appear so from the special niche that highland ethnic populations occupy.

The visitor to Chiapas, in making the trip from lowlands to highlands, may well remark on the apparent marginality of the farmlands that native farmers utilize. Indian fields cling to steep slopes, and, in the spring, before seeding, the farmland's rocky character is all too evident. Nevertheless, these lands are farmed intensively by the Indians. Ladinos. however, no longer farm intensively in the highlands, partly because their larger holdings were expropriated under land reform to benefit the Indians, but also because the lowlands offer richer harvests. Even Zinacantecos, corn-farming specialists of the highlands, concentrate the bulk of their efforts on lowland farming of rented fields. Why is it, then, that they continue to farm in the highlands? Why do their neighbors in Chamula continue to farm overworked lands?

Zinacanteco highland farming, although intense, is at a level that supplies only about one-fifth of the township's corn harvest, the remainder coming from fields that Zinacantecos rent in the lowlands of the Grijalva basin (map 11). Zinacanteco expansion into the lowlands has been dramatic within the last two decades. Cancian's studies (1972) of Zinacanteco lowland farming show it to be a complex operation whose changing cost components vary according to location but are within a range that permits substantial profit to the Indian who will farm on a large scale. Large-scale farming of lowland fields that render high yields per acre makes it seem, at first, an attractive alternative to highland farming. But a comparison of the costs of the two operations shows that the price Zinacantecos pay for scale of operation is a poorer return to labor and to necessary cash outlays, explaining in part why Indians exhaust available highland farm sites rather than abandoning them altogether in favor of lowland farming.

Zinacantecos contract for lowland rentals in groups, selecting one from among them to negotiate with a rancher for an area that they then divide for independent use. Swidden farming techniques are similar to those employed in the highlands. But the location of rental lands at least a day's travel from the highland hamlets, the larger scale of lowland farming, and environmental differences influencing plant growth all combine to require greater organization and more complex preparation for work. Rains begin later in the lowlands. delaying seeding until May, but tropical heat promotes more rapid corn and weed growth, making weeding in mid-to-late June essential. Since most men plant more corn than they can weed before unwanted growth strangles the corn, they hire workers who must be transported to the fields, fed, and supervised in their work. Men cannot afford needless trips to and from the hamlets, and lowland farming requires careful preparation of provisions and equipment for farming expeditions that may last a month or more. After a second weeding in July, beans are planted in September, cultivated shortly after, and harvested with the corn in November and December. Rent is usually paid in kind at the harvest, and the remaining crop is sold to middlemen or a government agency or is transported home by truck or mule for consumption or later sale (plate 18).

The contrasts between highland and lowland farming boil down to differences in productive output and in labor and capital inputs. At best, highland fields produce about 50 units of harvest for each unit of seed, while the return on lowland seed may reach 150 to 1 under favorable conditions. Highland farming requires a labor input with very little capital outlay, but lowland farming requires capital outlay for workers' wages, land rent, and transport costs, as well as increased labor investment in travel, field fencing, and work organization.

18. A Lowland Farm Camp. At their lowland harvest camp these Zinacantecos have abandoned their ethnic garb for nondescript work clothes. (Photo by author)

TABLE 13. *Farming Budgets*

		Farmer's Labor in Days	Total Expenses in Pesos	Gross Harvest in Pesos	Net Harvest
Lowland operations	1.	112	1,795	3,312	1,517
	2.	50	372	828	456
	3.	100	369	1,656	1,287
	4.	175	832	2,075	1,243
	5.	97	1,415	2,144	729
	6.	203	364	1,560	1,196
	7.	106	1,128	1,899	771
	8.	31	126	388	262
	9.	50	1,722	3,456	1,734
Highland operations	A.	34	38	432	394
	B.	77	512	1,800	1,288
	C.	58	182	792	608
	D.	23	55	336	281
	E.	38	19	696	677

Note: Highland budgets are lettered, and lowland budgets are numbered in the same manner as in figure 15.

When these additional labor and capital costs of lowland farming are aggregated, they go far to offset the larger lowland harvests. Table 13, for instance, shows the aggregated costs and returns for nine typical lowland farm budgets and five typical highland farm budgets collected from residents of *Apas* for 1965. The first column shows the number of days that the farmer himself devoted to organization, travel, and actual field work in each example. The second column sums the many categories of his expenses, converted into a peso value (1 peso = U.S. $0.08). Included are hired labor, food, the cost of seed, outlays for ritual, transport costs, gifts to the landowners and workers, fiscal taxes, and other minor outlays. The third column gives the cash value of the corn and bean harvest less the value of field rent (paid in kind out of the harvest). The final column shows the net value of the harvest after deducting farming expenses.

The scale of these examples is variable, generally small for the highland examples and somewhat larger for lowland examples. Lowland farming gave a higher net profit than did highland farming, but at a cost of much greater labor and expenses. The relative return to

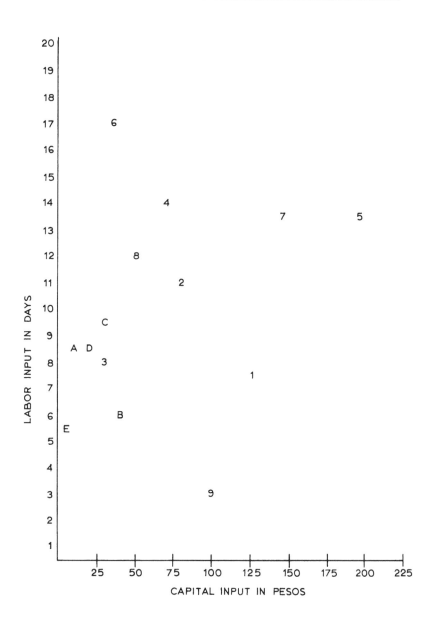

Fig. 15. Labor and Capital Inputs to Farming. Amounts of labor and capital inputs of the five highland and nine lowland operations producing 100 pesos of net harvest. The highland operations are lettered and the lowland operations numbered in the same manner as the budgets shown in table 13.

labor and capital inputs of each farming operation can be evaluated by computing the amount of each required to produce a net harvest value of 100 pesos. These data are graphed in figure 15. In almost every case, production of 100-pesos worth of lowland net harvest required substantially more of the *Apas* farmer's labor and expenses than did production of the same amount in the highlands. In short, lowland farming permits an increased scale of farming and profit but at a cost of a poorer return to labor and cash investment.

This conclusion is reinforced by Cancian's comprehensive study of Zinacanteco lowland rental farming (1972). By 1966 Zinacantecos had taken advantage of newly constructed lowland roads and improved marketing facilities by expanding rental operations from their traditional sites off the escarpment near Acala and Chiapilla to more favorable distant areas as far as Pujiltic and Porvenir (see map 11). Cancian's data show Zinacanteco lowland rental farming to be at a larger scale and with a higher net profit than in the highlands, yet to have consistently poorer returns to capital investment, even in the most profitable lowland zones.

Lowland production is typically at a larger scale than is possible in the highlands (where parcels are small and limited in number). *Apas* men seeded an average of 2.93 almuds (an almud is 15 metric liters) in the lowlands in 1966 (see table 14). By contrast, the average highland operation involved only 1.7 almuds of corn seed.

Under normal conditions, lowland farmers can expect higher net profits than in the highlands. Lowland operations differ from zone to zone and in their scale. Cancian computed profits expectable at the scales of 2, 4, and 6 almuds seeded in zones 2, 6, and 9 (see map 11) in order to encompass the range of alternatives employed by Zinacantecos in 1966. Table 15 illustrates the net profits expectable of these operations. Profits increase with scale and by the distance of farming zone from the heavily used traditional sites. The profits expectable (834 pesos) at the smallest scale (2 almuds) in the zone nearest *Apas*

TABLE 14. *Lowland Farming Scale*

Almuds of seed	1	2	3	4	5	6	7	8
Numbers of farmers	18	32	31	11	4	8	3	1

Note: Amount seeded in lowlands in 1966 by *Apas* farmers (from Cancian 1972, p. 99).

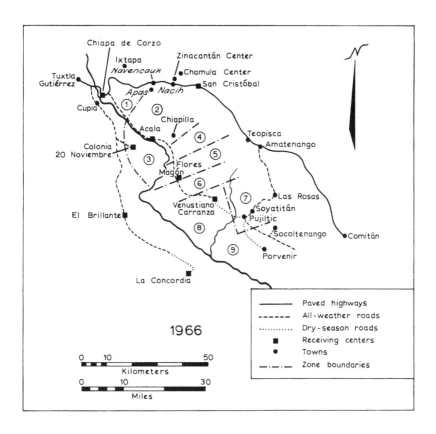

Map 11. Zones for Zinacanteco Lowland Rental Farming in 1966. Zones are numbered according to increasing distance of travel for Zinacanteco lowland rental farmers. (After Cancian 1972, p. xiii)

(zone 2) substantially exceeded that of the average highland operation (650 pesos) in 1966.

On the other hand, Zinacantecos incur costs that require substantial cash outlays when they farm in the lowlands. Table 16 summarizes the cash outlays made for hired labor and transport for the lowland farming alternatives. The ratio of net profits to these costs are the returns to capital investments from normal lowland farming (table 17).

TABLE 15. *Lowland Profits*

Scale of Operation (in almuds seeded)	Farming Zone 2	6	9
2	834	1.268	1.385
4	988	1,950	2,217
6	1,154	2,647	3,015

Note: Net profits (in pesos) for Zinacanteco lowland farmers (from Cancian 1972, p. 105).

TABLE 16. *Lowland Farming Costs*

Scale of Operation (in almuds seeded)	Farming Zone 2	6	9
2	444	442	613
4	1,568	1,470	1,779
6	2,680	2,483	2,979

Note: Costs, in pesos, of hired labor and transport for Zinacanteco lowland farmers (from Cancian 1972, p. 105).

TABLE 17. *Returns*

Scale of Operation (in almuds seeded)	Farming Zone 2	6	9
2	188	287	226
4	63	133	125
6	43	107	101

Note: Net return, in excess of costs, in pesos per hundred pesos of costs for Zinacanteco lowland farmers. The figures are obtained by dividing costs (table 16) into net profits (table 15) and multiplying by 100. The return to highland farming is 402 pesos per 100 pesos of cost.

They compare unfavorably with an overall return of 402-pesos profit per 100-pesos investment in highland operations in 1965. Thus, all the normal lowland rental alternatives yield substantially poorer returns to capital outlays than does highland farming.

At first glance, then, it would seem that highland farms should not be considered marginal. To the Zinacanteco, farming in the highlands is categorically preferable to farming in the lowlands, requiring substantially lower inputs of both labor and capital. For him, the marginal costs of lowland farming greatly exceed those of highland farming. Paradoxically, we might be tempted to conclude that the lowlands were more marginal for agriculture than the highlands.

Such a conclusion, however, would be in error. For the Zinacanteco farmer, profits differ largely because of the high costs associated with rent and with transport from the distant lowland farm site to his home.[1] Cancian's data on transport costs and rent allow computation of the returns from capital outlays by hypothetical lowland residents.

Transport costs (see table 18) include both those for bringing highland hired labor to lowland fields and those for shipment of the harvest home. A lowland resident farming near his home would have lower costs and higher profits because of their elimination. Consequently, the return to his cash outlays would be higher (see table 19) than for the Zinacanteco farming next to him.

Moreover, a lowland resident might own his farmland, avoiding the rental fees Zinacantecos pay in kind at harvest time (see table 20). Elimination of rent would increase his profit and consequently the return to his cash outlay (see table 21).

In either case, the lowland resident farming at a scale of 2 almuds of corn seeded would reap a return from cash outlays approaching or

TABLE 18. *Transportation*

Scale of Operation (in almuds seeded)	Farming Zone 2	6	9
2	123	198	293
4	203	324	492
6	284	445	710

Note: Transportation costs, in pesos, for Zinacanteco lowland farmers (from Cancian 1972, p. 105).

1. Hired labor enters into lowland farming costs only when the scale of farming exceeds the acreage a man can weed alone. Labor costs bite deeply into profits when the scale exceeds two almuds of seed, as can be seen easily in table 16.

TABLE 19. *Partially Adjusted Returns*

Scale of Operation (in almuds seeded)	Farming Zone		
	2	6	9
2	298	601	524
4	87	198	210
6	60	152	164

Note: Increased net return, in pesos, per 100 pesos of cost for lowland resident having no transport costs.

TABLE 20. *Rent*

Scale of Operation (in almuds seeded)	Farming Zone		
	4	6	9
2	432	432	576
4	864	864	1,152
6	1,296	1,296	1,728

Note: Rental fees, in pesos (although paid in kind), for Zinacanteco lowland farmers (from Cancian 1972, p. 39).

TABLE 21. *Fully Adjusted Returns*

Scale of Operation (in almuds seeded)	Farming Zone		
	2	6	9
2	433	778	704
4	151	274	300
6	114	215	240

Note: Increased net return, in pesos, per 100 pesos of cost for lowland resident having no transport costs and paying no rent.

exceeding the return from highland farming by Zinacantecos. Were Zinacantecos to farm in the highlands at a scale of 4 or 6 almuds of seed, wage-labor costs would surely reduce their profit-to-cost ratio from 402 pesos per 100-peso investment to levels far lower than the ratio for similar operations by lowland resident landowners or renters. (The return from an unusually large highland operation of 3.5 almuds seeded, for instance, was only 252 pesos per 100 pesos of cost.) Thus, it seems certain that lowland farming is more profitable for the lowlander than is highland farming for the highland native. A free agent, capable of placing himself at will within the agricultural system, would select a lowland farming site.

This observation leads us to a more acceptable connotation for the construct "marginality." The highlands are marginal to the lowlands for agriculture in terms of characteristics deriving from location within an economic system. Analysis of the economics of highland and lowland farming from the point of view of the Zinacanteco alone obscures the fact that Zinacantecos are themselves placed in the system in a certain way. Given complete mobility and free convertibility of his resources, a Zinacanteco would abandon life in the highlands in order to become a resident lowland farmer.

In taking the perspective offered by looking at Zinacanteco farming within an economic system. we are led again to the questions: Why does the Zinacanteco "choose" to live in the highlands? Why is he willing to live an economically marginal life?

The narrow answer is that Indians are placed within the economic system in a special niche—that of highland resident—within which lowland farming is not an attractive alternative to tilling their own marginal fields. But the answer can be broadened by analyzing the niche as a unit within a larger social landscape, one whose delimiting features are ethnic as well as economic and physiographic gradients.

In general, anthropologists have noted that ethnic boundaries are apparent cultural barriers to social mobility. The Indian is bound to his community by ties of language, custom, and deeply seated tradition. Opportunities open to him are limited, in short, by his ethnic-group membership. But this point of view is subject to serious criticisms, for it assumes that ethnicity is necessarily a kind of barrier. While it is true that ethnicity can be thought of as a kind of boundary relationship delimiting a group, the boundary cannot be assumed to be a barrier. Rather, we must ask what kinds of communcation can cross the boundary and with respect to what domains does the boundary exist.

In the discussion to follow we will explore the boundaries of the ethnic niche occupied by Indians in highland Chiapas. The principal features of Chiapas ethnicity belie its interpretation as the effect of cultural barrier mechanisms. Ethnic boundaries are often thought to break down when natives acquire knowledge of the outside world or become mobile. Yet we will see that ethnic patterns in Chiapas are not eroded either by astute native awareness of the state and nation or by migration that has gone on for centuries. Ethnic boundaries sometimes can be correlated with specialized economic resources. But highland Chiapas craft production using special resources seems to be a re-sponse to deep-seated ethnic patterns rather than their cause.

The strands of ethnicity and marginality are woven together explic-itly in a model of the refuge region propounded by Gonzalo Aguirre Beltrán (1967). According to the model, regions like that of highland Chiapas, which were marginal to the developing colonial economy, evolved special forms of social organization in which a rural elite (La-dinos) exploited a subordinate group (Indians). Ethnic pluralism is maintained between the two castes in the face of pressures from the nation to reform and develop its marginal hinterlands. Ethnicity thus reinforces a relationship between two part systems in which the posi-tion of Indians is analogous to that of prey in a natural food chain: Indians produce the harvest surpluses, which the Ladino elite, through commerce, ultimately reaps. Finally, the interconnections between Indianism and Mexican nationalism are compared to ethnic move-ments in other parts of the world, which appear to be an adaptive re-sponse to the rise of nationalism.

CHAPTER SEVEN

ETHNICITY

PAST discussion has stressed the importance of external factors that condition the internal state of local systems. Thus, lowland rental farming relieves the pressure of rising population, allowing the swidden patterns of farming to continue in *Apas*'s highland tracts; this, in turn, maintains the high value placed on property, the precondition for a stable equilibrium in Zinacanteco processes of social organization. In a similar fashion, distant wage-labor markets were seen to condition land-abuse sequences in Chamula by encouraging rapid population growth. In both cases, analysis of the local community led to identification of conditioning factors in a larger system.

In the last chapter, Indian groups were depicted as specially placed in structural positions of marginality to a broader economic system. The ties to a traditional homeland, the difficulties of using Spanish as a commercial language, and the lack of ready access to distant opportunities put the Indian at a disadvantage and encourage special adaptations of his life to suit the fringes of the larger system. Almost every relation that engages the Zinacanteco or the Chamula with the larger system is colored and structured by his being an Indian. In short, ethnic status is the special position that Indian groups hold in the economically marginal highlands. By exploring the characteristics of highland Chiapas ethnicity, we build a stepping stone to a more comprehensive understanding of the manner in which external factors influence the internal dynamics of the Indian community.

Ethnicity can be thought of as a boundary distinguishing one population from another. We will now explore ethnic boundaries of two types. The first is the major vertical cleavage of Indians and Ladinos into subordinate and dominant "castes." The second is the differentiation found among Indian townships, giving each a distinct character. Chiapas has had ethnic boundaries of both types since the time of the Spanish Conquest.

The persistence of ethnic characteristics among the highland Indian communities is not something to be attributed simply to static traditional life ways. Indeed, we shall see that, among the Tzotzil, ethnic patterns persist in spite of features commonly thought to break them down. For one, knowledge of the outside world might be thought to

erode barriers and enhance integration with it. Yet astute native local-
level leadership uses astonishingly comprehensive knowledge of the
non-Indian world to fortify and entrench Tzotzil ethnic differentiation. For another, migration is commonly thought to erode ethnic
boundaries by intermixing—and thus homogenizing—distinctive
populations. Yet highland Chiapas ethnic boundaries along township
lines have been distinct and stable despite substantial migration and
mixture of Indian populations since the 1500s. At the same time, differences between townships do not seem based in resource differentiation and production specialities commonly thought to underlie ethnic
differentiation. Lacking a clear-cut economic base, Tzotzil ethnicity
would long ago have been eradicated by migration alone were not
ethnic differentiation a dynamic and continuing process permitting
native interaction with the outside world in a selective and structured
manner.

Tzotzil ethnic boundary relations are dynamic. As in other recent
approaches to ethnic boundaries (Barth 1969), these are seen not as
barriers to communication for the local system but rather as an interface across which interaction is structured and selective. Like the walls
of a living cell, ethnic boundaries define and protect a local subsystem
that is, nevertheless, dependent upon the larger system for the resources that give it integrity.

THE INDIAN-LADINO ETHNIC INTERFACE

In Tzotzil society, there are several roles that involve Indians in
explicit and direct interaction with the non-Indian world. One of these
roles is that of corn-farming work-group leader described in earlier
chapters. Another is that of native lawyer, the voluble advocate who
will argue his clients' cases both within the framework of native legal
institutions and before the Ladino judiciary. A third set of roles is
linked to township government and includes officials required by the
state constitution to effect government.

Men in these roles usually speak Spanish well, and they are known
for their personal contacts with influential Ladino landowners, lawyers, and government officials. Consequently, they are sought out by
neighbors and acquaintances who need help in dealing with non-
Indians. Sometimes they have large and loyal followings that are
aligned in opposition to one another in intramunicipal factional politics. Indeed, the most successful of these men are local-level political
bosses comparable to the "cultural brokers" or "cultural middlemen"

who articulate ethnic groups with the larger society in many parts of the world.[1]

This section reviews what is known about the history of land tenure in Zinacantán in order to argue that such roles are not new to Indian society but are a characteristic fixture of highland Chiapas ethnicity. The section first will review land-tenure history. It will conclude by focusing on the Indian's special position in highland Chiapas society.

Land-Tenure History in Zinacantán

Discussion of the history of Zinacanteco land tenure will make occasional reference to map 12, which depicts three classes of land found today in the township. The first class is called "communal" and refers to land thought of by Zinacantecos as ancestral private property. The second class, ejido, was acquired by expropriation under the aegis of Mexican land reform during the 1930s. Finally, there are small tracts of ranchland held as private property by Ladinos within the confines of the township.

Indian land tenure before Mexican independence has been described best for central Mexico and other areas close to the hub of colonial administration. By mid-sixteenth century, Indians were conceived of as special wards of the crown, and their townships were accorded special forms of communal land, corporately owned and inalienable. Policy for tenure by non-Indians, however, developed more by default than by explicit plan. At first, Spaniards were uninterested in land acquisition, devoting their efforts to mining. But, as the mining industry boomed in the mid-sixteenth century, support industries of agriculture and cattle herding (for food and for hides) flourished, and Spaniards began to claim grazing rights. In the seventeenth century, these claims became legitimized as actual property rights even when they encroached upon the supposedly inviolable Indian communal tracts. Indeed, the tenure history of the colony can be viewed as a process in which Indians fought a continual rear-guard battle in the courts and on the ground to defend communal tracts that were gradually eroded by encroachment (see table 22).

Archival documents suggest a history of colonial land tenure in Zinacantán roughly in accord with this general pattern. At the close of the eighteenth century, the township held several communal tracts,

---

1. Nonethnic communities also often have middlemen who can articulate the interests of local-level clients to patrons in the larger social system (cf. Foster 1963; Kenny 1960; Boissevain 1966).

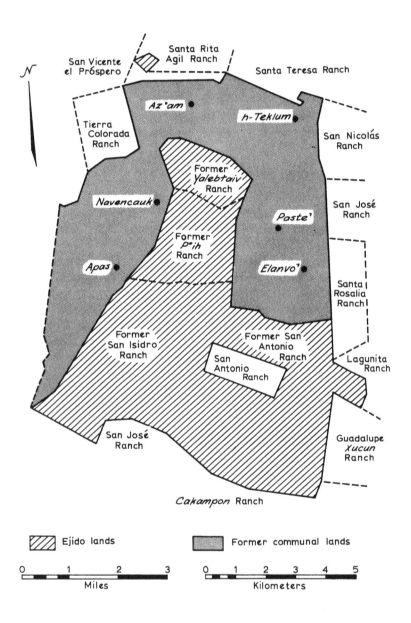

Map 12. Ejido Lands in Zinacantán. (After plan of partial definitive
donation of ejido to Zinacantán, Chis., Department of Asuntos Agrarios
y Colonización, Tuxtla Gutiérrez, Chiapas)

TABLE 22. *A Condensed Chronology*

16th and 17th centuries	Clerics and colonists debate the status of Indians
	Mining boom in New Spain
	Rapid decline of Indian population
	Cattle ranchers encroach on Indian lands; their illegitimate claims largely validated after 1620
1712	Tzeltal rebellion
1760	*Repartimiento* system of commercial redistribution practiced in highland Chiapas
1821	Mexican independence
1824	Chiapas secedes from Guatemala, joins Mexico
1826, 1827	Chiapas enacts colonization laws
1840s	Tzotzil groups entitle their communal tracts under colonization laws
1863	Juárez comes to power
	Enactment of Leyes de Reforma strips church and Indian towns of corporate lands
	Many Indians forced into debt-indentured labor in lowlands
	Liberals, in power in Chiapas, move state capital to Chiapa de Corzo
1860s	Zinacantecos acquire *Ibestik* tract
1869	Chamula Caste War rebellion
1876–1910	Dictatorship of Porfirio Díaz
1891	State capital moved to Tuxtla Gutiérrez
1908	Zinacantecos purchase tract of national land in Grijalva basin
1910	Mexican Revolution begins
1914	Revolutionary forces under Carranza take power in Chiapas
	Ley de Obreros enacted, freeing indentured Indian laborers
	Indians return from indentured lowland labor to the highlands
1917	Mexican constitution adopts agrarian plank with far-reaching land-reform provisions

TABLE 22. *A Condensed Chronology* (continued)

1920s	First Tzotzil petitions for land restitution made and largely ignored
1934–1940	Presidency of Lázaro Cárdenas Land reform begun in earnest Chamula scribes participate in labor reforms State Department of Indian Affairs established Chamulas and Zinacantecos buy up some highland ranches
1941	Zinacantecos acquire ejido donations under land reform
1948	First Chamula stills in operation
1952	Ladino liquor monopolists battle with Chamula distillers until the Department of Indian Affairs intervenes

but encroachment by Ladinos had begun in the form of ranches within the township confines.

After Mexican independence, policy makers faced two problems in the realm of land tenure. The first was to legitimize land titles from the colonial period. The second reflected acute awareness of the inequities of wealth distribution in the nation, conceived of as a problem in the distribution of people rather than of land. Population was concentrated in just a few small areas of Mexico. Rather than redistribute property, lawmakers attempted to redistribute people by means of "colonization" laws that offered incentives to those who would leave areas of dense population to colonize the north or the relatively undeveloped Isthmus of Tehuántepec. The same laws allowed for legitimization of colonial deeds for land that townships could re-entitle as though newly colonized.

In Chiapas, colonization laws were passed in the late 1820s. By the mid-1840s, Zinacantecos had taken advantage of these laws to entitle all the major tracts now thought of as "communal" (plate 19). The titles themselves are still extant and retain great significance in Zinacanteco eyes. Older men in several hamlets secretly guard title copies, which are recognized as validating Zinacanteco rights to their private property. The titles are believed to have magical powers conferring wealth upon their guardians. When improperly cared for, the titles become a cause for township-wide alarm. In 1967, the public's wrath

19. Boundary Marker. Boundary marker for Chamula "communal" tract probably dates from the 1850s. (Photo by author)

was aroused when one title guardian tried to use it as collateral for a bank loan. Township officials and hundreds of spectators retrieved the title and deposited it for safekeeping with another elder.

Zinacantecos believe that the titles for the communal tracts were purchased from the state governor by three men who later sold off portions of the property to other Zinacantecos. The titles do in fact name the men who initiated the petitions for the titles, using municipal funds to pay the state the fees for communal lands stipulated by law, and it is easy to imagine that other Zinacantecos viewed the procedure as a negotiation for land purchase from the state governor.

By the mid-nineteenth century, a fundamental change had come about in the economic and political philosophy behind Mexican land policy. For one, control of Mexican politics had shifted back and forth between liberals and conservatives during the 1830s and 1840s, and the Catholic church had increasingly been drawn into politics on the conservative side. Politically, the church became a target in debates about its enormous rural real estate holdings. For another, nineteenth-century economic liberalism had swept through Mexican intellectual circles. Increasingly, mechanisms were sought to create in rural Mexico a middle class of propertied farmers whose independent, competitive economic endeavors would bring rural development.

In 1856, the liberal Juárez regime came to power and passed laws to reorganize rural land tenure. Although interrupted by the Maximilian intervention, the Juárez laws, effective by 1863, expropriated rural church estates and required that all Indian communal tracts be turned over to natives as private property. Both measures would free rural peasantry from the grip of tradition, either in the form of church influence or deriving from antiquated communal mechanisms, and thus enhance the development of rural free enterprise.

Through much of Mexico, the Juárez laws, also known as the Leyes de Reforma, struck a crushing blow to Indian defenses against Ladino land encroachment. No longer could townships defend their lands corporately, utilizing communal funds. Furthermore, lands now required to be held individually could be purchased piecemeal from impoverished Indians and consolidated into larger non-Indian estates. In many areas, Indian communal organization disappeared, and Indians became simple debt-indentured peasants on new rural ranches. In Zinacantán, several formerly communal tracts were acquired in such a manner by Ladinos, and inhabitants of some hamlets did enter into debt-indentured labor arrangements in the ranches of the Grijalva Valley. Nonetheless, other Zinacantecos took advantage of the private-property option by purchasing a large tract of highland ranch from

Ladinos in the late 1860s. Modern accounts of the purchase indicate that three men acquired the tract and then sold off portions to other Zinacantecos, who came from several hamlets to settle on the land. Their descendants later abandoned the settlement and returned to other hamlets in the 1940s, but today they bear as lineage surnames the nickname of the original purchasers, a label that facilitates their unity in some contemporary factional disputes.

In the two decades before Mexico's revolution, Mexican liberalism was transformed into the positivist dictatorship of Porfirio Díaz, who brought rapid development through incentives to foreign investment in railroads and in rural economic enterprise—but at a price of strong-arm political cronyism and growing disparity between the wealth of the rich and the poverty of the rural masses. In this endeavor, Díaz's policy was to seek revenue for the government through the sale of national lands to surveying companies and other investors. Zinacantecos took advantage of this policy to acquire a lowland tract in the Grijalva Valley in 1908. Although they later abandoned their claim because they did not wish to settle a colony on the land as required by law, the transaction is proof that the Indian community was not rendered ineffective even by loss of communal lands and by drainage of its population into lowland debt peonage at the height of the Porfiriato.

After Mexico's revolution, the 1917 constitution included provisions limiting the size of private property holdings and outlining procedures for donating land to communities needing it. The land-reform program known as the "ejido" was based on these provisions but was not effected in Chiapas until the presidency of Cárdenas from 1934 to 1940.

To participate in the ejido,[2] villagers had to select a representative committee to petition for restitution of lands lost by the community through application of the Juárez Leyes de Reforma after 1856 and for donation of additional lands to alleviate property shortage. Review by a state agrarian commission established the validity of the petitions and designated lands to be expropriated for the purpose of donation. Approval by the state commission allowed petitioners to occupy the affected lands until official federal approval granted them full rights under ejido law. When this happened, the village selected an administrative body to distribute ejido lands and collect ejidal taxes.

In Zinacantán, the first petitions for land restitution and donation were made by separate hamlets during the 1920s but in the context

2. The summary of Zinacanteco participation in the ejido program is abstracted from Edel (1962).

of nationwide unwillingness to implement land reform. Not until the Cárdenas regime were subsequent efforts in Zinacantán successful. Then a flurry of petitions to the state commission for land restitution and donation were made by several hamlets. The commission merged the petitions into two groups comprising the eastern and western portions of the township, completed required surveys and censuses by the late 1930s, and finally granted land to petitioners by 1941 (plate 20).

While the land-reform planks of the 1917 constitution were to fulfill widespread desires of the landless Mexican peasant, it is clear that Zinacantecos did not embrace the program with complete enthusiasm. Many individuals refused to participate in submitting the initial petitions and in cooperating with subsequent administrative efforts for the ejido. Some feared that they would be conscripted if they signed petitions, and others were unwilling to share in the costs of petitioning for land. A few felt that land reform would jeopardize farming arrangements with existing ranches. In fact, Zinacantán's ejido participation seems to have been largely the result of the organizing efforts of a few determined men. These leaders stimulated the early petitions of several hamlets, rallied political support within the community, and put constant pressure on engineers and agrarian-commission officials to ignore the requests of private landholders that their properties be treated specially so as to avoid expropriation.

One man, in particular, was involved in the ejido effort from start to finish. Once the state had granted the ejido to Zinacantán in 1940, this man was selected president of the township ejido committee. Throughout the 1940s, he perpetuated his tenure of one or another ejidal post and used his position to build a political following so strong among ejido participants that he was able to dominate Zinacanteco political life until recently, repeatedly selecting township presidents and other civil officials who would favor his interests.

The Indian in Highland Chiapas History

It is a commonplace that, after the Spanish Conquest, Indians were a subordinated and exploited class in colonial Latin America. The facts. however, are more complicated. Indeed, the Indian was exploited and abused in many respects. But it is much more interesting to recognize that Indians occupied a special position in the colony, which gave them a voice and a certain degree of influence within colonial society. This position was most clearly articulated during the sixteenth-century debate between clerics and colonists over basic human rights of Indians, which resulted in explicit crown policies to protect the interests of the Indian in a form of indirect rule. The mechanisms of communal land tenure, the formally legitimized statuses of an Indian nobility, the establishment of a separate judiciary for Indians that would bypass local civil jurisdictions—all these were elements of a fundamentally pro-Indian philosophy on the part of the Spanish crown.

There is good evidence that Indians in highland Chiapas took advantage of this special status in a manner similar to that of Indians elsewhere in Mexico. Archives of court litigation show that, time and again through the colonial period, Tzotzil and Tzeltal groups could articulate their ethnic status into sanctions and action on their behalf against colonist exploiters and even clerics. Upon occasion, Indian uprisings and rebellions served to emphasize the numerical power of Indians, which was not inconsequential in remote areas like central Chiapas. The most notable example was the Tzeltal rebellion of 1712, in which Indians from many townships became followers of a cult that would establish a native ritual clergy to administer the Catholic rites and lead efforts to exterminate the colonists. The rebellion seems to have developed because of widespread dissatisfaction with changes in the activities of Catholic clergy, who began to extort inordinate fees for services and to manipulate commodity prices abusively.

It is true that Indians played the role of a subordinated labor force during the latter part of the colony and after independence. Throughout that period, over half of Chiapas's Ladino population lived in San Cristóbal and Comitán, the most important commercial centers. From there, they directed operations on countless ranches in all zones to raise sugar, cacao, cotton, coffee, and cattle for trade with Mexico or Guatemala. Indians were usually the labor force on these ranches, particularly after 1856 when Ladinos came to control more and more of the lands traditionally owned by Indian groups. In this period, Indians maintained special relationships to the ranches. Seventy or more Indian families might live as indentured laborers on such a ranch, bound to the land to work off debts of hundreds of pesos at the rate of an eighth of a peso per day. In addition to their wage, Indian workers were given housing and a monthly ration of corn and beans. Often, they developed ties of ritual kinship (*compadrazgo*) with the ranch owner or foreman, who would sponsor their children's baptism. On the outskirts of the ranches were groups of *baldíos*, Indians willing to provide the landowner with their work one week out of every four in return for use of the land. Such relationships of Indians to the ranches were sought out by Indians with no resources other than their labor or were actively solicited by agents of the ranch owners, who offered Indians cash in return for indentured status.

Even while these patterns were prevalent, however, Indians could respond to their categorically special position within society. The best example is the Chamula rebellion of 1869. In the few years prior to 1869, Chiapas politics had been rent with liberal-conservative factional disputes paralleling national issues. The land aristocracy of San Cristóbal were proclerical conservatives who had tacitly supported the French intervention. Now, under Juárez, liberals had removed state government to lowland Chiapa de Corzo. When an Indian saint cult emerged similar in nature to that which had fostered the terrible Tzeltal rebellion of 1712, San Cristóbal conservatives appealed to the liberal government to suppress the cult. Liberals responded that the separation of church and state protected Indians' right to worship as they pleased. Thus, Indians, as a bloc, were in a position of playing off the local Ladino elite against liberal nationals in a manner reminiscent of the tripartite division of Indians, colonists, and clergy in the sixteenth century.

Matters came to a head when a dissident liberal schoolteacher entered Chamula to convert the cult into a militaristic movement that would rise to destroy the Ladino suppressors on the model of the violent Caste War in the Yucatán. In 1869, the Chamula cultists killed a cleric and precipitated an armed rising that nearly overran San Cristóbal. Although the movement was put down, the uprising has served as clear warning to administrators and government officials ever since to respect the potential power and tacit rights of Indians.

The Porfiriato brought changes to Chiapas that, if not directly affecting Indian society, had profound impact on the structure of regional society. Although the seat of state government had been returned to San Cristóbal in the 1870s, the liberal-conservative political axis did not change, the highland capital remaining the locus of power of a cultured oligarchy of conservative clergy, army chiefs, and rich property owners. Liberals, however, continued to favor another lowland town, Tuxtla Gutiérrez, for the locus of government. The ascendancy of Díaz brought support to the lay elite of Tuxtla Gutiérrez which did not share its power with the church and could accept the positivism of the Porfiriato. Because Díaz's support in Chiapas had always come from Tuxtla Gutiérrez, he turned, when in power, to the Tuxtla Gutiérrez faction for the control of Chiapas politics. Furthermore, economic factors strongly favored Tuxtla as a political center. San Cristóbal had always turned to Guatemala for the bulk of its trade and had developed only a small industry catering to Indian demands for fireworks, candles, and cloth. It thus feared Díaz's program to promote a rising middle class based on commerce and industry centered in Tuxtla Gutiérrez, a natural communications center much closer than San Cristóbal to the expanding plantation area of the Soconusco, soon to be linked by rail with the rest of the country.

The definitive transfer of the capital took place in 1891 with immediate detriment to San Cristóbal's economic and political status. Former businessmen and lawyers there turned to agriculture in the most backward area of the national economy. At the turn of the century, San Cristóbal remained as dependent on a landed oligarchy and on exploitation of the Indian as it had been in the 1860s, while other areas flourished economically under Díaz's stimulating (if tightfisted) control. San Cristóbal's loss of economic and political power had no immediate impact on the status of Indians, but it paved the way for more dramatic loss of control by highland Ladinos over Indian communities after the Revolution, when Tuxtla Gutiérrez continued to retain economic and political control of the region.

In 1914, followers of Carranza entered Chiapas and began the work of the Revolution with anticlerical measures. More significantly, they passed the Ley de Obreros, which abolished company stores and set up a minimum wage, norms for health and accident compensations, freedom of residence, and cash wages for workers—all measures to help free indentured workers. The Carrancistas demanded these changes with arms in hand, entering many ranches and forcing the departure of even those peons who did not want to go. San Cristóbal landowners attempted military countermoves to forestall their ruin, but these efforts failed. The result was abrupt change in the economy of Chiapas ranching after 1914. With debt-indentured slavery abolished, Indian families left the ranches to return to their former villages. Elder Zinacantecos recall the period as one in which their fathers returned from the lowlands to beg land and housing from their wealthier compatriots who had not entered into labor indenture, working for them for a period of years and finally purchasing land from them.

Once the economic grip by highland Ladinos over Indians was broken, natives entered actively into local-level politics. We have seen above how land reform in Zinacantán led to political reorganization of the community after 1940. In nearby Chamula (Prokosch 1963), the land reform and labor-organizing activities of the Cárdenas era also proved catalytic to development of political bossism. In 1944, Chamula had not reconciled traditional government with a new body of municipal officials required by state law. The amorphousness of political control was further complicated by a body of eleven scribes, young men associated with but not part of the civil leadership who, because of their ability to read and write, participated in most affairs involving the community with the state. Yet by 1962 power clearly lay in the hands of four men, energetic young scribes of 1944 whose progressive outlook led them to be trusted by Chamulas as well as state officials. After 1944, each was able to perpetuate his tenure of one political office until he found another position of power. One man became secretary of the state-sponsored labor syndicate, a critical position of power, since land-hungry Chamula relies heavily on wage labor for its sustenance. Two others secured positions on the Chamula ejido committee, and a fourth collaborated with the National Indian Institute to start a cooperative store and trucking line. By cooperating with the outside, these leaders bettered their own interests as well as those of other Chamulas and developed a political base that allows them, like their counterpart in Zinacantán, to hand-pick municipal officials and thus control the community's internal politics.

Land reform had the additional effect of freeing much of the highlands from Ladino control. An unknown number of their ranches, carved from Indian lands after passage of the Juárez laws, were returned to Indians by the ejido movement. Additional holdings were expropriated to donate to the ejidos, and, in many cases, remaining private holdings were sold outright to Indians by their Ladino owners, who saw no economic future for drastically reduced highland holdings. Thus, land reform transformed Indian communities from a patchwork of small Indian hamlets interspersed between Ladino properties into an area of consolidated and continuous Indian control.

Eric R. Wolf (1959, p. 230) has described the Indian community as being in a symbiotic relation with the hacienda, the former dependent on seasonal labor for its sustenance in lieu of land and water, the latter dependent on a convenient, ready, and cheap labor supply for its economic growth. Such a description seems appropriate to the late nineteenth-century highland Chiapas situation. The ranches of the San Cristóbal elite contained all the viable highland agricultural areas. Debt peonage was the prevalent form of labor recruitment. Indian communities, shorn of their lands by the Leyes de Reforma, had no alternative to the symbiotic existence that Wolf describes.

Indian communities in Chiapas today have a totally different character. Their symbiosis with the hacienda no longer exists. Replacing it is a community that has retained and reemphasized its Indian identity, vesting its political power in the leadership of a few energetic and forceful men, dealing with the outside world not as a dominated caste but as a collectivity negotiating with a state government that mediates between society's elements.

It is easy to note that these changes had their roots in the political and land reforms of the Cárdenas era. And it is clear that the shifting locus of state political power during the Porfiriato facilitated the change by forcing Indian communities to restructure their lines of communication to a government no longer favoring San Cristóbal's landed interests. Yet the view of the nineteenth-century Indian community as a passive participant in a symbiosis with the hacienda is a deceptive one. The initiative and organization of Indian community leaders in the 1930s and 1940s had not been absent under the hacienda system. How could Zinacantecos have obtained three large tracts of communal land, purchased a sizeable ranch, and attempted to secure a huge tract of lowland national land at the height of the Porfiriato without that kind of initiative? Indeed, accounts by informants, who say that these efforts were spearheaded by a few capable men who secured land in order to sell it to their compatriots, suggest a political opportunism at least on a par with that of native political leadership today. In fact, given the evidence of a categorically special position of the Indian in regional social structure dating from the sixteenth century, it seems clear that such leadership is characteristic of interaction across the Indian-Ladino ethnic interface.

The connection of native leadership to activist roles in relation to land may be general to communities of the closed-corporate peasant type. Wolf (1955, 1957) has described such communities as limiting access to land to legitimate community members in various ways. "Open" communities, by contrast, do not have communal jurisdiction over land. Such jurisdiction is related to ritual, economic, and cultural mechanisms that constitute a "barrier against the entry of goods and ideas produced outside the community" (1957, p. 6). Natives whose mediation with the outside world reinforces corporate jurisdiction over land thus play a crucial role in the continuance of the closed-corporate community. Although other local officials share middleman status in the domains of administration, conflict resolution, and religion, land leaders often hold center stage in local-level politics. The dramatic events of the Mexican Revolution and subsequent agrarian reform have highlighted leaders of agrarian revolts, such as Zapata (Womack 1969) and Primo Tapia (Friedrich 1970), but the less dramatic evidence from earlier periods is also of native leaders who fought for their community lands.

Agrarian leaders thus use their knowledge of the outside world to structure the relations of the local community to it in a manner that

20. Zinacantán Center. The ceremonial center of Zinacantán was
surrounded by Ladino-owned ranches, visible as grazing land on the
periphery and in the far end of the valley, until affected by land
reform after the 1930s. (Photo courtesy of Harvard Chiapas Project
and Cía. Mexicana de Aerofotos, S.A.)

heightens ethnicity. In this case, knowledge does not erode ethnic boundaries but rather reinforces them. In fact, it seems doubtful that the Indian community, even in its phases of greatest "closure," ever lacked the knowledge of external realities directly bearing on its most important interests.

MOBILITY AND ETHNICITY

Our examination of highland Chiapas ethnic boundaries will continue within the context of demographic trends. Both widespread depopulation in the early colonial period and dramatic population growth in recent times have resulted in redistribution of ethnic peoples above and beyond that associated with the domestic cycle or with gradual readjustment to microecological conditions. The evidence is that natives can and do cross ethnic-group boundaries and thereby redefine their ethnic identity. Yet patterns of ethnicity are little changed as a result, exhibiting greater durability than the patterns by which people are tied to locality.

Resettlement at the Local Level

Tzotzil and Tzeltal settlement patterns are much more effectively described as being in systematic flux than by means of any static representation. The most regular settlement-pattern changes are associated with social universals of the domestic cycle and take the form of constant relocation of small numbers of individuals. In a much more gradual cycle, resettlement of larger aggregates, as when hamlets are formed or abandoned, appears as response to microecological change (plates 21, 22, and 23).

Domestic-cycle settlement changes are such as were described in earlier chapters. Marriage and maturation usually occasion these domestic shifts, which commonly are within one hamlet, sometimes between adjacent hamlets of one township, but rarely across township or ethnic boundaries. Because the relative proportion of families in various stages of the domestic cycle is fairly stable, these shifts in residence occur regularly.

Residence changes in themselves, while they may reflect no more than the dynamics of domestic-group maturation, can be economically or ecologically motivated. A young man without land may move to live with his wealthier in-laws to farm his wife's inherited land. Construction of a new highway may induce young couples to use the occasion of a domestic-group split to set up a roadside store on purchased land. Again, moves tend to be short, usually within a hamlet and rarely across ethnic or township boundaries.

From time to time, entire hamlets have resettled for reasons having to do with economic opportunity or microecological constraints. One Zinacanteco hamlet was formed in the late nineteenth century to exploit newly purchased ranch lands. Three generations of farming, however, resulted in exhausted fields and reduced corn yields. More significantly, the capacity of local soils to hold water was reduced by overly intense farming to the point where wells that had been year-round water sources began to dry out in early spring. Within a few years, the settlement was abandoned and its population redistributed among other Zinacanteco hamlets with permanent water supplies. Another example is that of a Chamula hamlet that is seasonally transhumant, taking advantage of rainy summer to herd sheep on grasslands of its older settlement where wells succumbed to abusive land-use practices, reducing the springtime water table and precluding permanent settlement.

Although many hamlets have supported populations continually since the Conquest, the number of abandoned or depopulated settlements is large enough to suggest a slow cycle in which agriculturalists gradually have shifted across the highland landscape so as to exploit tracts and then abandon them to extended regrowth. Such a pattern would be compatible with long-range stability in the man-land interaction if land use did not, as in Chamula, result in irreversible abuse.

For purposes of this chapter, domestic-group shifts and more gradual resettlement at the local level are considered as characteristic of highland Chiapas settlement flux. Both occur largely within the constraints of locality implied by ethnic territoriality and would appear to explain the loosely aggregated character of settlement throughout the Maya area. In this regard, they contrast with population regrouping of the early colonial period and expansive colonization of recent times, motivated by depopulation and population explosion, respectively.

Colonial Depopulation

Population trends in colonial New Spain have been reconstructed from census records and tribute roles. Although highland Chiapas was administratively part of the Audiencia de Guatemala, documentary clues point to population trends there that were parallel to those reconstructed farther to the north.

Controversy in Mesoamerican historical demography revolves around the widely divergent estimates of aboriginal population at the Conquest. The best evidence points to an Indian population at least as large as that found today. The dramatic depopulation of most areas after the Conquest, however, is not controversial. In the first century after the Conquest, native population fell to one-fifth of its aboriginal level or less; it continued at that level through the seventeenth century and then ascended gradually through the last century of the colony and more rapidly since independence to reach the high levels found today.

Many factors contributed to rapid depopulation in the sixteenth century. Natives had little or no resistance to many European diseases; smallpox, measles, and other epidemic diseases took heavy tolls. and venereal disease probably lowered fertility. Polemicists have pointed to specific abuses by the colonists as causing population decline, but it is more likely that indirect effects of colonization had a greater demographic impact. For one, herding of European livestock replaced agriculture in many areas that were fallow at the Conquest, reducing the land area available for swidden agriculture. In effect. cattle herds replaced people, the geometric growth of the former being as spectacular as the decline of the latter. In turn, a reduced land base meant a diminished food supply, poorer nutrition, and greater susceptibility to disease. Finally, the mechanisms of labor recruitment for mining, transport, construction, and, later, plantation agriculture dislocated native communities and relocated their inhabitants in novel, sometimes hostile, environments.

Rural depopulation presented colonists with tremendous administrative headaches. To begin with, depopulation undermined Spanish efforts to restructure native settlement patterns. Civilized life in medieval Spain, even in rural areas, was in tightly nucleated towns, and colonists could not comprehend the native pattern of scattered settlement, considering it an aberration of an otherwise sophisticated social system. To further its civilizing goal, and also to facilitate evangelization and administration, the crown established the practice of aggregating scattered native groups into nucleated townships. Tribute quotas were levied on such townships in proportion to their population. Depopulation often undermined these resettlement efforts. decimating many townships to the point where the surviving populace would flee to widely dispersed rural settlements to avoid inequitable tribute levies. Renewed efforts to concentrate rural natives would meet with comparably desultory results.

The unsystematic record of highland Chiapas ethnohistory reflects the prevalence of these patterns of depopulation. Drought, famine, epidemic disease, and emigration all occasioned specific instances of dispersal and subsequent regrouping of natives for administrative control. Locally distinguishable ethnic entities were merged into larger aggregate units and sometimes recombined at a later date. Over the long run, tribal intermixture must have been considerable. Nevertheless, certain overall patterns of ethnicity changed little. Many Indian townships, Chamula and Zinacantán, for instance, endured as ethnic entities through the colonial period to modern times, often with significant continuities in their internal organization. Intertribal relations also retained much of their aboriginal mold, as in the case of ritual linkages between Zinacantán, neighboring Ixtapa, and lowland San Lucas. And the subdivision of highland natives into Tzeltal- and Tzotzil-speaking groups has been geographically stable.

Thus, ethnic-group boundaries were not destroyed by mobility in the colonial period resulting from depopulation. Rather than serving as barriers to mobility, ethnic lines delimit classes of native peoples whose membership can change and, at the same time, create a framework for enduring intergroup relations.

Population Growth

Depopulation abated gradually by the close of the colonial period. Trends of the nineteenth century were toward population growth, which continues today. National census compilations show unabated growth among the Tzotzil and Tzeltal in recent decades. While population growth may have had indirect economic stimulus, the aggregate effect of growth has been pressure on resources sufficient to motivate migration, and in some instances aggressive colonization by highlanders. Once again, however, we find ethnic patterns to be more durable at the level of intergroup relations than for individuals.

Table 23 displays official census enumerations for the eight native townships nearest San Cristóbal de las Casas. The statistics show an annual population growth rate of 1.6 percent for the 1950–1960 decade, 2.6 percent for the 1940–1950 period, and 6.1 percent from 1930 to 1940. Although the earlier figures seem to reflect underenumeration, the latest census appears internally consistent and reasonably accurate.

Analysis of the population growth rate requires a breakdown to evaluate how births offset deaths. Direct measures of mortality in these townships are not available but may be inferred from figure 16; the population pyramid for the Tzeltal and Tzotzil townships contrasts

TABLE 23. *Population Trends*

Township	1930	1940	1950	1960
Amatenango del Valle	—	2,136	2,529	3,179
Chamula	8,677	16,010	22,029	26,789
Chenalhó	3,958	5,289	7,481	10,553
Huistán	4,205	5,090	7,383	7,421
Larraínzar	3,707	8,521	8,807	7,337
Mitontic	1,449	3,572	3,880	4,677
Tenejapa	2,931	5,378	7,750	9,768
Zinacantán	2,129	4,509	6,312	7,650

Note: Census enumerations in eight Tzotzil and Tzeltal townships from 1930 to 1960.

with that for the United States in the high mortality associated with all ages, especially infancy, requiring a very high birth rate simply to maintain a constant population.

The fact of steady population growth is not to be explained by declining mortality. It is true that some immunization and other public health services have become available in this century, but primarily to Ladinos in urban centers. Differential birth rates among the Tzotzil and Tzeltal apparently are best explained by variations in marriage patterns. Table 24 shows that the populations with the largest proportions of children aged four years and younger are populations in which the higher proportions of women under age twenty are married. Presumably, economic conditions favoring increases in manpower could elicit earlier marriage and higher fertility, and it is suggestive to note that the three townships with highest proportions of young children and young brides (Amatenango, Chamula, and San Andrés Larraínzar) are also heavily dependent upon wage labor. By contrast, in communities where land is the significant resource, young men tend to wait for land inheritance, permitting some measure of self-support before entering marriage; consequently, their courtships are longer and their brides probably older at first conception.

In the long run, population growth increases demographic pressure on local resources and may stimulate migration. Unfortunately, census and other records do not afford suitable measures of migration rates within the Chiapas highlands, but notable examples of migration have been described ethnographically. In general, native migration is of two kinds: (1) sporadic resettlement by individuals who subsequently change their ethnic identity, and (2) chauvinistic, invasive

Tzotzil pyramid

U.S. pyramid

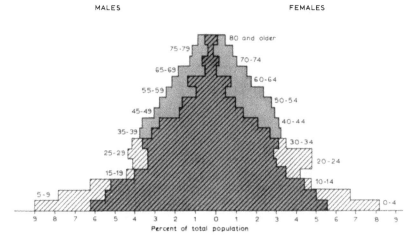

Fig. 16. Population Pyramid for Tzotzil and Tzeltal Townships

TABLE 24. *Early-Marriage and Birth Rates*

Township	Variable (see key on page 160)			
	1 (%)	2 (%)	3 (%)	4 (%)
Amatenango del Valle	2.96	17.8	42.1	17.2
Chamula	9.28	18.5	40.4	26.9
Chenalhó	2.92	17.1	39.2	21.6
Huistán	3.82	16.9	39.0	19.3
Larraínzar	4.39	17.4	49.8	32.5
Mitontic	4.41	16.0	45.4	19.9
Tenejapa	2.31	15.3	25.6	11.7
Zinacantán	1.88	14.5	36.6	17.3

Township	Rank of Variable			
	1	2	3	4
Amatenango del Valle	4	7	6	2
Chamula	8	8	5	7
Chenalhó	3	5	4	6

TABLE 24. *Early-Marriage and Birth Rates* (continued)

Huistán	5	4	3	4
Larraínzar	6	6	8	8
Mitontic	7	3	7	5
Tenejapa	2	2	1	1
Zinacantán	1	1	2	3

Spearman Rank-Order Correlation between Variables			
Variables	2	3	4
1	0.643	0.714	0.666
2		0.595	0.524
3			0.643

Note: The table uses available census data to explore the relationship between early marriage and fertility. The incidence of children under one year and under five years as a percentage of total population is taken to reflect fertility. Two variables measure marriage and childbearing in the 14–19 age range of women. The high rank-order correlations between all four variables suggest that high fertility is linked to early marriage.

Key to variables: Variables are computed from official census figures of the *VIII Censo General de Población. 1960.* Secretaría de Industria y Comercio, Dirección General de Estadística, Mexico City, 1963.

1. Children under one year of age as a percentage of total population (from table 6 of the census).
2. Children aged up to 4 years as a percentage of total population (from table 6).
3. Women aged 14–19 and married, as a percentage of all women aged 14–19 (from table 8).
4. Percentage of women aged 15–19 who have borne one or more children (from table 31).

colonization by an ethnic group of neighboring lands.

In times of plenty, population can expand to the limits of local resources. Paradoxically, it is the reduction of these resources in periods of scarcity (rather than population growth itself) that forces an over-expanded population into migration. In such circumstances, individuals seek food and shelter where they may, often in another township. In Zinacantán, there are many such individuals who took up residence in the lean years subsequent to the Revolution. Over the years they married, bore offsping, and gradually entered into community life. The most notable example is that of a small hamlet on ranchland purchased cooperatively by Zinacanteco and Chamula farmhands in the 1930s. Although mixed in ethnic origin, hamlet dwellers now deny their Chamula ancestry, having assumed all the accouterments of Zinacanteco ethnic role behavior, including active participation in the expensive *cargo* system. Other notable examples are poor Ladinos who have abandoned their putatively superior cultural heritage to become Zinacantecos. Admittedly, the numbers of these ethnic transplants are not great, but they do illustrate the notion that ethnic identity need not be a barrier to mobility.

Chauvinistic, invasive colonization to augment farmland resources may pit one tribal group against another or against Ladino ranchers. Natives of Chamula have a reputation for aggressive colonization that dates at least to the mid-nineteenth-century incursive colonization by Chamulas of lands of neighboring Mitontic. In more recent times, Chamulas have been known to occupy nearby ranchlands with blitzkrieg efficiency overnight, moving families and livestock into a hastily constructed hamlet settlement and invoking legal sanctions afforded to settled communities by the Agrarian Code. A successful invasion will require effective leadership in the litigation bound to ensue and local-level politicking of the kind that has characterized interethnic relations from time immemorial. Finally, it should be noted that, while Chamulas have a well-deserved reputation for incursive colonization, having established ethnic enclaves in many parts of the state, other groups have been successful colonizers as well.

Both chauvinistic colonization and more sporadic migration by individuals are responses to demographic pressure that might be thought to lead to ethnic homogenization and ultimate breakdown of interethnic differences. In their sensitive analysis of ethnic relations in the Ixil region of Guatemala, for instance, Benjamin Colby and Pierre Van den Berghe (1969) argue that Indians who leave their homeland as migrants have an anomalous status. They belong neither to the predominant Indian group nor to the superordinate Ladino group in areas to which they migrate. In such a situation, they reason, Indians can easily choose to "pass" into the superordinate status. Clearly, the outcome of migration in highland Chiapas is otherwise. Individuals may change their ethnic group identity, or they may carry their old identity with them chauvinistically, but ethnic patterns are not eroded by either process. In the long run, ethnic patterns have survived both severe depopulation and dramatic population growth. The explanation of ethnic patterns requires inquiry into realms other than demographic.

ETHNICITY AND OCCUPATIONAL SPECIALTY

Variations in environment are commonly thought to underlie the dif-

21. An Ejido Colony. A substantial segment of the population of
Aguacatenango has resettled in the ejido colony of El Puerto. (Photo
courtesy of Harvard Chiapas Project and Cía. Mexicana de Aerofotos,
S.A.)

22. Aguacatenango Center. A substantial segment of the population of
Aguacatenango has resettled in the ejido colony of El Puerto.
(Photo courtesy of Harvard Chiapas Project and Cía. Mexicana de
Aerofotos, S.A.)

23. A Small Ejido Colony. Settlers in this recently established colony have obtained legal title to the tract whose boundary can be seen traversing the town edge and forest. (Photo courtesy of Harvard Chiapas Project and Cía. Mexicana de Aerofotos, S.A.)

ferentiation of ethnic groups that are economically interdependent. Examples that come to mind are reindeer herders in Scandinavia and pastoralists in Africa that produce protein foods at the fringes of agricultural zones to trade to sedentary populations. This section explores occupational specialties in highland Chiapas, which are of interest for two reasons: they are thought to be ethnically differentiated and sometimes have the reputation of being monopolized by certain townships. Yet they are crafts whose ethnic monopolization is more apparent than real, their production being quite widespread. Thus, the thrust of the discussion will be to rule out a simple correlation between the distribution of resources and ethnic boundaries in favor of a view of occupational specialties as the result (rather than the cause) of a dynamic system of ethnic differentiation.

Types of Occupational Specialty

Only certain products can be manufactured in highland Chiapas at costs that allow competition with nationally distributed goods. Distance from Mexico's urban core impedes importation to Chiapas of bulky goods but not compact products of heavy industry. Technologically backward and heavily reliant on extraction of raw materials (corn, sugar, lumber, and cattle), the state's economy favors commerce over manufacture, except manufacture utilizing local raw materials with low-level technology. Until recent establishment of a modern textile mill, industry in San Cristóbal has been limited to a scale at best one step up from household industry, such as tile, brick, and pottery making, baking, distilling, weaving, and other enterprises that may be large enough to employ several workers under a foreman responsible to family ownership. Service occupations, such as legal, medical, and educational professionalism, automobile repair, trucking, banking, mailing, and so forth, parallel manufacturing in scope.

By and large, these occupations are limited to Ladinos of San Cristóbal de las Casas who also dominate the commercial sphere (plate 24). Indian ethnic groups, however, are partially distinguished by small-scale craft production. Indian production is one order of magnitude farther removed than Ladino manufacture from that of the nation, utilizing the very simplest technology for the very crudest transformations of natural resources and relying heavily on human labor input, as in the following examples (plates 25, 26, and 27).

Pottery. The pottery industry of Amatenango has been described by Nash (1970). Amatenango produces a variety of containers, censers,

24. San Cristóbal. San Cristóbal dominates highland commerce. (Photo courtesy of Harvard Chiapas Project and Cía. Mexicana de Aerofotos, S.A.)

25. Chamula Instruments. Zinacanteco musician and instruments of
   Chamula manufacture. (Photo courtesy of Frank Cancian)

26. Amatenango Pots. Water pot from Amatenango at lowland rental
farm site. (Photo courtesy of Frank Cancian)

27. Bootleg Liquor. Zinacanteco shaman prays in ritual for which
participants consume bootleg liquor of Chamula manufacture. (Photo
courtesy of Frank Cancian)

and candleholders, which are transported into San Cristóbal and distributed through the market mechanism. Virtually all Indian groups, and poorer Ladinos as well, utilize the simply but distinctively ornamented Amatenango water jar.

Outsiders see pottery production as Amatenango's principal activity, despite the fact that potmaking is a full-time occupation only for poorer women. Although men market the town's crockery, most men are part-time agriculturalists who complement farming with agricultural or other forms of wage labor. While potmaking contributes 15 to 20 percent of the township's aggregate income, proceeds from other sources are substantial.

While Amatenango has a wide market for its distinctive ware, it is not without competition from other townships. Chamula, for instance, has a hamlet with a specialty in ceramic cookware of which any Zinacanteco home contains many pieces. *Cargo* holders, in particular, prize the larger cookpots, whose capacity can exceed thirty gallons. There is some evidence that Chamula has supplanted Amatenango production of the larger ceremonial cookware. The craft has grown in importance since Pozas's study (1959) of Chamula, men now being active in a sphere that formerly was women's work; meanwhile, manufacture of such cookware in Amatenango has died out. Furthermore, ceramic production from the parish of San Ramón in San Cristóbal supplies the region with a widely used glazed bean bowl. Finally, even in hamlets of Zinacantán without craft specialties, women make pottery griddles for home use and occasional sale. Thus, potting is an activity more diffuse than it would appear to be from ethnic-group reputation. While Amatenango is thought of as the potters' town, in fact it produces only a few of the distinctive wares found in the central highlands.

Wool Weaving. When Chamula's ejidal commissioner travels to Mexico City on official business, he packs a bag of the finest traditional garb. Perhaps his most elegant garment is a thick, finely woven, glistening black tunic, an unusual specimen in size and quality of another product specialty, woven woolens.

Although most highland Indians herd sheep, Chamula weavers have the reputation for the finest wool products. For while women of other groups weave for home demand, only Chamula women weave on a scale keyed to export. At the daily market in San Cristóbal, in the regular weekly Chamula market, and at other regular market sites throughout the highlands, it is to Chamula women that Indians from other tribes go to purchase raw wool or to commission weaving.

Chamulas do not exercise a monopoly of the wool-weaving craft. Nevertheless, weaving for sale is a specialty that is marked for ethnic identity and that is, as well, coordinate with the widespread availability of grazing land in Chamula.

The Salt Trade. Before the Pan American Highway was constructed. San Cristóbal was linked to the west by horse and oxen trails through the ceremonial centers of Zinacantán and Ixtapa. Along this valley route are several salt wells that have been exploited for trade since colonial times or earlier. Sacred salt wells in one Zinacanteco hamlet are the source of salt distributed to *cargo* holders through the Esquipulas saint cult. Ixtapa wells are of much greater productive capacity and are the source of an export trade.

Four Zinacanteco descent groups have monopolized the salt trade for several generations. The active traders in each group purchase salt cakes in Ixtapa at bulk rates, pack them on mules, and trade along fixed noncompeting routes through the highlands. The traders pack other goods. mostly agricultural produce in season. to complement the income from salt. Sale is predominantly at the regular and periodic market sites that dot the remote hinterlands (plate 26).

Natives confuse Ixtapa salt with Zinacanteco salt and distinguish both from that available at competitive prices from the seacoast. While Ixtapa salt is "neutral," sea salt is "hot" and could have deleterious effects on certain illnesses. Thus. the Zinacanteco salt trade in the highlands is in a commodity that expanding commerce cannot readily replace and that other highland groups inevitably associate with Zinacantecos.

Distilling. In Tzotzil discourse. a suppliant cannot rely on the power of words alone to produce compliance but must lend force to his entreaty with a gift of liquor, which, when received and consumed by the listener, binds him to the terms of an agreement. Formal interaction, marked by stylized speech and systematic conversion of role-typed or status relations into relations of respect, pervades Zinacanteco life from petty contractual economic relations to the ritual spheres of curing and *cargos* and permeates the realm of conflict resolution and politics, as well. Since the gift of liquor is the most forceful sign of respect, its consumption is high, and its production, distribution, and sale are of great economic importance.

Although beer and commercial rum are coming into wider use. the traditional gift of liquor is locally distilled from cane sugar. In its purest form, *aguardiente* is colorless and about 80 proof. Except in most formal circumstances, it is diluted to about half-strength and bottled in liter. fifth, half-fifth, or quarter-fifth containers.

Until the 1940s, liquor production was monopolized by three or four Ladino families in San Cristóbal. Sugar, in the form of partially refined dark cakes, was transported from cane growers in the lowland area near Villa las Rosas and distilled in San Cristóbal. In distribution each distiller monopolized a discrete marketing area of the Indian hinterland.

Today, clandestine distilleries in Chamula compete for a large share of the native *aguardiente* market. The development of this production specialty can be traced to the late 1940s. At that time, three of the Ladino distillers in San Cristóbal sold out to the fourth, creating a larger liquor monopoly. The monopolist attempted to increase his profits by lowering the price he would pay to cane producers for sugar. When cane farmers resisted the pricing change, the monopolist purchased sugar from out-of-state, allowing the local crop to be left to rot unpurchased. Ironically, the price of sugar dropped so low locally that a few Chamula families were able to afford an initial investment in sugar and to build the first Indian distilleries.

By the early 1950s, clandestine Chamula production began to dent the monopolist's market. To suppress the competition, a mercenary force was sent to destroy Chamula stills. The force was ambushed in the Chamula hills and many were wounded, creating a wave of rumors and fear that Chamulas were ready to repeat the Caste War rebellion of 1869. To calm the tense situation, the state Office of Indian Affairs arranged a compromise in which Chamulas brought into their ceremonial center large numbers of stills for confiscation in return for a pledge that private policing of the township would cease. It would appear, however, that clandestine production quickly resumed at its former level and then expanded to meet a ready demand: the clandestine product sells for about one-half the cost of its commercial counterpart and is more tasty.

Only a circumscribed region in Chamula specializes in *aguardiente* distillation. Sugar is trucked or mule-packed to the still, mixed with water and spume from earlier batches, and allowed to ferment in large containers. The mash is cooked in a sealed metal drum, its vapor channeled off through a copper tube immersed in water to condense out the liquor. Larger stills, disguised as Indian huts, are built over channels of diverted streams so as to have a constant flow of cold water for efficient distillation. Localization appears related to a combination of factors. a year-round, stream-fed water supply, access to timber for fuel to fire the stills, and proximity to transport for importation of bulk sugar.

Chamula *aguardiente* is marketed as a five-gallon unit in the traditional stave barrel and in commercial glass jugs. Distribution is clandestine, usually by pack train or tumpline. Chamula vendors frequent the ceremonial centers of neighboring townships and cater to *cargo* holders. *Cargo* holders who wish to cut costs contract for delivery at the still and use their own or borrowed horses for transport. One *cargo* holder in Zinacantán, for instance, in the purchase of fifty gallons of *aguardiente* for his ritual role in the township's major fiesta alone, saved three hundred of the seven hundred pesos he would have to pay a Chamula vendor by taking delivery at the still.

Chamula *aguardiente* carries with it a distinction in aroma. flavor, and strength that marks it as a product of ethnic specialization. While there are many small-time clandestine distillers in other townships, their product is thought not equivalent in quality to that from Chamula. Like Amatenango pottery, Chamula *aguardiente* is in a class of its own, despite its imitators.

The Ethnic Facet of Specialization

Many other craft goods are produced as specialties by highland Chiapas natives, usually as crude imitations of material items of Ladino culture. A carpentry industry in Chamula, for instance, exports the cheap, unfinished miniaturized furniture for Indian homes, paralleling professional Ladino carpentry of finely finished, sturdy goods. Another hamlet manufactures musical instruments. again poor imitations of those utilized by Ladinos. By and large, these goods are associated in some way with ethnic product specialization. Can this association be explained?

Ethnicity is often equated with traditional behavior. Perhaps ethnic productive specialty can better be understood, if not explained, as an extension of occupational tradition. This notion would appear to have some merit: occupational specialization by township can be traced back into the eighteenth century at least and probably earlier.

Late in the colonial period, the Spanish crown commissioned a report on economic conditions in the New World. Travel and investigation, primarily in South America, of two military officers, Jorge Juan and Antonio de Ulloa, resulted in a secret report that the crown suppressed because of its revelations of exploitive abuses of a system called the *repartimiento*. Ironically, the suppressed report emerged in translation in rival England as the basis for a propaganda attack against Spain.

The *repartimiento* was practiced in highland Chiapas. The system was originated to generate cash revenue for Indians to pay their tribute and taxes. Associated with the office of *alcalde mayor* (equivalent to a regional governor) was the prerogative to commerce in goods of Indian townships. The official would purchase bulk goods at a fixed price in one township and sell them for a fixed profit to natives of another. The most important commodity was cotton, purchased in the lowlands and sold to certain townships for conversion into thread, purchased back at a slightly higher price and resold to be woven into cloth, again to be repurchased and sold in fixed quotas to yet other townships for clothing. Many products of agriculture and simple manufacture were linked by fixed quotas to specific townships. The *alcalde mayor* thus operated a vast, centralized redistributive cartel in which townships were guaranteed the revenue derived from simple crafts. The redistributive mechanism outlasted a given official's tenure, being the prerogative of the office and having a recognized annual profit, to which each new officeholder would acquire rights by purchase.

Thus, while only a few ethnically distinct crafts can be traced back definitively into the colonial period, it is clear that the pattern of ethnically specialized production is traditonal.

As such, craft specialization plays a part in the stereotyped conceptions that native groups have of one another. Many highland Tzeltal natives, for instance, stereotype Zinacantecos as salt merchants despite the overwhelming volume of Zinacanteco entrepreneurial corn farming. Similarly, Zinacantecos view Huistecos as herders because they see Huisteco plow teams on Ladino lands. Henning Siverts (1969*a*) has developed an abstract diagram of the marketing of specialized products (fig. 17), which concentrates on the redistributive mechanism of the San Cristóbal market. The diagram suggests that the source of ethnic stereotyping of specialization is in the images that Indian shoppers would carry away from a trading trip there, as well as from the highly structured trading between Indian townships not incorporated into Siverts's model. The ethnic component of crafts and special produce, therefore, may be an artifact of natives' view of the system.

The Niche of Production Specialties

The widespread association of particular crafts with particular townships suggests that specialties represent adaptation to distinctive phys-

28. Periodic Market Site. Several trails converge on the market site of
Yocib, in the foreground. The market is sometimes visited by
Zinacanteco salt merchants. (Photo courtesy of Harvard Chiapas
Project and Cía. Mexicana de Aerofotos, S.A.)

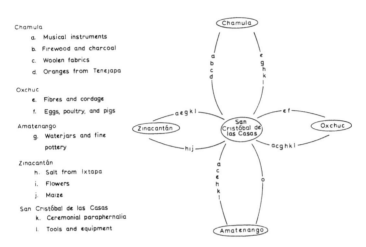

Chamula
  a. Musical instruments
  b. Firewood and charcoal
  c. Woolen fabrics
  d. Oranges from Tenejapa

Oxchuc
  e. Fibres and cordage
  f. Eggs, poultry, and pigs

Amatenango
  g. Waterjars and fine
     pottery

Zinacantán
  h. Salt from Ixtapa
  i. Flowers
  j. Maize

San Cristóbal de las Casas
  k. Ceremonial paraphernalia
  l. Tools and equipment

Fig. 17. Craft Marketing. The San Cristóbal market and a simplified representation of the flow of commercial goods. (After Siverts 1969*a*)

iographic niches. The efficient, larger *aguardiente* stills, for instance, utilize one of the few year-round streams in the highlands as coolant. The Chamula hamlets exploiting woven woolens are centered in the extensive Chamula grazing lands. And Ixtapa salt wells are unusually rich. These examples are in the minority, however, for monopolization of craft production is more apparent than real. Occupations like pottery making utilize local clay and firewood resources that are of wide distribution in the region. Local physiographic niches are thus only partially coextensive with specialization.

The concept of "niche," however, can be generalized to incorporate a larger locational field than that encompassed by local physiography. In biology, the niche is sometimes defined as the variables that impinge upon an organism; these variables may include the characteristics of a locality, but they incorporate, as well, such features as temporal relations (as in the annual cycle) and proximity to other organisms (as required for mating). By analogy, the niche of a productive specialty may include aspects of annual or other economic periodicities and the location of inputs, marketing and other distributional mechanisms, and regional demand. Product reputation (such as the aura of quality associated with Chamula *aguardiente*), distribution of competition (such as the nonoverlapping trading routes of Zinacanteco salt vendors), and even temporary conditions (the drop in sugar price that facilitated Chamula entry into distilling) could be considered part of the niche of a product specialty. Above all, ethnicity itself is a major component of the niches of specialized highland Chiapas crafts. The expectations general in the region—that Indian townships are distinct from one another and unique in some regards—foster the favoring of some townships' crafts as specialties. Ethnicity engenders specialization to a degree beyond that accounted for by physiography alone; and ethnic reputation protects a township's domination over particular craft markets. Thus, production specialties are more the product than the cause of ethnic differentiation.

CONCLUSION

In both its colonial and its modern phases, highland Chiapas has characteristics of a hinterland organized around a dominant seignorial city. The city (San Cristóbal) and its superordinate Ladino caste control most commercial activities and regulate the redistributive market mechanisms. The hinterland is differentiated into Indian townships producing cultigens and crude crafts. Language, clothing, technological level, ritual ideology, and social organization distinguish Indians from Ladinos. Distinctive dialects, costumes, crafts, and cults differentiate Indian townships from one another. The contrasts that these ethnic features represent are striking. We have seen them to be more than merely stable; indeed, they are vital, tenacious, and resistant to forces ordinarily thought to erode them.

Where is the locus of the vigor of ethnic patterns? Were ethnicity merely the static adherence to tradition, one could seek the causes of conservatism within the confines of the ethnic community. But, as we have seen, the boundaries of the local community are neither confining to migrant ethnic peoples nor constricting to the knowledge of their leaders. If anything, ethnic patterns are heightened by the contacts Indians have outside their townships. We have seen that Indian leaders fight to expand and entrench native access to land, thereby reinforcing the patterns separating Indians from Ladinos. And it seems likely, as in the case of craft production, that Indian townships stress uniqueness in most areas of life in opposition to their Indian near neighbors. Thus, both types of ethnic boundaries, between the region's castes and among subordinate Indians, appear the result of external contacts. The vitality of tradition comes from external processes encompassing the local community.

Ethnicity, then, is yet another example of internal features whose analysis leads to a consideration of external conditioning factors. In the chapters to follow, ethnicity will be seen as a characteristic of the central highland region that must be explained at yet again a more comprehensive level by looking at the position of the region in the state and nation.

CHAPTER EIGHT

THE REFUGE-REGION HYPOTHESIS

WE have explored several features of highland Chiapas ethnicity as background to the fundamental problem of the persistence of ethnic-group boundaries. Indian political activity during the colonial and national period suggests that Indians of the area not only were aware of the political milieu in which they lived but also proved themselves capable of acting to exploit political conditions for their own benefit. The Indian community was, in fact, linked communicatively with the outside world in a manner belying the traditional anthropological conception of the closed corporate peasant community. Ethnic-group boundaries are not a barrier to demographic mobility in times either of population decline or of growth but are as flexible with respect to individual ethnic self-identification as they are durable in overall configuration. Finally, we observed that the association of ethnicity with economic specialization was an idea more than a reality.

Requisites of an explanation of ethnicity, implicitly outlined in these chapters, are threefold. First, the explanation must view the ethnic-group phenomenon as a system of boundaries within a region reflecting aspects of its internal structure in the context of region-wide processes. Second, it must conceive of these processes as taking the form of interaction across internal boundaries. Finally, it must seek out the roots of ethnic immutability as well as suggest how change in ethnicity might come about. This chapter will review a model for regional social structure that has been proposed recently by Gonzalo Aguirre Beltrán and that incorporates many of these requisite characteristics.

Aguirre Beltrán's basic idea is that of the refuge region, a region that is physiographically and therefore economically, socially, and politically marginal to the mainstreams of national life and national development. In the history of Mexico's colonization, Spaniards quickly took control over the well-watered valley bottoms in central Mexico and Guatemala, pushing native populations aside into the refuge regions of the unarable tropical highlands and lowland rain forests. Yet colonization demanded that these marginal areas be brought under crown control, and settlements of colonists were established in the hearts of these marginal areas to effect this control. It is Aguirre Beltrán's thesis that economic, social, and political development in these refuge regions, consisting of seignorial Spanish settlements for control of a native hinterland, took on special forms that contrast with the forms of development in the less marginal areas. The ethnicity of Indian groups in refuge zones must be understood within the framework of these regional forms.

The overriding characteristic of the refuge region is its economic marginality. The highlands of Chiapas, for example, are not only remote from the centers of colonial development in Mexico and Guatemala but also physiographically limited in their potential for technological development. Plow agriculture is impossible on the steep mountain slopes, which are themselves barriers to the development of networks of communication, such as road systems. Even today, after federal programs have opened up road networks in the highlands, physiographic features almost rule out the possibilities for technological development in Chiapas. Aguirre Beltrán argues that the limited potential of refuge zones for development was the fundamental cause for the idiosyncratic emergence of social and political structures in these areas during the colonial period. The Spanish colonists of control towns, as bearers of a technological capacity of an order higher than that of the subjugated Indian groups, attempted to set up economic enterprises in refuge zones comparable to those of less marginal areas. To do so, they took over the less marginal highland valleys of the hinterlands for such operations as cattle raising and wheat farming. But, because of the intrinsic limitations imposed by the environment on development, they were forced to develop labor-intensive productive forms that turned to Indian populations as a labor source with exploitive mechanisms for labor recruitment. Still unable to compete with economic enterprises in less marginal areas, the Spanish-controlled economy of refuge regions reverted to consolidation of essentially extractive operations that could provide raw materials. such as corn and lumber, for externally developing economies.

Aguirre Beltrán relies on this economic argument to explain the castelike social structure of the refuge regions. Spaniards, and their mestizo and Creole descendants in refuge regions, had to develop mechanisms that would keep subjugated the Indian populations from which they could extract cheap labor for technologically uneconomic activities. Aguirre Beltrán calls these "dominical" mechanisms because they are used by the Spanish or mestizo caste to dominate the subject Indian caste.

One dominical mechanism that Aguirre Beltrán identifies is the concept of racial inferiority. Although Latin American concepts of race generally emphasize social and cultural criteria rather than genetic criteria, race constructs in refuge regions are distinctive in their equation of social and cultural with genetic attributes. In highland Chiapas, for instance, Ladino concepts of race construe the Indian as inherently inferior and intrinsically incapable of advancement. Aguirre Beltrán argues that such a concept developed so that Ladinos could rationalize economic exploitation of the subjugated caste.

A second dominical mechanism is political control of government by elites who not only reinterpret state and national policy in such a way as to enhance economic exploitation by the dominant caste but also pervert such policy so as to leave the subject caste in an underdeveloped state.

This is reflected in a third dominical mechanism, that of limiting the availability of social services to the dominant caste. In Chiapas, for instance, education and public health services have been virtually confined to the Ladino population centers. Finally, there are other dominical mechanisms by which the dominant caste maintains its social distance from the subjugated caste in a refuge region, through the formation of ritual and informal social institutions from which the Indian is either totally excluded or else included in a deliberately defined inferior status position.

Aguirre Beltrán makes the important point that dominical mechanisms are not confined to the dominant social caste. He sees ethnicity as the most important mechanism by which the subjugated caste maintains a precarious existence. Pushed into the most economically marginal zones, Indian groups quickly developed concepts of territoriality reflected on the level of the individual in private-property concepts and on the level of larger groups in concepts of tribal territoriality. Aguirre Beltrán argues cogently that ethnic dress, ethnic customs, and ethnic ritual were necessary forms developed from need to allocate the right to exploit economically marginal lands. As ethnicity developed, it not only enhanced pluralism within the subjugated caste (reflected in ethnic-group differentiation) but also enhanced the sense of social distance between castes by allowing the dominant group to equate ethnic characteristics with racial characteristics.

Aguirre Beltrán sees these dominical mechanisms, which focus attention on caste in the regional social structure, as masking a basic economic interdependence between castes. Technologically incapable of viable economic development, the dominant caste must rely on exploitation of the lower caste to survive. To this end, Ladino economic activity has developed and controlled a market system that skims off productive surpluses from Indian agriculture for sale in the national market. In return, Ladinos provide Indians with inferior local wares and cheap manufactured ritual goods, liquor, candles, and fireworks, which support the ritual systems by which Indians maintain their ethnicity.

This explanation of ethnicity incorporates the criteria we have deemed requisite in earlier chapters. Ethnicity is a dominical mechanism for maintaining boundaries (literally territorial) across which there are significant relations of interdependence (interchange of labor and commodities). Theoretically, such an approach is of interest because it delimits aspects of a region within which there is closure (eliciting inherent stability) yet across which open-ended processes flow (permitting greater systemic elaboration). The most cogent illustration of these constructs is in the realm of native ritual *cargo* systems.

As pointed out in chapter 1, Mesoamerican *cargo* systems have been analyzed by some writers as functioning to level wealth differences and by other writers (notably Cancian) as validating wealth and status differences within the native community. Both approaches treat of social processes within a closed ethnic system of interpersonal relations. *Cargo*-system functions are seen as integrative, defining the boundaries of the group, validating ethnic values, and compelling commitment to those values. In this view, *cargo*-system functions contribute to the stable behavior characteristic of system closure.

On the other hand, *cargo* systems can be viewed within the context of economic transactions in the region. Here, native labor yields a product siphoned off by the regional market system into Ladino channels. Ladino products destined for immediate ritual consumption are received in exchange for foodstuffs and other raw materials as tokens that are converted by Indians into prestige. From the point of view of energy, the system is an open one in which Indian agriculture is the source and Ladino elites are the ultimate consumers.

Ethnicity in ritual, taken as a whole, has aspects both of openness and of closure. Ritual behavior reinforces ethnic-group delimitation and at the same time enhances the mechanisms by which social distance between Indian and Ladino castes are maintained. In so far as ritual behavior reinforces closure by limiting participation in the Indian social system, it enhances internal social-structural equilibrium. On the other hand, the openness of the total economic system allows for ever greater elaboration and differentiation in so far as energy capture is constant or increases. Recent years, for example, have seen elaboration of *cargo* ritual in Zinacantán and other townships concomitant with the growth of Zinacanteco lowland entrepreneurial farming and of similar opportunities for other ethnic groups. Ethnicity thus provides the mold for system growth and elaboration.

The refuge-region model goes quite far in explaining the immutability of regional social structure, including ethnicity. For example, the model explains how the refuge-region process reacts to national programs for economic, social, and political development and change. National programs are formulated by technocrats and intellectuals in the mainstream of national development where they have a broad impact on the well-being of the lower classes. But, in refuge regions, the impact is transformed by local politicians and administrators committed to maintenance of the regional social structure to enhance the economic and social differences between castes. In the case of education and public health, for example—sectors in which the federal government has programs of broad scope—virtually all related facilities in highland Chiapas have been located in San Cristóbal, where they benefit the Ladino lower classes and elite but not the Indian caste (plates 29 and 30). Local-level political control by the dominant elite thus reinforces regional social structure.

The dominant caste, however, does not have a monopoly on political activity reinforcing intercaste social distance. Local-level native political leadership in highland Chiapas, in the native rebellions of 1712 and 1869 and in the far-reaching responses to the long history of changing land policies, was always such as to enhance Indian ethnicity, reinforce territoriality, and reaffirm native social structure either politically or ritually, and, in the case of the 1869 Caste War, both politically and ritually.

Finally, the refuge-region model, while explaining the characteristic social structure of the marginal region, points as well to differences in regional social structure found between areas like highland Chiapas and those elsewhere in rural Mexico. It is notable, for instance, that the castelike features of Indian-Ladino relations and the hyperethnic character of Indian-Indian relations in highland Chiapas are much weaker in central Guatemala and the valley of Oaxaca and virtually absent in central Mexican Nahuatl and Tarascan areas or in Yucatán. Redfield's study of acculturation in Yucatán (1941), for instance, showed native culture to be most traditional in areas farthest from the city of Mérida. By contrast, in highland Chiapas the gradients of ethnicity are reversed, the most elaborated and hyperethnic cultural entities being those nearest San Cristóbal, ethnicity grading off at the region's periphery. The refuge-region construct would emphasize the relative nonmarginality of the Yucatán economically in

29. Rural School. Rural schools, such as this one in Tenejapa, have been constructed by federal programs. (Photo courtesy of Harvard Chiapas Project and Cía. Mexicana de Aerofotos, S.A.)

30. National Indian Institute Regional Headquarters. Headquarters of the federal National Indian Institute district branch are on the outskirts of San Cristóbal. (Photo courtesy of Harvard Chiapas Project and Cía. Mexicana de Aerofotos, S.A.)

explaining the contrast with highland Chiapas. Yucatán's richer plantation economy, linked by ocean routes to the world commodity market, need not develop the complex apparatus of dominical mechanisms in order to make profitable use of rural labor. Correspondingly, rural natives of central Mexico have largely been integrated into the economic mainstream of the nation.

The refuge-region model, therefore, provides an answer to the question posed in chapter 6. Natives of Chiapas are willing to lead their lives in the marginal highlands because of the niche provided them by the ethnic component of regional social structure, which has evolved as a response to the entire region's marginality to the development of colonial society and the modern state. It would appear that ethnicity will perdure, and even elaborate, as long as highland Chiapas retains its character as a marginal hinterland focused on a seignorial city. Only in so far as the hinterland and its control city become articulated with the national economy will ethnic patterns erode.

CHAPTER NINE

NATIONAL INDIANISM AND INDIAN

NATIONALISM

THE refuge-region model attributes the character of ethnic systems to their marginal position in a larger society. The model sees traditional behavior not as a pre-existing condition but, rather, as one that develops as a consequence of colonization or other arrangements bringing isolated areas into a larger system's orbit. First, a relationship of core and periphery is brought into being; subsequently, ethnicity emerges as an adaptive response to marginality in the periphery. Yet this sequence is precisely the reverse of that accepted widely in social science literature on development and nationalism, literature that assumes that traditional, ethnic behavior is a pre-existing given that breaks down with integration in an encompassing system. In the view of this chapter, emerging national integration contributes to the rise—rather than the demise—of ethnicity by feeding upon and contributing to the sense of identity that ethnic groups display. Indianism is a major tenet of Mexican nationalist ideology, and its expression legitimizes Indian ethnicity by making it appear consonant with nationalist goals.

The view that ethnicity breaks down as national integration grows is typified by the writing of Karl W. Deutsch. For Deutsch, " 'tribalism' or any other social and political attachment to a small ethnic, cultural, or linguistic group" poses a "challenge" that must be "overcome" in the "process of national integration" (1963, p. 6). Integration may be nil, as when tribes "deny membership in the nation, refuse obedience to the state, and rise in war against other groups of . . . fellow citizens" (ibid.). Or tribes may be passive and compliant until given an opportunity to revolt and secede. Where integration is slight, such groups may become nonhostile and more compliant. Increasing integration brings tribes into more active political participation, although ethnic distinctions may remain. When fully integrated, groups share language and culture, and the "nation" is fully formed.

In this widely accepted view, tribalism is a pre-existing condition that is antithetical to emergent national integration because tribal and national allegiance are contradictory. For, on the one hand, the solidarity of tribalism springs from common ties of kinship, territory, language, race, religion, or other primary relations of a small group. By contrast, national integration involves a "civil attachment," a "moderate pluralistic concern for the whole" that "is not the spirit of the primary group" (Shils 1957. p. 144.).

Edward Shils was one of the first to question the antithesis of primordial and civil ties, first by noting the possibility of "integration of a large society through attachments which fell short of attachment to the central value system of the society" (ibid., p. 135) and, later, by exploring the manner in which the "primary group . . . endows a society with some of its values" (ibid., p. 137). Finally, Shils recognized the high degree to which societal integration is based precisely upon primary attachments: "As I see it, modern society is no lonely crowd, no horde of refugees fleeing from freedom. It is no *Gesellschaft*, soulless, egotistical, loveless, faithless, utterly impersonal, and lacking any integrative forces other than interest or coercion. It is held together by an infinity of personal attachments, moral obligations in concrete contexts, professional and creative pride, individual ambition, primordial affinities, and a civil sense which is low in many, high in some, and moderate in most persons" (ibid., p. 131). In short, primordial and civil ties are compatible with one another in the individual and are important for the integration of society.

Clifford Geertz extends Shils's argument to the arena of emerging nationalism. Peoples of new states are faced with the dilemma of forming an efficient bureaucratic unity in which collective civil sentiments recognize the identity of constituent groups that are often in competition for power. Because blood, race. language, locality. and other primordial ties are the only bases upon which "autonomous political units" can at first be "demarcated." such groups become "lift(ed) to the level of political supremacy" (1963a, p. 110). In short, tribalism quickly emerges as a set of opposed blocs that are not, however, opposed to the idea of the state. over which, after all, they compete for control. Moreover. tribalism or other parochial alignment is at first the only medium through which the state can "mobilize social resources for public ends" by extracting "legitimate authority" from the "inherent moral coerciveness" of primordial sentiments (ibid., p. 127). The problem for new states is the struggle to prevent parochial goals from overriding those essential to the civil polity. Geertz. like Shils, sees successful integration as bringing about compatible primordial sentiments and civil ties.

The "integrative revolution" coordinates primordial and civil sentiments by legitimizing ethnicity. Geertz argues that integration occurs through the aggregation of smaller into larger units on the basis of some principle, usually primordial. Thereby, primordial principles become generalized, and "primordial solidarity" or "consciousness of kind" is extended into "consciousness to the developing civil order" (ibid., p. 154). As this happens, tribal goals, symbols, and features are recast to stand for larger "ethnic blocs" that enter into "total relations with one another" (ibid.). In the end, ethnocentrism is "modernized," not destroyed. This means that: "At least as they have been conceived here, primordial and civil sentiments are not ranged in direct and implicitly evolutionary opposition to one another in the manner of so many of the theoretical dichotomies of classical sociology— *Gemeinschaft* and *Gesellschaft*, mechanical and organic solidarity, folk and urban society; the history of their development does not consist simply of the expansion of the one at the expense of the other" (ibid., p. 155). Moreover, the model explains the countless examples of rising ethnicity in new nations as a consequence of political integration.

Is modernized ethnocentrism a fixture or a phase of nationalism? Seymour M. Lipset and Stein Rokkan argue that outcomes such as those Geertz describes are transitional and will give way to other alliances and cleavages as industrialization proceeds. Michael Hechter, by contrast, argues that industrialization, when it proceeds unevenly over a territory, can further reinforce and entrench ethnicity.

Lipset and Rokkan distinguish two dimensions of cleavage. The first is territorial and embodies conflicts over allocation of resources that crosscut territorial alignments. They outline three phases in national building in which cleavages and alignments tend to shift from territorial to functional as industrialization proceeds. In the first phase, cleavages are territorial because "the thrust of penetration and standardization from the national center increase territorial resistances and raise issues of cultural identity" (1967, p. 9). Thus, tribal, ethnic, or other cultural alignments emerge in the first phase. In the second, territorial cleavages become generalized into a *"variety of alliances across communities of the nation"* (ibid.), especially alliances of the kind that Geertz identifies as ethnic blocs. Geertz's "integrative revolution" is similar to the second of these two phases, which together constitute the *"National Revolution"* (ibid., p. 14). But a subsequent *"Industrial Revolution"* (ibid.) brings transition to a third phase in which territorial considerations give way to functional considerations. Industrial production redefines individuals according to their function in the productive process and thus engenders class interests that crosscut territory and region. Conflict between core and periphery in earlier phases gives way to conflict over allocation of resources or over

class ideology. In this phase, then, functional cleavages and alignments replace territorial and cultural ones: ethnicity gives way to
social class.

The thrust of the Lipset and Rokkan argument is to modify the accepted stance toward tribalism and parochialism and to conceive of
these as characteristics of only the early phases in the rise of the
modern state. Hechter's further modification of their reasoning is
inspired by the startling "flourish of national consciousness among
ethnic and regional minorities in advanced industrial societies" (1971,
p. 21). Hechter elaborates the model of internal colonialism (González
Casanova 1965; Stavenhagen 1965), which sees domination of a
periphery by a core elite within a national system as analogous to the
overseas colonial situation: economic and structural differences,
through which core elites dominate peripheral groups, underlie entrenched cultural differences between them—for example, ethnicity.
Hechter observes that industrialization is not likely to spread evenly
through a system but will favor core areas to the relative detriment of
peripheral areas; consequently, structural differences between core
and periphery are increased, and ethnicity is heightened (1971, pp.
42–45).

What general conclusions regarding ethnicity can we draw from
these viewpoints?

First, we might accept the proposition that ethnicity, tribalism,
parochialism, and related alignments are not primarily pre-existing
conditions to be overcome when a relation between peripheral and
core area is brought into being. Although they build upon pre-existing
attributes of primordial character, they themselves are new processes
through which core and periphery are related. They are expectable
in the context of newly formed states.

Second, we might accept the proposition of Geertz, supported by
Lipset and Rokkan, that alignments of ethnic, tribal, or parochial
character tend to become heightened and generalized to blocs of increasing scope in newly formed systems.

Third, we might accept Hechter's treatment of the uneven spread
of industrialization from core to periphery as the rule rather than the
exception. Cleavages of ethnic character are not likely to be displaced
(as Lipset and Rokkan would argue) and may even be heightened by
industrialization, and they may thus continue in older states.

On the other hand, we might modify Hechter's use of the "internal
colonialism" model to explain the rise of structurally based ethnic
alignments in which a dominant core elite and a subordinate peripheral group are in direct opposition. We might adhere to Aguirre's

refuge-region model in which peripheral elites have an instrumental role in the maintenance of ethnic alignments.

Finally, we might accept Geertz's proposition that those in power must strive to reconcile the dilemma of recognizing the identity and legitimacy of society's constituent blocs while ensuring the furtherance of perceived overall goals.

Taken together, these propositions have implications for ethnicity in a nation like Mexico that go beyond those of the refuge-region hypothesis. Within that national arena, ethnic groups have a role to play, albeit a role that is modified by an entrenched position within the refuge region. Those in power will recognize the legitimacy of the Indian bloc in Mexico and will strive to heighten and generalize principles of that bloc so as to conform with nationalist goals. This phenomenon we may call "national Indianism." In response, those of the Indian bloc will attempt to bend such recognition at the national level to the securing of their entrenched position at the regional level, a stance that we may call "Indian nationalism." The following sections will attempt to sketch national Indianism in Mexico and Indian nationalism in Chiapas.

NATIONAL INDIANISM

Indianism became a tenet of Mexican national ideology only after the Revolution of 1910. Before that time, Indians were often the objects of national policy, but their interests were never deemed central by leaders except in a phase of remarkable colonial Indianist policy of the sixteenth century. Both contemporary and colonial Indianism merged groups of great diversity into a bloc, often submerging their differences and their distinctive needs.

Colonial Indianist policy flowered briefly in the mid-sixteenth century. In the first decades of colonization, Indians were the objects of haphazard—and often disastrous—subjugation under the institution of encomienda (Simpson 1966; Chamberlain 1939a), which delegated to colonists the crown's right to tribute in return for their military services. Thereafter, the crown attempted to curb the prerogatives of colonists by defining Indians as a bloc with legitimate interests to be promoted and protected by special institutions. Indianist policy reformed encomienda under the New Laws of 1542; reformed tribute schedules and labor recruitment for Indians (Miranda 1951, 1952); redefined the juridical status of Indians to make them direct wards of the crown; set up special mechanisms for Indian education and evangelization (McAndrew 1965); restructured the settlement pattern of Indian communities under the plan of *reducción*; and redefined and legitimized native statuses of local political authority (López Sarrelangue 1965; Chamberlain 1939*b*). For a period, this active Indianist policy stemmed the tide of rapid decline of the Indian community in many areas. Later, however, the growth of ranching increased colonist control of rural areas (Chevalier 1963) while the crown became preoccupied with European affairs, and the Indianist cause withered.

The effect of this phase of Indianism policy was to merge Indians into a bloc in colonial society. Although concerned with regional differences and aware of cultural differences among Indian groups, the crown formulated policies that, in principle, were to be applied uniformly and that, in practice, hastened the obliteration of pre-existing native institutions. Moreover, the ideological inspiration for sixteenth-century Indianism sprang not from Indians themselves but from scholastic philosophers like Fray Bartolomé de Las Casas, who espoused the Indian cause but really understood little about the Indian condition (cf. Las Casas 1909). Indianist policy thus created and legitimized an ethnic bloc in New Spain without recognizing—much less reifying—many of the primordial attributes of groups merged within the bloc. Subsequently, many of the primordial differences among these groups were effaced as the Indian community entrenched itself around land-tenure, ritual, and political institutions more Mediterranean than aboriginal.

Indianist policy was largely nonexistent after the sixteenth century. In the later colonial period, it was Creoles (elites of Spanish descent born in the colony) whose bloc interests sought recognition. Creoles defined themselves in opposition to *gachupines*, the Spanish-born who monopolized the highest statuses in colonial government. At first thoroughly European in their orientation, Creoles began to promote Americanisms in their identity. They revived an interest in the Indian past, but the purpose of such interest was to distinguish the status of provincial life ways by attributing to them elements of a uniquely American heritage. After independence, Creoles took power, vacillating between federalism and centralism, issues that had little to do with rural villagers. Agrarian policy, which sought first to redistribute population through colonization laws and later to reform rural agriculture by divesting church and townships of corporate and communal holdings, did affect Indian villagers profoundly by undermining the security of their access to land. Although not so intended, nineteenth-century liberal land policy was anti-Indianist in its near effacement of the Indian ethnic bloc.

The Mexican Revolution opened an era in which Indianism once again was elevated to a national goal. Intertwined in this Indianism were two related but distinguishable themes. One sought in Indian society the inspiration for reform of the larger society. The other sought, rather, means by which national policy could better the status of Indians.

Among those who looked to Indian models for society at large were writers, artists, social scientists, and other intellectuals. The mural art of Diego Rivera, one of many executing remarkable public art in the 1920's, evoked the delicacy and beauty of Aztec agriculture, social organization, and ritual and depicted with horror the transformations of the Conquest. Manuel Gamio wrote of "the originality, the significance, and the rare beauty in the work of art which pre-Columbian mythology created" (1943, p. 388); he inspired a generation and more of Mexican anthropologists to pursue the study of ancient and contemporary Indian life ways as examples of what had been and what might yet be. These leading Indianists had more than an antiquarian or scholarly interest; the Indian was the heritage of the nation and in him survived positive values and patterns of thought that might be revived for society.

Those concerned more with devising national policy to raise the status of the Indian were not always inspired with the value of Indian culture. José Vasconcelos, architect of Mexico's vast rural education program in the 1920s, saw that the task of the nation was to bring the Indian into the mainstream of its life, to modernize him by incorporating him into a system as much Spanish as Indian in origin, and to combine the features of both into a better hybrid blend (cf. Vasconcelos 1948).

The distinction between these viewpoints was not always clear-cut, although the tension between them was sometimes great. Many Indianist policies reflected both goals simultaneously. In land reform, the far-reaching policies written into the constitution of 1917 and effected gradually in the 1920s and rapidly under Cárdenas after 1934, had explicitly Indianist provisions of both kinds. On the one hand, the policy sought to further communal social forms thought partly indigenous by restoring to rural towns communal lands lost under Juárez's laws of 1856 and 1863, by excluding private forms of tenure under land-reform grants, and by encouraging cooperative administration of the ejido by participating towns. Here, "Indian" ideals were to be generalized through rural agriculture. On the other hand, the provisions of land reform were intended to better the economic status of the Indian and to enable his participation in rural development. The distinction can also be traced in rural educational policy. On the one hand, some saw education as a means of incorporating the Indian into the nation, especially by stressing literacy in Spanish. Others, however, conceived the challenge of rural education to be to "make the world intelligible to the Indian" and thereby to give the Indian "a sense of his own value, to justify his world to him, and ultimately to erase the myth of inferiority from the national conscience" (Ruiz 1963, pp. 137–138).

Indianist philosophy was articulated actively in the 1920s and most thoroughly put to practice in the 1930s, affecting education, public health, justice, and rural development profoundly. Since the presidency of Cárdenas, the visionary goals of inspiring the nation through its Indianism have given way gradually to those seeking to raise the Indian's status through incorporation; and Indianism itself has declined somewhat in political appeal and national funding. Nevertheless, Mexico's leaders frequently reiterate their Indianist orientation. National Indianism still thrives.

INDIAN NATIONALISM

Indianism as a tenet of Mexican nationalism engendered social action within the Indian bloc. Indians were made aware of the goals of Indianism and exposed to specific programs designed for their benefit. Yet their use of those programs was often at odds with nationalist goals for rapprochement between the Indian and the larger society. Frequently, Indians used nationalist programs to strengthen and entrench their ethnicity, thereby heightening their distinctiveness from their mestizo counterparts and reinforcing their commitment to a peripheral niche in the social system.

An example of Indian social action that takes advantage of the climate of national Indianism to further ethnic goals is an ongoing colonization effort of a group of Zinacantecos from *Apas* and other hamlets. The colonization effort involves the lowland tract—mentioned in chapter 7—that was purchased in 1908 from national lands in the Grijalva Valley under Porfirio Díaz's revenue-generating policy.

The disruptive years of the Revolution, the general flow of indentured Indian laborers back to the highlands after 1918, and the subsequent tensions between lowland ranchers and land claimants contributed to Zinacanteco unwillingness to settle the tract. In the 1930s the tract was abandoned as Zinacantecos focused their efforts on land reform in the highlands.

But it was not forgotten. Although temporarily diverted by the success of highland reform, families that had participated in the purchase tried to revive the claim in the 1950s. They had been apprised of new provisions in the national ejido policy permitting communities with existing ejidos to expand their grants where land was available. The lowland tract appeared possible to incorporate into the ejido in this manner. But the Zinacantecos found that adjacent ranchers had doctored their property titles to incorporate the tract; they had taken over the land for grazing. Zinacantecos butchered one of the steers, but they were caught and forced to pay for it. They took their claim to the district agrarian office and were advised that it was not valid. Consequently, they joined other Zinacantecos in an effort to extend the ejido to incorporate this and other tracts through expropriation. The effort met with minor success in adding some highland property to the ejido, but not the former national lands.

In 1968 the issue was revived. Some eighty families, including descendants of the original claimants and new opportunists, carefully hatched a plot to invade the tract, settle a village there, and renew the claim in state and federal agrarian offices. Protected by a small arsenal of hunting rifles and shotguns, they established a settlement of crude dwellings on the claim. Unable to move lock, stock, and barrel to lands they well might lose, they agreed to inhabit the settlement in shifts, availing themselves of the legal protection afforded bona fide settlers. Under the dynamic leadership of Marcos Bromas, they initiated legal action to secure the claim under the Agrarian Code.

Qualities of leadership abound in the group. Included in it are relatives of Zinacantán's wily ejido boss, whose established connections in the agrarian bureaucracy are vital to a colonization ploy. Two members of the foremost family of *Navencauk*, strong traditionalists who have passed prestigious ritual *cargos* with élan, contribute to the respectability of the group. Another up-and-coming young participant, orphaned in childhood, educated unusually well by patrons for whom he worked in Tuxtla Gutiérrez, has connections of friendship with crafty and influential lawyers there. Marcos Bromas is the skilled broker of these combined assets, a man respected because of his literacy, his active ritual *cargo* participation, his success as arbiter within his hamlet and as spokesman in the township court, and his charm and diplomacy with Mexican bureaucrats in past endeavors that took him to Mexico City.

Group efforts on behalf of the claim began in Tuxtla Gutiérrez. Marcos Bromas hired an engineer to make a survey of the claim and a lawyer to prepare petitions, which were submitted to the agrarian office. Meanwhile, Ladino ranchers submitted their own titles with supporting surveys. When promises of quick action from the agrarian office extended into months of delay, the Indians suspected that officials there had been bought off.

Bromas then traveled to Mexico City and somehow prevailed upon federal officials to order action in Tuxtla Gutiérrez. In the months that ensued, Indians engineered a new survey and filed additional briefs at considerable cost. When they discovered that definitive action would have to await the term of newly elected state officials, Bromas joined the political entourage of the campaigning governor-to-be, whose signature ultimately approved state-level action favorable to the Indian suit.

Definitive resolution of the claim has still to come from federal bureaucratic machinery. Meanwhile, Zinacantecos have begun to cultivate lands of the new colony with some assurance of success. But the pending action still requires the continued pressure and presence of group leaders.

I was lucky enough to accompany these men on a trip to Tuxtla Gutiérrez in the summer of 1970. The purpose of the trip was to secure a lawyer's intervention to prod state agrarian officials into action. The experience proved to be an object lesson in the subtleties of ethnic role behavior. The two-hour drive from San Cristóbal to Tuxtla Gutiérrez traverses Zinacantán before the escarpment drops to the lowlands. We picked up group members, eleven in all, on the roadside near their hamlets. As I drove, they planned their day. A meeting with the lawyer had been prearranged. But discussions (in Tzotzil) turned on the personal habits of various officials, their customary schedules, their bureaucratic relation to one another, and the manner in which each should be approached. The Zinacanteco knowledge of Ladino bureaucratic role behavior would have impressed Erving Goffman (1955).

In Tuxtla Gutiérrez we found that the lawyer was not, as promised, in his office. In a quick huddle, the Indians decided that he should be tracked down at home. One of the group, a clean-cut youth who spoke enough Spanish to joke with the typist, was left at the lawyer's office. Another man, not well known to agrarian officials, was sent to their headquarters to keep tabs on comings and goings there. We traveled across town, leaving two more of the group to watch the house of the lawyer's brother. A fifth man was dispatched to the office of the survey engineer lest the lawyer make an appearance there.

Then we drove to the lawyer's suburban home. His wife invited us in. No, he was not at home but was expected shortly from his ranch. We sat down, in the parlor, to coffee, and two of the group engaged the woman in an hour of almost perfect Spanish parlor conversation while others whispered in Tzotzil about the changed plans.

As noon approached, the decision was reached to find the lawyer on his farm; for by 2 P.M. offices close, and the day would be lost. Leaving two of the group in earnest chitchat, we excused ourselves and made the half-hour drive to the ranch. Too late; the lawyer had just left for a nearby town. We retraced our steps, gathered up members of the group, and made another appointment with the lawyer's secretary.

To Indians of the group, the day had been a loss. But to me the experience was a poignant demonstration of the unusual facility and insight with which Indians approach their counterparts in the Ladino world. Their persistent pursuit almost had overcome the notorious languor of Mexican bureaucracy.

The establishment of the Zinacanteco colony is, without question, an example of Indian social action that is made possible by national Indianism. Some of the colonists had helped mastermind township-wide ejido efforts in the 1930s, thereby acquainting themselves with federal agrarian bureaucracy. Many had represented the township in programs subsequently sponsored by the National Indian Institute. Three had traveled to Mexico City to petition federal agencies for support for a variety of projects. These experienced men had availed themselves of knowledge to use national Indianism for practical ends.

Yet an assessment of the colonization effort should take stock of the participants' goals, costs, and achievements. One goal was to expand the land base for subsistence swidden farming of hamlets whose land has been subdivided too many times among a growing population and exhausted through overuse. Colonists are expanding their farmlands in the direction of the lowlands, shifting their niche to take advantage of the economies of lowland corn production.

Another goal was to further Zinacanteco patterns of kinship. Property and inheritance generate expectations between fathers and sons, resulting in the formation of localized patrilineal descent groups. Zinacanteco colonizers, reactivating the property claims of their fore-bears of 1908, are planning for the maturation of their own offspring. Many of the participants have proudly pointed out plots they will give to their children; they will cement their own descent groups in this manner.

While these goals may be fulfilled, the costs of colonization are high. For five years, eighty families have each invested many months and hundreds of pesos in fees, bribes, and other expenses. For those and many years yet to come, the considerable talents and scant resources of the leading families of Zinacantán have been absorbed in the battle to secure a tract that can be used only for traditional corn farming.

In the final analysis, the achievements of the colony will be similar to those of other traditional Zinacanteco settlements. Colonizers will entrench themselves in the traditional way of life, probably erecting a chapel and incorporating it into the Zinacanteco *cargo* system. Through commerce, the Ladino elite will continue to skim the cream of Indian harvest surpluses. The struggle to defend the colony against local elites will continue, for even officials of the federal agrarian office in Tuxtla Gutiérrez can be prevailed upon by local elites to hamper the legal redistribution of land resources. Indian colonizers will assume the defensive posture that maintains the social distance between Indian and Ladino worlds. The achievement of the colony will be the entrenchment of the Zinacanteco ethnic niche.

This prognosis does not mean that Indians are not integrated into the nation. The colonization effort reflects "personal attachments, moral obligations in concrete contexts, . . . creative pride, individual ambition," and "primordial affinities" of exactly the kind Edward Shils (1957) sees integrating modern society. Moreover, widespread participation of these and hundreds of other Indian groups in land reform since the 1920s has engendered a civil consciousness like that Geertz sees springing initially from primordial consciousness of kind. Indians accept federal schools, conform with the demands of national politics and the electoral process, send token groups of youths for military conscription, and otherwise comply with the civil order largely because the benefits of land reform have committed them irrevocably to national participation. Indian nationalism thrives in the refuge region.

Taken together, national Indianism and Indian nationalism fit the conclusions drawn at the beginning of the chapter. Indian ethnicity is not a pre-existing condition but a dynamic process, instead, that is reinforced by Indians' role in the developing nation. Indians have emerged as a bloc with nationally recognized legitimate interests. Despite the industrialization of Mexico's economic core, its uneven spread has not altered the peripheral character of the niche Indians occupy. Within the niche, protected and promoted by astute invocation of national Indianist policy, Indians engage as a bloc in total relations with their refuge-region Ladino counterparts. That the total relations are ethnic relations does not divorce them from the national context. Tzotzil tradition is, indeed, a form of modernized ethnocentrism for which the nation, as much as the region, is an immediate and significant environment.

CHAPTER TEN

CONCLUSION

L ET us now review the features of Tzotzil tradition as we have delineated them in family descent group, hamlet, township, caste, and region and make clear what we think to be the bases of tradition at each of these levels.

Farmland and dwelling sites, in their use, ownership, and transmission by inheritance and sale, were shown to be fundamental to the Tzotzil domestic cycle, giving shape to interpersonal relations within families and to the characteristic aggregates of families at the most local level of Tzotzil society. We described the paradigm that governs Tzotzil family relationships: the obligation of a father to transmit property to those of his sons who obey his authority and respect his control. We delineated the complex of behaviors and beliefs in which the paradigm is expressed in daily domestic routines, the cycle of agriculture, and the crisis of death. We described the variation in extent and effective organization of local-descent groups that form through the domestic cycle and attributed this variation to the differentials in property among the constituent groups of Tzotzil local settlements. The characteristic mix of neighborhoods (some tightly integrated around a reigning, prestigious local-descent line, others only loosely integrated, if at all, around families of lesser means and status) proved to be understandable in terms of a long-run redistribution of property within the locality. Clearly, property is at the root of Tzotzil tradition as it manifests itself in family and local organization.

We delineated a variety of factors that affect the relative value of land. Where population density is high, per capita holdings may be so small as to be "worthless" to most individuals for farming or for inheritance. But worthlessness is a relative matter depending upon the alternatives to highland farming: wage labor, craft production, and lowland rental farming. The relative worth of these alternatives differs from township to township. First, because of ethnic barriers, resettlement is largely within townships, making per capita holdings relatively uniform within them but different between them. Second, tribes' ethnic reputations are connected to the alternatives to highland farming, as in Zinacanteco lowland rental farming and Chamula distilling. Third, all members of a township have roughly equal chances to benefit from different geographical location—for example, Zina-cantecos have easy access to the Grijalva Valley. Fourth, ritual *cargo* systems rank status in a manner that is uniform for a township's inhabitants who share standardized criteria for relative success in ritual and economics. Finally, the organization of land reform and other politically inspired activities affecting production often relies on the administrative integrity of the township. These five factors allow us to think of the township as a niche for a characteristic kind of local organization.

Generally, where land is abundant and a free good, swidden farmers do not have descent organization, but, where land is scarce and a valued commodity, descent emerges to systematize rights to land. When, however, landholdings are overly used and excessively fractioned by inheritance, farming tends to give way to other occupations, and land ceases to motivate descent-based kinship. These stages form an evolutionary sequence because of the tendency of population to rise. In Chiapas, the sequence is related to the alternatives to farming that become attractive when farming resources are depleted. Yet in most townships, highland Indians cling to traditional farming patterns (and to the descent-based kinship to which traditional farming gives rise), because they can supplement farm income through wage labor, sale of simple crafts, and so forth. Were Indian tribes to be closed off from these sources of income, they would not survive; correspondingly, these external linkages are part of the basis of internal traditional patterns.

In a similar manner, the engagement of Indian tribes in a regional system of interethnic relations bears upon tribal adherence to traditional life ways. We have already observed how tribal territoriality holds Indians to their land. Relations between Indians and Ladinos also have this effect. By definition of their ethnic status, production open to Indians is limited to that suited to the marginal highlands. Indians produce only by the most direct means, that is, by farming with simple tools on their own lands, while Ladinos monopolize commerce and technology. Correspondingly, the mountain lands are most valued by the Indians who live within them; Ladinos have relatively little desire to invade the Indian preserve. Ladino preference for life in towns, Ladino fear of Indians' ritual alcoholism, Ladino attribution of violence and uncivilized manners to the Indian, and other similar attitudes inherent in the system of interethnic relations contribute to the geographical separation of Indians in a distinctive zone whose tradition reflects the social distance between them and the larger society.

This system of interethnic relations, in itself, is a traditional form that has its basis in a range of broader influences on its participants. Were it not for Indian *cargo* ritual, Ladinos would have to seek totally new markets for commercial goods and new sources of foodstuffs. Ladino coffee plantations would have to transform production were Indian wage workers not available for long-distance hire. Ladino ranchers would have to invest in equipment to convert their marginal scrub forests into ranching land in the Grijalva Valley if they could not clear the land by renting it to Indians for slash-and-burn agriculture. The extractive economy of the zone rests on the exploitation by a peripheral elite of a subordinate caste's labor in a manner that would not have arisen in an area more centrally engaged to the national economy.

We see the perpetuation of the region's traditional forms even in its linkages to the nation. As a legitimate and recognized bloc in national politics, Indians elicit the flow of federal resources into Chiapas. Yet Indians do not have the vision or the power to use these resources to break away from their subordinate position. Instead, they expand their traditional farming base under land reform, leaving to Ladinos the benefits of schools, clinics, road construction, irrigation works, and other social services intended for the rural zone. The differential flow of these external resources perpetuates the gap between the Indian and the Ladino.

These final considerations complete our scheme. We have shown that tribal adherence to swidden-style agriculture on marginal highland township lands gives form to the processes of Tzotzil social organization. We have studied the factors holding tribal populations in an ongoing relation to township lands. These include structured interethnic relations that endure because they contribute to the flow of resources Indians must have to ensure survival in their marginal niche, and they directly benefit the dominant Ladino caste by permitting production for the national sector that would otherwise be uneconomic. Even the relations of the marginal region to the national economy reinforce this state of affairs.

This interpretation of the bases of Tzotzil tradition may properly be termed *ecological* in the sense of attributing tradition to a special environmental adaptation. An ecological approach identifies the environment as those attributes of man's location in a system that have direct and immediate effects upon him, and it studies these effects. Implicit in this approach is a simplifying assumption about what is important to study and an interpretation of how the environment is to be conceived.

The ecological approach deals only with direct and immediate effects. Contrary to popular view, ecologists do not usually deal with the entire web of life; to do so would be impossibly complex. Rather, they focus on the flow of energy and resources and other processes having the most direct bearing on an organism (Andrewartha 1961). Ecological studies in anthropology ordinarily focus on subsistence and technology because food getting is a basic process around which so many others are built. Studying subsistence is a simple way of being sure to study problems of fundamental importance. This simplification, for instance, is implicit in Julian H. Steward's concept of the culture core—"the constellation of features which are most closely related to subsistence activity and economic arrangements" (1955, p. 37)—and it is explicit in the work of Walter Goldschmidt, which "stresses the priority of some aspects of society over others. To translate a theme from George Orwell's *Animal Farm*, all social institutions are basic, but some are more basic than others. That is to say, some aspects of the situation have immediate, direct and consistent influences on the total structure of society, whereas others are peripheral. . . . Furthermore, certain areas of life activity lie closer to such external factors as environment or such internal ones as technical change and are therefore more vulnerable to their pressure" (1959, p. 107).

In this book, all the direct and immediate effects described have been economic factors that influence Tzotzil subsistence. We have studied the attributes of Tzotzil lands, the style and strategy of swidden farming, and the activities with which Indians supplement farming with wage labor, rental farming, and crafts. We have explored the marginality of the highland zone relative to the lowlands and the reasons for Indian adherence to this marginal niche. We have seen that attributes and processes of the region and the nation, especially those evoking and maintaining ethnicity, reinforce this adherence.

Such single-minded attention to economic factors need not lead us to exclude noneconomic considerations. Indeed, this book has explored many facets of Tzotzil organization at the levels of family, hamlet, township, and interethnic social relations. But the starting point for each of these explorations has been the quest for factors bearing upon Tzotzil subsistence, and this quest has virtually guaranteed that related social and political organization be central to Tzotzil life. The claim is not made that the ecological approach leads us to consider every important facet of Tzotzil society but rather that the starting point of interest in subsistence leads us closer to a total synthesis than any other simplifying assumption.

Yet this study has gone further than most cultural ecological stud-ies—with a few exceptions—because of the manner in which it has conceived of the environment. Ecologists make a useful distinction between an organism's habitat and its niche. Habitat is the locale in which an organism lives. A niche is the range of conditions within which it can survive. Most organisms survive within characteristic ranges of food, weather, and relations to other animals, and they must have a place in which to live (Andrewartha 1961). In order to under-stand the organism's survival, one must look beyond the habitat to the entire set of these conditions. Together they form a set of values in a system of variables that we can think of as the environment of the organism. In a hostile environment the variable values are out of the range that the organism requires, the conditions of its niche are not satisfied, and the organism cannot survive. None of these variables are necessarily local, and, in the case of man, with his capacity for communication and his social and cultural superstructures, very few of them are likely to be local. This conception of the environment, therefore, leads us to look beyond man's habitat to the wider systems of variables that affect him.

This conception of the environment has not been common in cul-tural ecology. With the exception of a few studies of complex social systems from an economic viewpoint (see Steward et al. 1956 or Sahlins 1961), most studies in cultural ecology have been limited by an overly concrete conception of the environment, stressing locality and thereby confounding habitat and environment.

This can be seen in three well-known examples. The first is Harold C. Conklin's approach to swidden agriculture, both in the Philippines (1957) and elsewhere (1961). Conklin's approach is microecological in the extreme, attempting the nearly impossible web-of-life type of understanding of the complex interaction of soils, plants, and animals involved in the swidden farming of a locality. Conklin's approach leads to understandings of great subtlety but of limited scope; it en-genders a conception of swidden agriculture as an isolable process that can be adequately studied locally. Obviously Conklin does not believe that placement in a larger socioeconomic system is irrelevant to swidden agriculturalists, and yet his comprehensive bibliography on swidden agriculture virtually ignores exogenous factors, such as land reform, wage labor, or trade, which bear upon the manner in which swidden cultivators farm. The second example is Edmond R. Leach's study *Pul Eliya* (1961), a Ceylonese village agricultural system based on complicated irrigation works. Leach uses the example of Pul Eliya to argue the case for environmental determinism. Locality is the only enduring feature of the Pul Eliya system, and regularities of social organization in the town should be attributed to the inflexible character of locality rather than to values, norms, or social rules. This equation of locality and environment ignores all the factors holding Pul Eliya's population to their wet-rice irrigation system. These constraints are part of the environment of the system, and their study would lead Leach farther afield to a more comprehensive view of the Ceylonese landscape. Finally, we have Roy A. Rappaport's study of the Maring of New Guinea (1968). Rappaport studies the homeostatic flow of nutrients in a biotic community in which human and pig populations are balanced off by ritual feasts (in which pigs are consumed) and warfare (in which men are killed). Rappaport assumes that the biotic community is localized and is a closed system with regard to nutrient flow. This assumption leads him uncritically to assert that the elimination of warfare under colonial rule had no fundamental impact on the Maring-pig homeostasis, whose analysis, nevertheless, extends to the interaction of groups in war. The elimination of warfare obviously must have transformed the interaction of groups at the local level so as to affect the homeostasis in nutrient flow. The assumption of closure in the analysis of the Maring is a useful analytic device, but not when it leads to a view of their social system as one of timeless, ahistorical cycling. In all three examples, then, the equation of environment with locality has led to analyses of limited scope that explain local processes but do not enhance our understanding of how these are conditioned by their fit into a larger social and economic landscape.

This book stands with a handful of studies of broader systems of variables influencing man-land processes. Some of these take intergroup relations as a starting point and thus naturally analyze external factors conditioning group internal processes. Gunnar Haaland's Fur and Baggara (1969), Harald Eidheim's Lapps and Norwegians (1968, 1969), and Barth's Pathans (1956, 1959, 1969) are economically differentiated from one another or from encompassing social systems because of such intergroup relations. Others take the processes of large social systems as a starting point to explain internal variations, as in Geertz's *Agricultural Involution*, in which Dutch colonial exploitation accounts for Indonesian farming variants. Both types of explanation lead from the outside in and naturally assume a broad perspective. This book differs by going from the inside outward, beginning with the local and seeking its external conditions and causes. A conception of environment as a system of conditioning variables inevitably leads us outward in this manner from the study of local processes to more comprehensive syntheses. This conception of the environment may serve as a corrective to the sometimes narrow approach of cultural ecology.

The ecological approach of this book frames answers to our introductory questioning of the isolation usually attributed to traditional Indian groups in Latin America. Isolation means the complete separation or detachment of a system from external influences. A subsystem cannot be isolated from a larger system because a part-to-whole relation requires some kind of integrative process by which part and whole interact. Isolation of a system implies not only that there be no interchange between it and other systems but also that there be no external constraints that inhibit interchange, for such constraints would signify some kind of attachment to other systems. Therefore, the concept of isolation has no place in an approach that is strictly ecological. It follows from the approach that there are no strictly isolated human systems.

Nevertheless, we can think of isolation in relative terms as the degree of detachment that a system exhibits. One of the purposes of this book was to demonstrate that Tzotzil tribal groups are much less detached from intertribal, regional, and national processes than we had heretofore assumed. The assumption of isolation bears reexamination for all tribal groups in the Americas. None of them are substantially detached from larger social systems. The distinctive social and cultural characteristics of these groups require explanations other than isolation that take into account the interactions of groups with a larger social landscape.

The ecological approach impels the study of important processes at whatever level they occur and thus bypasses the pitfall of studying populations only at the level at which they appear to be distinctive aggregates. The emphasis that has been given to the distinctiveness of tribal groups in Latin America is an error in method caused by a failure to conceive of social groups as subsystems embedded within encompassing systems of increasing scope. Most Mesoamericanists have selected aggregates for study because of their distinctiveness and consequently have limited themselves to the study of processes internal to tribes or townships. Yet anthropological theory clearly has moved toward identifying processes at many different levels, pinpointing other kinds of units, both larger and smaller than the community, appropriate for understanding community processes. We have, for instance, the domestic unit and its developmental cycle (Goody 1958). We have the genetic unit (Romney 1957) for the study of the dispersing language family. We have ethnic studies (Barth 1969), which see distinctiveness of communities not as the limits of an entity but rather as the interface of structured interaction between related groups. And we have Leach's *Political Systems of Highland Burma*, which deliberately looked beyond the community and the cultural boundaries that ordinarily limit ethnographic research in order to analyze as variants of one encompassing system the diverse patterns of Burmese political leadership. We have studies of peasants (Foster 1953; Wolf 1966) as occupying a special position within the state. Each of these levels of process may be of importance to man-land studies. Even if our intellectual starting point is a local system and our goal is its understanding, the ecological approach leads us to this understanding by examining the relevant facets of encompassing systems.

We have clarified the ecological nature of our approach in this book and explained why the ecological approach takes us away from the characterizations of Tzotzil tribes as isolated and distinctive. What, then, can we say about the ecological bases of tradition? This study is meant to leave the reader with the definite impression that the bases of Tzotzil tradition are similar to the bases of traditional, ethnic behavior elsewhere in being a dynamic, active, and adaptive response to peripheral placement in a larger system. The system must be differentiated so as to have central and peripheral regions. The system must be integrated to the degree that peripheral populations participate in it. The example of Chiapas suggests that peripheral elites will participate in such a system by exploiting other peripheral groups. Ethnic tradition is an adaptive response by which exploited groups establish and defend a protective niche, a niche whose distinctiveness peripheral elites recognize and support because it contributes to their position of dominance. The prerequisites for this kind of peripheral ethnicity appear to have been met in those parts of the world where colonialism brought rural peoples of marginal areas into the orb of larger systems whose cores were defined as central and whose representatives came to dominate peripheral peoples. Where more centrally situated rural groups became peasants, dominated peripheral groups became ethnic. Partly because nationalism itself can encourage the revival of tradition, peripheral ethnicity has survived the transition from colonialism to the emergent new state. Interethnic patterns continue to be the best adaptation of marginal peoples to peripheral placement in a larger system.

APPENDIX

METHODOLOGY

HIGHLAND CHIAPAS ETHNOGRAPHY

Although early ethnographic exploration of the central Chiapas highland was contemporaneous with that in Guatemala and Yucatán, intensive research began in the 1950s, involving a variety of institutions and programatic strategies. The Mexican National Indian Institute (Instituto Nacional Indigenista, INI) established a regional center in San Cristóbal de las Casas. By the mid-1950s INI was actively eliciting the involvement of Indian leadership in programs of education, road construction, agricultural improvement, and public health. The institute encouraged ethnographic research in the area, gave valuable local sponsorship to Mexican and North American ethnographers, and subsequently published a variety of research on the area (Pozas 1959; Holland 1963; Vogt 1966). During the same period, Franz Blom, archeologist, explorer, and scholar of Maya culture, and his wife, Gertrude Duby, established a research center and library in their home in San Cristóbal. They served as gracious hosts to researchers of many disciplines while pursuing an avocation of study of the Lacandon Indians in the eastern Chiapas lowlands.

Continuing the University of Chicago tradition of Mayan studies, the Man-in-Nature Project under Norman McQuown—a major effort of team research—engaged in fieldwork for a five-year period beginning in 1957. The project selected for study a transect passing from highland to lowland and including Tzotzil, Tzeltal, and Ladino populations. Geographers, botanists, linguists, archeologists, and ethnographers all contributed to the survey. All communities in the transect were visited by a linguist-and-ethnographer team to collect word lists and complete a cultural and technological schedule for comparative study. In addition, many participants selected communities and topics for dissertation research so as to further the multidisciplinary project goals. Preliminary results of the endeavor were distributed as a three-volume report (McQuown 1959), to which articles and monographs have been added (Hill 1964; McQuown and Pitt-Rivers 1970; Nash 1970).

The most intense and sustained institutional presence in the highlands has been that of the Harvard Chiapas Project, directed by Evon

Z. Vogt. A long-range study of Tzotzil culture change has been the core of the project since 1958 when baseline ethnographic study was begun by Vogt and his students. To coordinate the project, Vogt maintained a research laboratory at Harvard, an environment in which new and old participants could exchange data, ideas, and analysis. Graduate and undergraduate training programs were grafted to the core project and involved scores of students in field studies often leading to doctoral dissertations. Until 1964 the Harvard research was concentrated on the township of Zinacantán. But, with the advent of air-photo coverage of the entire highland zone, intensive study was extended to Chamula and other nearby areas as well as to facets of Ladino and regional social and economic organization. Products of the project have been Vogt's comprehensive ethnographic description of Zinacantán (1969), monographic treatment of various facets of Zinacanteco society (Cancian 1965, 1972; Colby 1966; J. Collier 1968, 1973), a collection of papers (Vogt 1966), and a variety of dissertations and papers (many in preparation for publication) that form the project bibliography to be found in Vogt's monograph (1969).

Many other projects of shorter duration have enriched ethnographic understanding of the region. An ethnomedical study by A. Kimball Romney involved Stanford personnel in the Tzeltal zone. Under Duane Metzger, a team effort to study drinking behavior led to methodological advances in formal elicitation and other replicable ethnographic techniques as well as to the fine ethnographic film, *Appeals to Santiago*. A major ethnobotanical survey of the highlands has been completed by Brent Berlin and Dennis Breedlove (cf. Berlin, Breedlove, and Raven 1968). And numerous individuals have conducted specialized studies reflecting the full range of problems currently of interest to the discipline.

Thus, although highland Chiapas was among the last of the Maya regions to receive ethnographic attention, it is today one of the better studied regions of the world, and its students constitute a significant proportion of the discipline.

THE CHIAPAS AIR-PHOTO SURVEY

In 1964 an aerial photographic reconnaissance of the central Chiapas highlands opened up theretofore unavailable opportunities for ethnography. The air-photo survey was inspired by Romney's team research on blood-group genetics in the township of Aguacatenango. The study required an exhaustive genealogical census of a township of considera-

ble size, and Romney recognized that aerial photographs of the settlement would speed up census collection. After amateur photography
from a rented plane proved useful for this purpose, Romney explored
the feasibility of a professional survey with the Itek Corporation of
California. Vogt and McQuown joined the discussions as it became obvious that a selective regional survey could benefit the three Univer-
sity-based projects in highland Chiapas.

Vogt, Romney, and McQuown received funding from the National
Science Foundation (grant no. GS–262) to contract for the reconnaissance with Itek. The goals of the endeavor (Vogt and Romney 1971)
were not only to develop a photographic data base for settlement-
pattern mapping and census work but also to explore novel applications, as in the tracing of Tzotzil ritual patterns through space, a task
which had defied the ingenuity of ethnographers on the ground.

In the spring of 1964 the reconnaissance was flown by the Compañía
Mexicana de Aerofotos, S.A., under technical supervision of Itek personnel, generating photography in three formats. First, the entire
6,400-sq.-km. zone received cartographic coverage in the 9-inch-square
RC-9 format at an approximate contact scale of 1:30,000, a format designed for planimetry and standard photogrametry. Second, the townships of Zinacantán, Chamula, Tenejapa, and Aguacatenango were
filmed with a special Itek camera in the Hyac 70-mm roll-film format,
providing a highly detailed imagery at a contact scale of roughly
1:5,000. Finally, aerial oblique shots in an 8-by-10-inch format focused on specific sites of ethnographic interest. Many of these aerial
obliques have been used to illustrate this book.

The National Science Foundation granted additional funds to Vogt
(grant nos. GS–976 and GS–1524) to establish a laboratory for photo
interpretation at Harvard. Itek delivered a training seminar on photo
interpretation, indexed and duplicated the photography, developed a
special reader-printer for the laboratory, and published a manual on
the use of the laboratory facilities (Kroeck 1966). By early 1965 the
laboratory was ready for use.

Studies from Air Photos

The aerial photographs served as a data base for a variety of studies
both in the field and at Harvard. Field studies could make the most
productive use of the photography because photointerpretation could
be with the aid of the best interpreters—native informants. Settlement-pattern mapping and census collection in several hamlets of Zinacantán and Chamula were easy to generate from photographs in

which individual houses were easily distinguished from one another. Tzotzil sacred geography could be explored and explained without months of exhausting trekking in the rugged highlands. Place names throughout the region could be pinpointed in photos, permitting the first systematic ethnogeographic mapping. And exhaustive land-use studies became feasible for the first time.

At Harvard, Vogt's students found it possible to complete a number of pilot studies from laboratory photo coverage. One student (Holmer 1974) completed a study of topographic features determining house-site selection and of trail-based communication networks without stepping foot in the field, and her findings were later corroborated by fieldwork. In 1969 a symposium on the uses of aerial photography in anthropology brought together many of these studies with those of researchers at other institutions, and the diverse collection is now in print (Vogt 1974).

The Photographic Study of Tzotzil Land Use and Tenure

Air photos contributed immeasurably to the research reported in this book, in the genealogical censusing of *Apas*, in the exhaustive survey of *Apas* landholdings, and in the study of the Chamula land-use sequence. In the course of these studies, photo interpretation was fitted to the exigencies of fieldwork and combined with a variety of traditional ethnographic approaches.

Genealogical censusing of *Apas* had been begun by Frank Cancian in 1962 in conjunction with his first studies of lowland corn-farming innovation. As I intended to do a study of *Apas* inheritance patterns, I continued census work in 1963, using as base map one of my several snapshots of the hamlet from the year before (see, for example, plate 7). My strategy was to train a key informant in photo interpretation and to work through him with other individuals. Censusing was carried to a new level of accuracy and completeness because of the photographic base map, but the highly detailed aerial photographs of 1964 brought an unexpected surprise. Over just a two-year period, a number of *Apas* houses had been moved. Tzotzil settlement pattern proved to be much more fluid than we had anticipated, and census work had to be adapted for the study of fluid residence-grouping processes. The key to this flexibility lay in computer processing of genealogical- and settlement-pattern census data, and in 1965 I developed an early version of the Kinprogram (G. Collier and Vogt 1965; G. Collier 1974*b*) to generate genealogies and link them to photograph-based settlement-pattern maps.

My dissertation research on *Apas* land tenure was begun in 1966. I brought to the field excellent photographic coverage in the form of RC-9 contact prints for stereoscopic viewing and Hyac high-resolution coverage of a major section of Zinacantán. Richard Price (1968) had just completed a field study of land-use patterns in nearby*Muk*ta hok*, and I adapted his research strategies to my own needs. We both found it easier to engage in photo interpretation with informants in the privacy of an office rather than in Zinacanteco fields themselves. The first task was to delimit the area of *Apas* land tenure and to develop a vocabulary for discourse with Tzotzil informants on land-use history. To this end, I elicited lists of local place names and texts on geography, inheritance, and land-use patterns. In order to familiarize myself with local topography, I built a plaster scale model of the *Apas* farmland region, based on stereoscopic examination of the cartographic photography. My key informant then helped me to delimit the study area and to relate the photographs to it.

The overall goal of the study was a complete parcel-by-parcel history of land tenure and use in this century. This goal could be approached by two techniques. First, the photographs permitted an exhaustive identification of land parcels; we had only to seek out individuals to tell us about them. Second, the exhaustive genealogical census identified almost all potential landowners and users. By cross-referring information on individuals with that on land parcels, we could come close to our goal in the year of field research.

To achieve this goal, I interviewed a large number of *Apas* landowners in Tzotzil, assisted by my key informant. I had hoped to use the scale model to elicit information from land users, but Zinacantecos were annoyed by inaccuracies in surface detail on the model and preferred to work directly with photographs. The types of data collected in conjunction with the interviewing are discussed below. Various strategies in interviewing that greatly facilitated air-photo interpretation are described in G. Collier (1974a).

The data for the Chamula land-use study were collected entirely from aerial photography with only a minimum of fieldwork to check on the accuracy of photo interpretation. My wife and I worked with enlargements of the RC-9 coverage, which we divided into a grid pattern of squares corresponding to land units of roughly one-half acre. We rated each of the thousands of these squares in relation to attributes visible in the photography—forest coverage, land slope, land use, settlement, trail, and erosion. Statistical analysis of the covariations of these attributes led to recognition of the land-use sequence so visible in the illustrations of chapter 5.

RESEARCH NOTES

Several chapters in this study report research findings in a descriptive prose that does not reveal underlying strategies of data collection and analysis. This discussion will review methods of research bearing on topics in the sequence with which they occur in the text.

Tzotzil-language interviews form the basis of data collection for all research materials related to *Apas* social organization and land tenure. I employed several strategies in interviewing. First, I relied heavily on key informants who were literate and trained to transcribe Tzotzil phonemically. These informants wrote texts on topics related to land tenure and social organization. Texts included a variety of forms, case histories, normative descriptions, lists of various kinds, and maps with descriptive keys. By translating Tzotzil texts myself, I enriched my vocabulary for discourse about land and related phenomena. Second, I worked with both literate and illiterate informants by using the frame method of formal elicitation (Metzger and Williams 1963, 1966). Topics and native categories appearing in texts were explored and defined through formal interviewing, which, in turn, often elicited new topics and categories that deserved textual illustration. Thus, text writing and formal elicitation complemented one another so as to build up a robust corpus of native language data. Finally, I interviewed a large number of informants in a less formal manner on a variety of subjects through loosely structured conversations.

Several topics dealt with in chapter 2, "Forms of Land Utilization," deserve amplification. The discussion of the agricultural cycle is in terms of stages defined both by Zinacanteco farmers and by other researchers. The stages of highland farming are compared with those of lowland farming discussed in Cancian's monographs (1965, 1972). Man-day labor estimates are averages reported by a sample of highland farmers who supplied detailed farming budgets analyzed in chapter 6.

The enumeration of desirable field attributes is based on statistical analysis of the characteristics of all field parcels in the study area. Each parcel was rated on a schedule of size, grade, altitude (determined by altimeter), state-of-fallow, rate-of-regrowth, predominant flora, and rockiness attributes by informants who owned or had worked on the plots. Accuracy of the schedule was verified by spot checks in the cornfields. The attributes discussed in chapter 2 are those whose covariation with others was strong enough to suggest important functional relationships.

The discussion of trends in farming intensity derives from an analysis of the fallow cycle. I collected parcel-use histories over the period 1940–1966 for almost all study area plots and for some back to the turn of the century. The year-by-year sequence of use or fallow for a given parcel was modeled as a Markov process in an attempt to uncover the regularities in the fallowing patterns. Controlling for altitude and rockiness reduced the variation to be explained, but modeling ruled out any systematic principle for farming and fallowing decisions. Graphic presentation of trends in aggregate farming acreage is confirmed by a statistical comparison of use of the parcels in several successive decades. This can be seen in the quantitative data of tables 25 and 26, which correspond to the histograms in figure 5 in chapter 2. Table 25 describes the distribution of fields according to their use and fallow status; percentages in this table correspond proportionally to column sizes in figure 5. Table 26 describes the disposition of fields in the year subsequent to observation by indicating the probability of use for each status. These probabilities correspond to the proportion of each column that falls below the horizontal baseline in figure 5.

The following test was made to determine whether the likelihood of use changed through time: The decisions for each combination of land category and fallow state were grouped into a contingency table showing the number of fields in each time period cultivated or not. Then the standard Chi-square test for uniformity was applied. One such table, for instance, included 230 decisions concerning "rapid" regrowth fields in use for only one year prior to the decision (see table 27). Here, deviations from expected values computed from the margins are recorded in parentheses. Chi-square with 2 degrees of freedom was 13.55, and the null hypothesis that the likelihood of use was invariant was rejected at the 0.01 level of significance. The test corresponds to the leftmost column of the subtable of figure 5 and tables 25 and 26 dealing with land of "rapid" regrowth. A similar test was made for each subtable column. This and other similar approaches to testing the parameters of probabilistic models, such as the Mth order Markov models, are discussed in Goodman (1959) and Anderson and Goodman (1957).

The map locating the distribution of firewood types was constructed from interviews with women (who are responsible for collecting fuel in *Apas*).

The morphology of social groups in *Apas* presented in chapter 4 is readily apparent in the census of *Apas* begun by Cancian in 1962 and perfected through the 1963–1965 field seasons. Census collection is described above in conjunction with aerial photography.

The normative description of inheritance is based on texts and in-

TABLE 25. Status of Fields

| Time Period | In Use for | | | Percentage of Fields Fallow for (Years) | | | | | | Number of Observations |
	1	2	3+	1-2	3-4	5-6	7-8	9-10	11+	
Fields of rapid regrowth										
1963–1967	10.4	9.2	4.8	23.9	21.3	14.4	7.4	2.9	5.8	729
1957–1962	14.0	9.0	5.0	21.2	18.7	13.8	9.1	4.7	4.7	709
1953–1956	16.7	6.1	2.7	30.1	19.8	12.2	6.1	2.1	4.2	329
Fields of gradual regrowth										
1963–1967	7.8	4.9	2.7	22.6	21.5	15.6	11.9	6.6	6.3	410
1957–1962	13.2	8.8	3.7	22.5	20.7	12.7	6.9	5.0	6.4	377
1953–1956	16.0	8.6	5.7	24.0	13.2	14.8	10.3	4.6	2.9	175
Fields of retarded regrowth										
1963–1967	4.6	4.3	3.0	18.0	19.5	20.2	12.6	8.0	9.9	635
1957–1962	15.1	8.9	5.3	21.1	18.4	12.0	7.1	3.6	8.4	450
1953–1956	16.8	7.3	0.5	24.6	15.2	7.9	8.9	4.7	14.2	191

Note: In these tables, fields are cross-classified by rate of regrowth, time period of observation, and status during a given year of observation. Cells show the percentage of the total observations in a table row corresponding to each status category. Thus, percentages summed across rows total 100%.

TABLE 26. *Use of Fields*

				Probability of Being Used								
	In Use for				Fallow for							
Time Period	1	2	3+		1–2	3–4	5–6	7–8	9–10	11+		
					(Years)							
Fields of rapid regrowth												
1963–1967	.685	.343	.486*		.017	.116	.190	.240	.286	.119		
1957–1962	.777*	.344	.228		.027	.083	.163	.292	.212	.091		
1953–1956	.437*	.450	.556		.020	.031	.050	.150	.000	.000		
Fields of gradual regrowth												
1963–1967	.531*	.300*	.364		.000	.046	.078	.061	.111	.115		
1957–1962	.760*	.272*	.358		.012	.064	.229	.308	.158	.167		
1953–1956	.465*	.667*	.100		.000	.000	.000	.111	.125	.400		
Fields of retarded regrowth												
1963–1967	.552	.185	.368		.000	.040	.039	.100	.039	.048*		
1957–1962	.706*	.475*	.417		.011	.048	.093	.125	.063	.264*		
1953–1956	.470*	.214	.000		.000	.035	.000	.059	.000	.111		

Note: In these tables, fields are cross-classified in the same manner as in table 25. Cell entries correspond to the observed probability that a field of a given status would be put to use in the next season. Thus, the cell entries are the conditional probabilities of use given a certain status. As such, they are independent of one another and thus do not sum to 1.000. Asterisks mark probabilities that were statistically significant from corresponding probabilities in other time periods.

TABLE 27. *Fields of Rapid Regrowth Previously
Used Just One Year*

Time Period	Decision Made to Cultivate		
	Yes	No	Total
1963–1967	52	24	76
	(+ 1)	(− 1)	
1957–1962	77	22	99
	(+11)	(−11)	
1953–1956	24	31	55
	(−12)	(+12)	
Total	153	77	230

terviews. Informants wrote texts both on ideal inheritance patterns
and on actual case histories that illustrated or violated customary inheritance principles. In addition, careful interviews with many household heads, typically lasting through three days of discussion, led to a
detailed reconstruction of the development and dispersion of domestic
groups and the concomitant property distributions. Finally, the ongoing domestic-cycle process could be observed in fieldwork by direct
contact with families undergoing such changes.

The phenomenon of nicknaming became evident in censusing and
in later fieldwork. The system of paired Spanish and Tzotzil surnames
is actually little used by Zinacantecos in unofficial discourse, and reference to individuals in fieldwork and interviews was almost always
by nickname. Victoria Bricker's independent discovery of the role of
nicknames in Zinacanteco ritual humor led to our collaboration in an
article on the topic (Collier and Bricker 1970).

Finally, it should be noted that reference to specific individuals
throughout the book, such as to "Romin Heronimo" in chapter 4, is
through fictitious names and with other precautions to conceal the
true identity of individuals.

The relation of aerial photography to the study of stages in the sequence of Chamula land use (chap. 5) is described above. As mentioned in the text, it is important to realize that the stages can be illustrated, to a greater or lesser degree, within almost every highland
township.

Because of the general conclusions sought from the Chamula study,
examples of Tzotzil ideology were not drawn directly from the excellent corpus of materials collected by Gossen (1970, 1974). More recent fieldwork by Priscilla Rachun Linn also adding to our under-

standing of Chamula world view is being prepared as a doctoral dissertation.

The book's initial discussion of marginality incorporates a comparison of highland and lowland farm budgets. Budgets were collected from interviews with farmers who reconstructed a day-by-day account of their farming activities during the 1966–1967 farming cycle. The interview schedule incorporated a detailed breakdown of costs that have been aggregated in the text to facilitate discussion.

The farming budgets can be analyzed usefully in other ways. It is notable, for instance, that net returns to farmers' labor average slightly more than thirteen pesos in the highlands and eleven pesos in the lowlands per day of farming activity. These returns are very close to the actual wage rate (about 12 pesos per day in 1967) for hired labor throughout central Chiapas and reflect the close attunement of corn farming to a larger economic system.

The latter half of the book combines library research on ethnohistory with fieldwork on social history. The treatment of land-tenure history in Zinacantán is based on a careful examination of the ejido archives of Zinacantán, graciously made available to me in Tuxtla Gutiérrez by the Departamento Agraria Mixta. The archives contain typescripts of many original documents and land titles still in private hands, items that were brought forth as legal evidence during the land-reform era. Local archives, such as those available for study in Tuxtla Gutiérrez, constitute an extremely valuable, but little-exploited source of data on social history of Mexico in the last century.

General information on Chiapas in the nineteenth century was gleaned during a year of postdoctoral study on Mesoamerican local-level native leadership in which I engaged at the Latin American Library at Tulane University. Tulane's collection includes unusually rich materials that apparently once constituted the personal library of Flavio Paniagua, an important nineteenth-century liberal from Chiapas. In addition, the Tulane collection includes a variety of unusual materials on the Tzeltal and Tzotzil uprisings of 1712 and 1869, cited in the Bibliographic Notes.

Finally, the discussion of demographic trends in chapter 7 must be considered embryonic. Census materials from 1970 will soon be available for comparison with those of 1960 and should provide a basis for accurate study of recent trends in vital rates that cannot be inferred directly from vital statistics because of inaccuracies in reporting.

BIBLIOGRAPHY

NOTE: Citations in the Bibliography refer to many sources not cited directly in the argument of the book. These citations have been classified into categories related to the unfolding of the argument, which can be considered a guide to the more detailed background to the study.

Physiography: Adams 1961; Berlin, Breedlove, and Raven 1968; Beard 1955; Florescano and Moreno 1966; Garbell 1947; Helbig 1964*a*, 1964*b*; McBryde 1947; McQuown 1959; F. Miranda 1952–1953; F. Miranda and Sharp 1950; W. W. Reed 1923; Servicio Meteorológico Mexicano 1945; Stevens 1964; Vivó 1958, 1959, 1964; Vivó and Gómez 1946; Vogt 1969; P. Wagner 1964; Waibel 1946.

Political Geography: Aguirre 1953, 1967; Calnek 1961, 1962; Colby and Van Den Berghe 1961, 1969; Edel 1962; Gilman 1964; Hill 1964; McQuown 1959; Nash 1970; Pozas 1959; Siverts 1960, 1969*a*, 1969*b*; Tax 1937; Vogt 1969; Wolf 1955.

Indian-Ladino Relations: Aguirre 1953, 1967; Colby 1966; Colby and Van Den Berghe 1961, 1969; McQuown 1959; B. Metzger 1960; Pozas 1948, 1959; Siverts 1969*a*; Tumin 1952.

Culture-Area Concepts and Constructs for the Study of Maya Social Organization: Bullard 1960; Eggan 1954; Goody 1958; Guiteras 1947; *The Maya and their Neighbors* 1940; Miles 1957; Redfield 1941, 1953; Romney 1957; Tax 1952; Vogt and Ruz 1964; Wissler 1926.

Farming and Other Land Exploitation: Berlin, Breedlove, and Raven 1968; Cancian 1972; Conklin 1961; Diener 1971; Florescano and Moreno 1966; D. Metzger and Williams 1966; Price 1968; Reina 1967; Stadelman 1940.

Kinship and Social Organization in Zinacantán: Bricker 1968, 1973; Cancian 1965, 1972; G. Collier and Vogt 1965; J. Collier 1968, 1970, 1973; Holmer 1974; Laughlin n.d.; Price 1968; Vogt 1961, 1965, 1966, 1969.

Chamula Erosion and Tzotzil Ideology: Adams 1961; Cook 1949; Gossen 1970, 1974; Guiteras 1961; Holland 1963; Vogt 1965, 1969.

General Historical Sources on Mesoamerica: Aguirre 1953; Borah 1951; Borah and Cook 1960; Caso et al. 1954; Chamberlain 1939a, 1939b; Chevalier 1963; Cook and Simpson 1948; Fábila 1941; Gamio et al. 1958; Gibson 1952, 1955, 1964; Gussinye 1960; Hanke 1949; Juan and de Ulloa 1918; López 1965; McAndrew 1965; Mendieta 1946; J. Miranda 1951, 1952, 1966; N. Reed 1964; Roys 1943; Scholes and Roys 1948; Simpson 1937; Spores 1967; H. Wagner 1967; Wilkie 1970; Wolf 1955, 1959; Zavala 1948.

Sources on the History of Chiapas: Adams 1961; Aguirre 1967; Archivo General de Chiapas 1953a. 1953b; Cáceres 1946, 1962; Calnek 1961, 1962; Casahonda 1963; Castillo 1961; Chamberlain 1948; Comisión Agraria Mixta n.d.a, n.d.b; Departamento Agrario n.d.a, n.d.b; Edel 1962; Fuentes 1882; Gilman 1964; Gossen 1970; Las Casas 1909; Locke 1964; Lowenthal 1963; B. Metzger 1959, 1960; Moscoso 1960; Orozco 1911; Paniagua 1870; Pozas 1948; Remesal 1932; Reyes 1961, 1962; Trens 1957; Villa 1961; Ximenes 1929.

Local-Level Indian Leadership in Chiapas and Mesoamerica: Aguirre 1953, 1966, 1967; Calnek 1962; Caso et al. 1954; J. Collier 1970; Edel 1962; Fernández 1961; Friedrich 1970; Gamio et al. 1958; López 1965; Prokosch 1963; N. Reed 1964; Roys 1943; Scholes and Roys 1948; Siverts 1958, 1960, 1964, 1965, 1969a, 1969b; Spores 1967; Vásquez 1940; Villa 1947; Wilson 1966; Wolf 1955; Zavala 1948; Zorita 1942.

The Tzeltal and Tzotzil Rebellions of 1712, 1869: Archivo General de Chiapas 1953a, 1953b; Archivo General de la Nación 1948; Baluarte de la Libertad 1867–1870; Bricker n.d.; Calnek 1961, 1962; Flores 1939; Klein 1966; Molina 1934; Núñez 1692; Pineda 1888; N. Reed 1964.

Population Trends in Chiapas and Mesoamerica: Aguirre 1967; Borah and Cook 1960; Calnek 1961; Cook 1949; Cook and Simpson 1948; Dirección General de Estadística 1963; Gossen 1970; Hill 1964; Marina 1961; Pozas 1952; Reyes 1962; Vogt 1969.

Occupational Specialties, Topical and Theoretical Considerations:

Aguirre 1967; Arbuz 1963; Archivo General del Gobierno 1937;
Berry 1961; Bunnin 1966; Cancian 1965; Hagget 1966; Haviland
1966; Helbig 1964*a*, 1964*b*; McQuown 1959; Nash 1970; Plattner
1969; Pozas 1959; Siverts 1969*a*; Skinner 1964.

Adams, Robert M. 1961. "Changing patterns of territorial organization
in the central highlands of Chiapas, Mexico." *American Antiquity*
26:341–360.
Aguirre Beltrán, Gonzalo. 1953. *Formas de gobierno indígena*. Mexico
City: Imprenta Universitaria.
———. 1966. "Las funciones del poder en la comunidad indígena."
La Palabra y el Hombre 40:547–562.
———. 1967. *Regiones de refugio*. Ediciones Especiales, no. 46.
Mexico City: Instituto Indigenista Interamericano.
Anderson, T. W., and L. A. Goodman. 1957. "Statistical inference
about Markov chains." *Annals of Mathematical Statistics* 28:
89–110.
Andrewartha, H. G. 1961. *Introduction to the study of animal
populations*. Chicago: University of Chicago Press.
Arbuz, Georges. 1963. "La construction de la guitare et du violon a
Chamula." Manuscript, Harvard Chiapas Project.
Archivo General de Chiapas. 1953*a*. "Los frailes domínicos del pueblo
de Chiapa de la Real Corona despojan a los naturales del templo de
Santo Domingo en 1776." *Documentos Históricos de Chiapas* 1:
21–58.
———. 1953*b*. Motín indígena en Tuxtla. *Documentos Históricos de
Chiapas* 2:25–52.
Archivo General de la Nación. 1948. "Sublevación de los Indios
Tzendales. Año de 1713." *Boletín del Archivo General de la Nación*.
19:497–536.
Archivo General del Gobierno. 1937. "Año de 1763. Autos formados
sobre la Real Cédula, para que esta Real Audiencia con la brevedad
y reserva posible remita una relación individual de los Corregi-
mientos y Alcaldías Mayores de este Reyno." *Boletín del Archivo
General del Gobierno* 2:448–486.
Ashby, W. Ross. 1960. *Design for a brain*. 2d rev. ed. London:
Chapman and Hall.
El Baluarte de la Libertad. 1867–1870. [Weekly newspaper published
in Chiapa de Corzo, Mexico, with partial copies on file in Latin
American Library, Tulane University.]

Barth, Fredrik. 1956. "Ecological relationships of ethnic groups in Swat, North Pakistan." *American Anthropologist* 58:1079–1089.
———. 1959. *Political leadership among Swat Pathans.* London: Althone Press.
———. 1969. *Ethnic groups and boundaries.* Boston: Little, Brown and Co.
Beard, J. S. 1955. "The Classification of tropical American vegetation types." *Ecology* 36:89–100.
Berlin, Brent, Dennis E. Breedlove, and Peter H. Raven. 1968. "Covert categories and folk taxonomies." *American Anthropologist* 70: 290–299.
Berry, Brian, J. L., and A. Pred. 1961. *Central place studies: A bibliography of theory and applications.* Philadelphia: Bibliographic Series, no. 1. Regional Science Research Institute.
Bohannon, Laura, and P. J. Bohannon. 1953. *The Tiv of central Nigeria.* London: International African Institute.
Boissevain, Jeremy. 1966. "Patronage in Sicily." *Man* 1:18–33.
Borah, W. 1951. *New Spain's century of depression.* Ibero-Americana, no. 35. Berkeley: University of California Press.
Borah, W., and S. F. Cook. 1960. *The population of Central Mexico in 1548.* Ibero-Americana, no. 43. Berkeley: University of California Press.
Bricker, Victoria R. N.d. "A Maya passion." Manuscript, Tulane University.
———. 1968. "The meaning of laughter in Zinacantan: An analysis of the humor of a highland Maya community." Ph.D. dissertation, Harvard University.
———. 1973. *Ritual humor in highland Chiapas.* Austin: University of Texas Press.
Bullard, William R. 1960. "Maya settlement pattern in northeastern Petén, Guatemala." *American Antiquity* 25:355–372.
Bunnin, Nicholas F. 1966. "La industria de las flores en Zinacantan." In Vogt 1966, pp. 208–232.
Bunzel, Ruth. 1952. *Chichicastenango: A Guatemalan village.* Seattle and London: University of Washington Press.
Cáceres López, Carlos. 1946. *Chiapas: Síntesis geográfica e histórica.* Mexico City: Editorial Forum.
———. 1962. *Chiapas y su aportación a la república durante la reforma e intervención Francesa, 1858–1864.* Mexico City: Sociedad Mexicana de Geografía y Estadística.
Calnek, Edward E. 1961. "Distribution and location of the Tzeltal

and Tzotzil pueblos of the highlands of Chiapas from earliest times to the present." Mimeographed. Also in McQuown 1959.

———. 1962. "Highland Chiapas before the Spanish Conquest." Ph.D. dissertation, University of Chicago.

Cancian, Frank. 1965. *Economics and prestige in a Maya community.* Stanford: Stanford University Press.

———. 1972. *Change and uncertainty in a peasant economy: The Maya corn farmers of Zinacantan.* Stanford: Stanford University Press.

Casahonda Castillo, José. 1963. *50 años de revolución en Chiapas.* Tuxtla Gutiérrez: Instituto de Ciencias y Artes de Chiapas.

Caso, Alfonso; Silvio Zavala; José Miranda; Moises González Navarro; Gonzalo Aguirre Beltrán; and Ricardo Pozas A. 1954. *Métodos y resultados de la política indigenista en México.* Memorias del Instituto Nacional Indigenista, no. 6. Mexico City.

Castillo Tejero, Noemi. 1961. "Conquista y colonización de Chiapas." In *Los Mayas del Sur y sus relaciones con los Nahuas Meridionales,* pp. 207–220. VIII Mesa Redonda, San Cristóbal de las Casas, Chiapas. Mexico City: Sociedad Mexicana de Antropología.

Chamberlain, Robert S. 1939a. *Castilian backgrounds of the Repartimiento-Encomienda.* Contributions to American Anthropology and History, no. 25. Washington, D.C.: Carnegie Institution of Washington.

———. 1939b. "The concept of *señor natural* as revealed by Castilian law and administrative documents." *Hispanic American Historical Review* 19:130–137.

———. 1948. *The governorship of the Adelantado Francisco de Montejo in Chiapas, 1539–1544.* Contributions to American Anthropology and History, no. 48. Washington, D.C.: Carnegie Institution of Washington.

Chevalier, François. 1963. *Land and society in colonial Mexico: The great hacienda.* Berkeley: University of California Press.

Colby, Benjamin N. 1966. *Ethnic relations in the Chiapas highlands.* Santa Fe: Museum of New Mexico.

Colby, Benjamin N., and Pierre L. Van Den Berghe. 1961. "Ethnic relations in southeastern Mexico." *American Anthropologist* 63: 772–792.

———. 1969. *Ixil country: A plural society in highland Guatemala.* Berkeley: University of California Press.

Collier, George. 1966. "Familia y tierra en varias comunidades Mayas." *Estudios de Cultura Maya* 6:301–335.

————. 1968. "Land inheritance and land use in a modern Maya community." Ph.D. dissertation, Harvard University.

————. 1974*a*. "The impact of airphoto technology on the study of demography and ecology in highland Chiapas." In Vogt 1974.

————. 1974*b*. *The KINPROGRAM: A package of PL/I programs for the processing of genealogical censuses*. Stanford: Department of Anthropology, Stanford University.

Collier, George A., and Victoria R. Bricker. 1970. "Nicknames and social structure in Zinacantan." *American Anthropologist* 72: 289–302.

Collier, George A., and Evon Z. Vogt. 1965. "Aerial photographs and computers in the analysis of Zinacanteco demography and land tenure." Paper presented to the 64th annual meeting of the American Anthropological Association, Denver.

Collier, Jane Fishburne. 1968. *Courtship and marriage in Zinacantan, Chiapas, Mexico*. Middle American Research Institute Publication 25, pt. 4. New Orleans.

————. 1970. "Zinacanteco law: A study of conflict in a modern Maya community. Ph.D. dissertation, Tulane University.

————. 1973. *Law and social change in Zinacantan*. Stanford: Stanford University Press.

Comisión Agraria Mixta, Archivo. N.d.*a* File 138. "Zinacantan." Tuxtla Gutiérrez.

————. N.d.*b* File 661. "Apas, Municipio de Zinacantan." Tuxtla Gutiérrez.

Conklin, Harold C. 1957. *Hanunóo agriculture: A report on an integral system of shifting cultivation in the Philippines*. Rome: Food and Agricultural Organization of the United Nations.

————. 1961. "The study of shifting cultivation." *Current Anthropology* 2:27–61.

Cook, S. F. 1949. *Soil erosion and population in central Mexico*. Ibero-Americana, no. 34. Berkeley: University of California Press.

Cook, S. F., and L. B. Simpson. 1948. *The population of central Mexico in the sixteenth century*. Ibero-Americana, no. 31. Berkeley: University of California Press.

Departamento Agrario, Archivo. N.d.*a* File 138. "Zinacantan." Tuxtla Gutiérrez.

————. N.d.*b* File 661. "Apas, Municipio de Zinacantan." Tuxtla Gutiérrez.

Deutsch, Karl W. 1963. Introduction to *Nation Building*, edited by Karl W. Deutsch and W. J. Flotz. New York: Atherton Press.

Diener, Paul. 1971. "The role of domesticated animals in a

Mesoamerican subsistence economy." Ph.D. dissertation prospectus, Stanford University.

Dirección General de Estadística. 1963. *VIII censo general de población, 1960. Estado de Chiapas.* Mexico City: Secretaría de Industria y Comercio, Estados Unidos Mexicanos.

Edel, Matthew D. 1962. "Zinacantan's ejido: The effects of Mexican land reform on an Indian community in Chiapas." Mimeographed. Columbia-Cornell-Harvard-Illinois Summer Field Studies Program, Harvard.

Eggan, F. 1954. "Social anthropology and the method of controlled comparison." *American Anthropologist* 56: 743–763.

Eidheim, Harald. 1968. "The Lappish movement—an innovative political process." In *Local-level politics*, edited by M. Swartz. Chicago: Aldine Publishing Co.

———. 1969. "When ethnic identity is a social stigma." In Barth 1969.

Evans-Pritchard, E. E. 1940. *The Nuer.* Oxford: Clarendon Press.

Fábila, Manuel. 1941. *Cinco siglos de legislación agraria (1493–1940).* Mexico City: Los Talleres de Industrial Gráfica.

Fernández de Recas, Guillermo S. 1961. *Cacicazgos y nobiliario indígena de la Nueva España.* Instituto Bibliográfico Mexicano, no. 5. Mexico City: Biblioteca Nacional de México.

Flores Ruíz, Timoteo. 1939. *La guerra de castas en el año de 1869.* San Cristóbal de las Casas, Chiapas: privately printed.

Florescano, Enrique, and A. Moreno Toscano. 1966. *Bibliografía del maíz en México.* Jalapa: Universidad Veracruzana.

Fortes, Meyer. 1945. *The dynamics of clanship among the Tallensi.* London: Oxford University Press.

———. 1949. *The web of kinship among the Tallensi.* London: Oxford University Press.

———. 1953. "The structure of unilineal descent groups." *American Anthropologist* 55: 17–41.

Foster, George M. 1953. "What is folk culture?" *American Anthropologist* 55: 159–173.

———. 1961. "The dyadic contract: A model for the social structure of a Mexican peasant village." *American Anthropologist* 63: 1173–1192.

———. 1963. "The dyadic contract in Tzintzuntzan, II: Patron-client relationship." *American Anthropologist* 65: 1280–1294.

Friedrich, Paul. 1970. *Agrarian revolt in a Mexican village.* Englewood Cliffs, N.J.: Prentice-Hall.

Fuentes y Guzmán. D. Francisco Antonio de. 1882. *Historia de*

Guatemala, o Recordación Florida. 2 vols. Madrid: Biblioteca de los Americanistas.

Gamio, Manuel. 1943. "Static and dynamic values in the indigenous past of America." *Hispanic American Historical Review* 23:386–393.

Gamio, Manuel, et al. 1958. *Legislación indigenista de México.* Ediciones Especiales, no. 38. Mexico City: Instituto Nacional Interamericano.

Garbell, M. A. 1947. *Tropical and equatorial meteorology.* New York and Chicago: Pitman Publishing Co.

Geertz, Clifford. 1963a. "The integrative revolution: Primordial sentiments and civil politics in the new states." In *Old Societies and New States,* edited by Clifford Geertz. Glencoe, Ill.: Free Press.

————. 1963b. *Agricultural involution: The processes of ecological change in Indonesia.* Berkeley and Los Angeles: University of California Press.

Gilman, Antonio. 1964. "Municipio organization." Manuscript, Harvard Chiapas Project.

Gibson, Charles. 1952. *Tlaxcala in the sixteenth century.* Stanford: Stanford University Press.

————. 1955. "The transformation of the Indian community in New Spain, 1500–1810." *Journal of World History* 2:581–607.

————. 1964. *The Aztecs under Spanish rule: A history of the Indians of the valley of Mexico, 1519–1810.* Stanford: Stanford University Press.

Goffman, Erving. 1959. *The presentation of self in everyday life.* Garden City, N.Y.: Doubleday and Co.

Goldschmidt, Walter. 1959. *Man's way: A preface to the understanding of society.* New York: Holt, Rinehart, and Winston.

González Casanova, Pablo. 1965. "Internal colonialism and national development." *Studies in Comparative International Development* 1:27–37.

Goodenough, Ward H. 1955. "A problem in Malayo-Polynesian social organization." *American Anthropologist* 57:71–83.

————. 1956. "Malayo-Polynesian land tenure." *American Anthropologist* 58:173–175.

Goodman, L. A. 1959. "On some statistical tests for Mth order Markov chains." *Annals of Mathematical Statistics* 30:154–164.

Goody, Jack, ed. 1958. *The developmental cycle in domestic groups.* Cambridge: At the University Press.

Gossen, Gary H. 1970. "Time and space in Chamula oral tradition." Ph.D. dissertation, Harvard University.

————. 1974. *Chamulas in the world of the sun: Time and space in a Maya oral tradition.* Cambridge, Mass.: Harvard University Press.

Guiteras Holmes, Calixta. 1947. "Clanes y sistema de parentesco de Cancuc (México)." *Acta Americana* 5:12–17.

————. 1961. *Perils of the soul: The world view of a Tzotzil Indian.* New York: Free Press of Glencoe.

Gussinye, Miguel. 1960. *Código agrario y ley de colonización.* Mexico City: Leyes Mexicanas, Editorial Divulgación.

Haaland, Gunnar. 1969. "Economic determinants in ethnic processes." In Barth 1969.

Haggett, Peter. 1966. *Locational analysis in human geography.* New York: St. Martin's Press.

Hanke, Lewis. 1949. *The Spanish struggle for justice in the conquest of America.* Washington, D.C.: American Historical Association. Reissued 1965. Boston: Little, Brown and Co.

Haviland, John B. 1966. "Vob: Traditional music in Zinacantan." Manuscript, Harvard Chiapas Project.

Hechter, Michael. 1971. "Towards a theory of ethnic change." *Politics and Society* 2:21–45.

Helbig, Karl M. 1964a. *El Soconusco y su zona cafetalera en Chiapas.* Tuxtla Gutiérrez: Instituto de Ciencias y Artes de Chiapas.

————. 1964b. *La cuenca superior del río Grijalva: Un estudio regional de Chiapas, sureste de México.* Tuxtla Gutiérrez: Instituto de Ciencias y Artes de Chiapas.

Hill, David A. 1964. *The changing landscape of a Mexican municipio: Villa Las Rosas, Chiapas.* Department of Geography Research Paper, no. 91. Chicago: University of Chicago.

Holland, William R. 1963. *Medicina Maya en los altos de Chiapas.* Mexico City: Instituto Nacional Indigenista.

Holmer, Linnea K. 1974. "Settlement patterns and communications networks in highland Chiapas." In Vogt 1974.

Juan, Jorge, and A. de Ulloa. 1918. *Noticias secretas de América (siglo XVIII).* Biblioteca Ayacucho, vol. 1. Madrid: Editorial América.

Kenny, Michael. 1960. "Patterns of patronage in Spain." *Anthropological Quarterly* 33:14–23.

Klein, Herbert S. 1966. "Peasant communities in revolt: The Tzeltal republic of 1712." *Pacific Historical Review* 35:247–264.

Kluckhohn, Clyde. 1958. "The scientific study of values." In 3 *Lectures: University of Toronto Installation Lectures.* Toronto: University of Toronto Press.

Kluckhohn, F., and F. Strodtbeck. 1959. *Variations in value orientations.* Evanston, Ill.: Row, Peterson and Co.

Kroeck, Richard M. 1966. *A manual for users of aerial photography of the highlands of Chiapas, Mexico. Prepared for the Dept. of Social Relations, Harvard University*. Vidya Report, no. 233. Palo Alto, Cal.: Itek Corporation.

de Las Casas, Fray Bartolomé. 1909. *Apologética historia de las Indias*. Historiadores de Indias, edited by M. Serrano y Sanz. vol. 1. Madrid: Nueva Biblioteca de Autores Españoles.

Laughlin, Robert M. N.d. *The great Tzotzil dictionary of San Lorenzo Zinacantan*. Smithsonian Contributions to Anthropology. Washington, D.C.: Smithsonian Institution, forthcoming.

Leach, Edmund Ronald. 1954. *Political systems of highland Burma: A study of Kachin social structure*. London: London School of Economics and Political Science.

————. 1961. *Pul Eliya: A study of land tenure and kinship*. Cambridge: At the University Press.

Lipset, Seymour Martin, and Stein Rokkan. 1967. "Cleavage structures, party systems, and voter alignments: An introduction." In *Party systems and voter alignments: Cross-national perspectives*, edited by S. M. Lipset and S. Rokkan. New York: Free Press.

Locke, Nancy. 1964. "A case study in Mexican conservatism: Why the capital of Chiapas was moved from San Cristóbal to Tuxtla Gutiérrez in 1892." A.B. honors thesis, Smith College.

López Sarrelangue, Delfina Esmeraldo. 1965. *La nobleza indígena de Pátzcuaro en la época Virreinal*. Mexico City: Instituto de Investigaciones Históricas, Universidad Nacional Autónoma de México.

Lowenthal. Mary. 1963. "The elite of San Cristóbal." Manuscript, Harvard Chiapas Project.

McAndrew, John. 1965. *The open-air churches of sixteenth century Mexico*. Cambridge, Mass.: Harvard University Press.

McBryde, F. W. 1947. *Cultural and historical geography of southwest Guatemala*. Institute of Social Anthropology Publication, no. 4. Washington, D.C.: Smithsonian Institution.

McQuown, Norman A. 1959. "Report on the 'Man-in-Nature' project of the Department of Anthropology of the University of Chicago in The Tzeltal-Tzotzil speaking region of the state of Chiapas, Mexico." 3 vols. Mimeographed. University of Chicago.

McQuown, Norman A., and Julian Pitt-Rivers. 1970. *Ensayos de antropología en la zona central de Chiapas*. Mexico City: Instituto Nacional Indigenista.

Marina Arreola, Aura. 1961. "Población de los altos de Chiapas durante el siglo XVII e inicios del XVIII." In *Los Mayas del Sur y sus Relaciones con los Nahuas Meridionales*, VIII Mesa Redonda, San Cristóbal de las Casas, Chiapas, pp. 247–264. Mexico City: Sociedad Mexicana de Antropología.

The Maya and their Neighbors. 1940. Edited by C. L. Hays and others. New York: D. Appleton-Century Co.

Meggitt, M. J. 1965. *The lineage system of the Mae-Enga of New Guinea*. New York: Barnes and Noble.

Mendieta y Núñez, Lucio. 1946. *El problema agrario de México*. Mexico City. Editorial Porrúa.

Metzger, Barbara. 1959. "An ethnographic history of Zinacantan." Manuscript, Harvard Chiapas Project.

———. 1960. "Notes on the history of Indian-Ladino relations in Chiapas." Manuscript, Harvard Chiapas Project.

Metzger, Duane, and G. Williams. 1963. "A formal ethnographic analysis of Tenejapa Ladino weddings." *American Anthropologist* 65:1076–1101.

———. 1966. "Some procedures and results in the study of native categories: Tzeltal 'firewood.' " *American Anthropologist* 68: 389–407.

Miles, Susan W. 1957. *The sixteenth century Pokom-Maya: A documentary analysis of social structure and archeological setting*. Transactions of the American Philosophical Society, vol. 47, pt. 4. Philadelphia.

Miranda, F. 1952–1953. *La vegetación de Chiapas*. 2 vols. Tuxtla Gutiérrez: Departamento de Prensa y Turismo.

Miranda, F., and A. J. Sharp. 1950. "Characteristics of vegetation in certain temperate regions of eastern Mexico." *Ecology* 31:313–333.

Miranda, José. 1951. "La tasación de las cargas indígenas de la Nueva España durante el siglo XVI, excluyendo el tributo." *Revista de Historia de América* 31:77–96.

———. 1952. *El tributo indígena en la Nueva España durante el siglo XVI*. El Colegio de México. Mexico City: Fondo de Cultura Económica.

———. 1966. "La Propriedad comunal de la tierra y la cohesión social de los pueblos indígenas Mexicanos." *Cuadernos Americanos* 149:168–181.

Molina, Cristobal. 1934. *War of the castes: Indian uprisings in Chiapas, 1867–70*. Translated by Ernest Noyes and Dolores Morgadanes. Middle American Research Institute Publication, no. 5, pt. 8. New Orleans.

Moscoso Pastrana, Prudencio. 1960. *El Pinedismo en Chiapas, 1916–1920*. Mexico City: La Editorial Cultura.

Murdock, G. P. 1948. "Anthropology in Micronesia." *Transactions of the New York Academy of Sciences* 2:9–16.
———. 1949. *Social structure*. New York: Macmillan Co.
Nash, June. 1970. *In the eyes of the ancestors: Belief and behavior in a Mayan community*. New Haven and London: Yale University Press.
Núñez de la Vega, Fray Francisco. 1692. *Constituciones diocesanas del obispado de Chiappa*. Rome.
Orozco y Jiménez, Francisco. 1911. *Colección de documentos inéditos relativos a la iglesia de Chiapas*. Vol. 2. San Cristóbal de las Casas, Chiapas: Imprenta de la Sociedad Católica.
Paniagua, Flavio A. 1870. *Una rosa y dos espinas: Memorias del imperio en Chiapas*. San Cristóbal de las Casas, Chiapas: Porvenir.
Pineda, Vicente. 1888. *Historia de las sublevaciones indígenas habidas en el estado de Chiapas*. Tipografía del Gobierno, Chiapas.
Plattner, Stuart Mark. 1969. "Peddlers, pigs, and profits: Itinerant trading in southeast Mexico." Ph.D. dissertation, Stanford University.
Pozas Arciniega, Ricardo. 1948. *Juan Pérez Jolote: Biografía de un Tzotzil*. Acta Antropológica. vol. 3, pt. 3. Mexico City.
———. 1952. "El trabajo en las plantaciones de café y el cambio sociocultural del indio." *Revista Mexicana de Estudios Antropológicos* 13:31–48.
———. 1959. *Chamula: Un pueblo Indio de los altos de Chiapas*. Memorias del Instituto Nacional Indigenista, vol. 8. Mexico City.
Price, Richard. 1968. "Land use in Maya community." *International Archives of Ethnography* 51:1–19.
Prokosch, Eric. 1963. "Chamula government." Mimeographed. London School of Economics.
Rappaport, Roy A. 1968. *Pigs for the ancestors: Ritual in the ecology of a New Guinea people*. New Haven and London: Yale University Press.
Redfield, Robert. 1941. *The folk culture of Yucatan*. Chicago: University of Chicago Press.
———. 1953. *The primitive world and its transformations*. Ithaca, N.Y.: Cornell University Press.
Redfield, Robert, and A. Villa Rojas. 1934. *Chan Kom: A Maya village*. Washington, D.C.: Carnegie Institution of Washington.
Reed, Nelson. 1964. *The caste war of Yucatan*. Stanford: Stanford University Press.
Reed, W. W. 1923. "Climatological data for Central America." *Monthly Weather Review* 51:133–141.

Reina, Ruben E. 1967. "Milpas and milperos, implications for prehistoric times." *American Anthropologist* 69:1–20.

Remesal, Fray Antonio de. 1932. *Historia general de las Indias occidentales, y particular de la gobernación de Chiapa y Guatemala.* Vols. 4 and 5. Guatemala: Biblioteca "Goathemala" de la Sociedad de Geografía e Historia.

Reyes García, Luis. 1961. "Documentos nahoas sobre el estado de Chiapas." In *Los Mayas del Sur y sus Relaciones con los Nahuas Meridionales,* pp. 167–194. VIII Mesa Redonda, San Cristóbal de las Casas, Chiapas. Mexico City: Sociedad Mexicana de Antropología.

———. 1962. "Movimientos demográficos en la población indígena de Chiapas durante la época colonial." *La Palabra y el Hombre* 21: 25–48.

Romney, A. Kimball. 1957. "The genetic model and Uto-Aztecan time perspective." *Davidson Journal of Anthropology* 3:35–41.

Roys, Ralph L. 1943. *The Indian background of colonial Yucatán.* Carnegie Institution of Washington Publication, no. 548. Washington, D.C.

Ruiz, Ramón Eduardo. 1963. *Mexico: The challenge of poverty and illiteracy.* San Marino, Cal.: Huntington Library.

Sahlins, Marshall D. 1961. "The segmentary lineage: An organization of predatory expansion." *American Anthropologist* 63:322–343.

Scholes, France V., and Ralph L. Roys. 1948. *The Maya Chontal Indians of Acalan-Tixchel: A contribution to the history and ethnography of the Yucatan peninsula.* Carnegie Institution of Washington Publication, no. 560. Washington, D.C.

Servicio Meteorológico Mexicano. 1945. *Atlas climatológico de México.* Mexico City.

Shils, Edward. 1957. "Primordial, personal, sacred, and civil ties." *British Journal of Sociology* 8:130–145.

Simpson, Eyler N. 1937. *The ejido: Mexico's way out.* Chapel Hill: University of North Carolina Press.

Simpson, Lesley Byrd. 1966. *The encomienda in New Spain: The beginnings of Spanish Mexico.* Berkeley: University of California Press.

Siverts, Henning. 1958. "Social and cultural changes in a Tzeltal (Mayan) Municipio, Chiapas, Mexico." In *Proceedings of the 32nd International Congress of Americanists,* pp. 177–189. Copenhagen: Munksgaard.

———. 1960. "Political organization in a Tzeltal community in Chiapas, Mexico." *Alpha Kappa Deltan* 30:14–29.

————. 1964. "On politics and leadership in highland Chiapas." In Vogt and Ruz 1964.

————. 1965. "The 'Cacique' of K'ankujk': A study of leadership and social change in highland Chiapas, Mexico." *Estudios de Cultura Maya* 5:339–360.

————. 1969a. "Ethnic stability and boundary dynamics in southern Mexico. In Barth 1969.

————. 1969b. *Oxchuc: Una tribu Maya de México*. Ediciones Especiales, no. 52. Mexico City: Instituto Indigenista Interamericano.

Skinner, G. William. 1964. "Marketing and social structure in rural China: Part I." *Journal of Asian Studies* 24:1.

Spores, Ronald. 1967. *The Mixtec kings and their people*. Civilization of the American Indian Series, no. 85. Norman: University of Oklahoma Press.

Stadelman, R. 1940. *Maize cultivation in northwestern Guatemala*. Carnegie Institute of Washington, Contributions to American Anthropology and History, vol. 4, pt. 33. Washington, D.C.

Stavenhagen, Rodolpho. 1965. "Classes, colonialism, and acculturation." *Studies in Comparative International Development* 1(6):53–77.

Stevens, Rayfred L. 1964. "The soils of Middle America and their relation to Indian peoples and cultures." In *Handbook of Middle American Indians*, edited by Robert Wauchope, I, 265–315. Austin: University of Texas Press.

Steward, Julian H. 1955. *Theory of culture change: The methodology of multilinear evolution*. Urbana: University of Illinois Press.

Steward, Julian, R. A. Manners, E. R. Wolf, E. Padilla Seda, S. W. Mintz, and R. L. Scheele. 1956. *The People of Puerto Rico: A Case Study in Social Anthropology*. Urbana: University of Illinois Press.

Tax, Sol. 1937. "The municipios of the midwestern highlands of Guatemala." *American Anthropologist* 39:423–444.

————, ed. 1952. *Heritage of conquest: The ethnology of Middle America*. Glencoe, Ill.: Free Press.

Trens, Manuel B. 1957. *Historia de Chiapas desde los tiempos más remotos hasta caida del Segundo Imperio*. Mexico City.

Tumin, M. M. 1952. *Caste in a peasant society: A case study of the dynamics of caste*. Princeton: Princeton University Press.

Vasconcelos, José. 1948. *La raza cósmica: Misión de la raza iberoamericana, Argentina y Brazil*. Mexico City: Espasa-Calpe Mexicana.

Vásquez, Genaro V. 1940. *Doctrinas y realidades en la legislación para los Indios.* Mexico City: Departamento de Asuntos Indígenas.

Villa Rojas, Alfonso. 1947. "Kinship and nagualism in a Tzeltal community, southeastern Mexico." *American Anthropologist* 49: 578–587.

————. 1961. "Notas sobre la tenencia de la tierra entre los Mayas de la antiguedad." *Estudios de Cultura Maya* 1:21–46.

Vivó Escoto, Jorge A. 1958. *Geografía de México.* Mexico City: Fondo de Cultura Económica.

————. 1959. "Estudio de geografía y economía y demografía de Chiapas." *Boletín de la Sociedad Mexicana de Geografía y Estadística* 87(1–3):7–262.

————. 1964. "Weather and climate of Mexico and Central America." In *Handbook of Middle American Indians,* edited by Robert Wauchope, I, 187–215. Austin: University of Texas Press.

Vivó Escoto, Jorge A., and J. C. Gómez. 1946. *Climatología de México.* Mexico City: Instituto Panamericano de Geografía e Historia.

Vogt, Evon Z. 1961. "Some aspects of Zinacantan settlement patterns and ceremonial organization." *Estudios de Cultura Maya,* 1: 131–146.

————. 1964. "Ancient Maya concepts in contemporary Zinacantan religion." In *VIe Congrès International des Sciences Anthropologiques et Ethnologiques,* II, 497–502. Paris: Musée de l'Homme.

————. 1965. "Structural and conceptual replication in Zinacantan culture." *American Anthropologist* 67:342–353.

————, ed. 1966. *Los Zinacantecos: Un pueblo Tzotzil de los altos de Chiapas.* Mexico City: Instituto Nacional Indigenista.

————. 1969. *Zinacantan: A Maya community in the highlands of Chiapas.* Cambridge, Mass.: Harvard University Press, Belknap Press.

————, ed. 1974. *Aerial photography in anthropological field work.* Cambridge, Mass.: Harvard University Press.

Vogt, Evon Z., and Alberto Ruz L. 1964. *Desarrollo cultural de los Mayas.* Mexico City: Universidad Nacional Autónoma de México.

Vogt, Evon Z., and A. Kimball Romney. 1971. "The use of aerial photographic techniques in Maya ethnography." In *VIIe Congrès International des Sciences Anthropologiques et Ethnologiques,* XI, 156–171. Moscow: Izdatel'stvo "Nauka."

Wagley, Charles. 1941. *Economics of a Guatemalan village.* American Anthropological Association Memoir, no. 58. Menasha, Wis.

———. 1949. *The social and religious life of a Guatemalan village*. American Anthropological Association Memoir, no. 71. Menasha, Wis.

Wagner, Henry Raup. 1967. *The life and writings of Bartolomé de las Casas*. Albuquerque: University of New Mexico Press.

Wagner, Philip L. 1964. "Natural vegetation of Middle America." In *Handbook of Middle American Indians*, edited by Robert Wauchope. I, 216–264. Austin: University of Texas Press.

Waibel, L. 1946. *La sierra madre de Chiapas*. Sociedad Mexicana de Geografía y Estadística, Serie Geográfica, no. 2. Mexico City.

Wilkie, J. W. 1970. *The Mexican revolution: Federal expenditure and social change since 1910*. Berkeley: University of California Press.

Wilson, George Carter. 1966. *Crazy February*. New York: J. B. Lippincott.

Wissler, Clark. 1926. *The relation of nature to man in aboriginal America*. New York: Oxford University Press.

Wolf, Eric R. 1955. "Types of Latin American peasantry." *American Anthropologist* 57:452–471.

———. 1957. "Closed corporate peasant communities in Mesoamerica and central Java." *Southwestern Journal of Anthropology* 13:1–18.

———. 1959. *Sons of the shaking earth*. Chicago: University of Chicago Press.

———. 1966. *Peasants*. Englewood Cliffs, N.J.: Prentice-Hall.

Womack, John, Jr. 1969. *Zapata and the Mexican revolution*. New York: Alfred A. Knopf.

Ximenes, Fray Francisco. 1929. *Historia de la provincia de San Vicente de Chiapa y Guatemala*. Guatemala City: Biblioteca "Goathemala" de la Sociedad de Geografía e Historia.

Zavala, Silvio. 1948. *Estudios Indianos*. Mexico City: Edición de El Colegio Nacional.

Zorita, Alonso de. 1942. *Breve y sumaria relación de los señores de la Nueva España*. Biblioteca del Estudiante Universitario, no. 31. Mexico City: Universidad Nacional Autónoma.

Abuse of land. *See* Resources, declining
Adams, Robert M., 115
Administration of townships, 7, 79, 138, 146, 149–150
Adoption, 88
Aerial photography: in Chiapas, 214–217; mapping and, 215–216; in this study, 19, 110–111, 214–217
Aged, care of by children, 87–89
Agnation, in New Guinea, 50, 53, 56–58, fig. 11. *See also* Descent, unilineal; Patrilineal kinship
Agrarian ideology. *See* Ideology, agrarian
Agrarian reform. *See* Ejido program
Agricultural cycle, fig. 1; in *Apas*, 30–34; highland, compared to lowland, 34; and rain, 30, fig. 1. *See also* Burning of fields; Doubling of corn; Fallowing; Felling of forest; Harvesting; Reuse of fields; Seeding; Weeding
Aguardiente. See Liquor
Aguirre Beltrán, Gonzalo, 6, 16, 136, 183–185, 194
Almud, 130, tables 14–21
Altitude: as correlated with temperature, 25; as determining biotic zones, 19; effect of, on regrowth in fallowing, 19, 37–39, 110; and successional sequences, 25
Amatenango del Valle: family and land in, 60, 72–73, 76, 106, fig. 12, map 7, tables 1–3; population of, table 23; pottery produced in, 167, 173, plate 26
Ancestors, 62, 65. *See also* Souls
Anderson, T. W., 219
Animals, domestic, 87; foraging of, after harvest, 34; grazing of, 46; and spread of weeds in manure, 38. *See also* Mules; Sheep
—, wild, 46, 119
Apas, 19–47 passim, 66–67, 69–70, 79–108 passim; agricultural cycle in, 30–34; and *cargo* ritual, 69; clustering of households in, 81; communal lands in, 28, 88, 96, map 5; compared to *Muk*ta hok*, 37, 39; domestic groups in, 80–81, table 4; ejido in, 28, 35, 46, 88–89, 96–97, 103; family and land in, 60, 69–70, 73, 76–77, 79–107, fig. 12, map 7, plate 7, tables 1–3, table 10; genealogical censusing of, 216–217, 219; history of fallowing in, 36–43 passim; history of farmlands of, 28, map 5; inheritance in, 87–91, 98, 106; land and land use in, 19–47 passim, 109; leadership in, 46, 81, 105; local-descent group solidarity in, 87, 106; local organization of, 79–80, 81, 105, map 9; nicknaming in, 86, 91, 93–96, 98, 145, fig. 14, table 6; and other Zinacanteco hamlets, map 8; patrilocal residence in, 81, 95, 96, 98, table 7; patronymics in, 86; physiography of farmlands of, 28; population growth in, 35; *sna* in, 81, 105, map 9; study

of, through aerial photography, 216–217; water holes in, 81. *See also* Zinacantán

Archives used in this study, 223

Art and national Indianism, 197

Ascription. *See* Primordial tie

Asuntos Indígenas, Departamento de, 175, table 22

Authority in Maya family, 65, 69–73, 76, tables 1, 3. *See also* Ideology, of family and land

Baldíos, 147

Barth, Fredrik, 16, 138, 210

Beans, 32, 34, 126

Beliefs, 32. *See also* Ideology; World view

Berlin, Brent, 214

Bilateral kinship: in Amatenango del Valle, 72; in Chamula, 71; and genealogy, 52, fig. 10; among the Maya, 62

Birth rates. *See* Population, and fertility

Bloc. *See* Creoles as bloc; Indians as bloc

Blom, Franz, 213

Bootleg liquor. *See* Liquor

Borrowing of farmland from parents, 68

Bossism. *See* Leadership, as bossism

Boundaries, ethnic. *See* Ethnic boundaries

Boundaries, of fields, 111, 126

Breedlove, Dennis, 214

Bricker, Victoria R., 222

Bride price, 88, 121. *See also* Courtship; Marriage

Bride service in Chamula, 71

Brokers, cultural. *See* Leadership, as cultural brokerage

Bromas, Marcos, 199–200

Budgets: collection of, 223; for farming, 128–134

Bunzel, Ruth, 62, 64–65, 73

Bureaucracy, 200–201. *See also* Ejido program

Burial. *See* Funerals

Burning of fields, 30, 32, 38

Caciquismo. *See* Leadership, as bossism

Cancian, Frank: and *Apas* census, 219; and *cargo* ritual, 13, 186; and lowland corn farming, 34, 126, 130, 133, 218, map 11, tables 14–16, 18, 20

Candles, 149, 186

Capital of Chiapas. *See* Chiapas, relocation of capital of

Cárdenas, Lázaro: and Indianist policy, 197–198; and labor reforms, 149, table 22; presidency of, 145–146, 151, table 22

Cargo ritual. *See* Ritual, of *cargos*

Carpentry, 176, plate 25. *See also* Specialized occupations

Carranza, Venustiano, 149

Cash crops, 62, 68, 111

Caste, 137, 207, 181, 184–187. *See also* Indian-Ladino differences; Indian-Ladino relations

Caste War. *See* Rebellion

Catholicism, 12

Cattle ranching, 21, 207

Census, in study of *Apas*, 216–217, 219. *See also* Population

Chamula, 109–123; age at marriage in, 121; carpentry in, 176; colonization by, 160–161; as conditioned by regional factors, 109, 121–123, 137; depletion of resources in, 109–111, 115–116, 120–123; distilling of liquor in, 174–176, 178, 205; family and land in, 60, 70–73, 76, 106, fig. 12, map 7, plate 8, tables 1–3; government in, 149–150; Harvard Chiapas Project and, 214, 222–223; and labor reforms, 149, 150, table 22; land use in, 109–

116, 119–123, 155, plates 12–16; musical instruments from, 176, plate 25; physiography of, 109–110; population growth in, 109–111, 121–122; population of, table 23; rebellion of, in 1869, 148, 175, table 22; resettlement in, 110–111; specialized production in, 70, 72, 109, 121, 122; as studied by air photos, 217, 222; wool weaving in, 173–174; world view in, 118–119, 222–223

Chan Kom, family and land in, 60, 72–73, 76, fig. 12, map 7, tables 1–3

Chenalhó, 119, table 23

Chiapas: climate of, 21, 25, 30, 32–33, 120, 126, fig. 1; ethnography of, 213–214; mountains of, 20; in relation to Mexico, map 1; relocation of capital of, 148–149, table 22

Chichicastenango, family and land in, 60, 62–68, 73, 76, fig. 12, map 7, tables 1–3

Chimaltenango, family and land in, 60, 68–69, 73, 76, fig. 12, map 7, tables 1–3

Church: and Indians in colonial period, 146–148, 156, 196, table 22; and politics, 144, 148

Civil ties, 192–193, 202

Class, social, 193–194

Closed corporate community, 58, 151, 154, 183

Closed system, 8, 186, 210

Clothing, Indian, 10, 14, 185

Clustering of households: in *Apas*, 81; through domestic cycle, 65, 68–69, 71–73, table 2

Coffee, 20, 46, 207

Cognatic kinship. *See* Bilateral kinship

Colby, Benjamin N., 161

Colonialism, internal, 194, 212

Colonization, by Indians, 5, 158, 160–161, 198–202 passim

Colonization laws, 142, 196, table 22

Commerce: and *cargo* ritual, 186, 207; in colonial period, 176–177; of Indian crafts, 177, fig. 17; Ladino domination of, 12, 136, 147, 167, 206

Communal lands: of *Apas*, 28, 88, 96, map 5; in Chan Kom, 73; history of, 34, 139, 142, 144, 147, map 12, plate 19, table 22; as private property, 139

Compañía Mexicana de Aerofotos, S.A., 215

Conditioning factors: of Chamula region, 109, 121–123; of land use, 6, 47; of local organization, 105–106; of local systems, 137, 181, 206, 210; lowland rental farming as, 137; of production, 4; wage labor as, 109, 121–123, 137. *See also* Ecological explanation; Environment, as conditioning factors

Conflict. *See* Disputes

Conflict model, 49–50, 51, 53, figs. 6, 8. *See also* Curvilinear model; Solidarity model

Conklin, Harold C., 209

Conscription of Indians in military, 202

Conservatism in 19th century, 148. *See also* Liberalism, of 19th century

Controlled comparison: of Maya family and land, 60–87; method of, 50, 52, 59, 77

Cooking, 43, 46

Cooperation, 32

Core and periphery, 191, 193–194, 202, 207, 212. *See also* Marginality; Periphery; Refuge region

Corn: cooking of, with lime, 46;

doubling of, 34; farming of, 32–
34; marketing of, 81, 126. *See
also* Highland farming; Lowland farming
Corporateness: of kin groups, 62,
65, 68; of land ownership, 144;
in peasant societies, 58; and
unilineal descent, 52
Cosmology. *See* Ideology, of nature and man; Souls; World
view
Costumes, 10, 14, 185
Courtship: in *Apas*, 88; in Chamula, 121; length of, and population fertility, 158; in Maya area,
64–65, 68–82, table 1. *See also*
Marriage
Crafts. *See* Carpentry; Cash crops;
Liquor; Pottery; Salt; Specialized occupations; Sugar; Wool
Creoles as bloc, 196
Crown policy toward Indians. *See*
Indianism, in colonial period
Cults. *See* Rebellion; Ritual, of
cargos
Culture core, 208
Curvilinear model, 50, 50 n, 51,
59, 76–77, figs. 8, 12. *See also*
Conflict model; Solidarity model

Death. *See* Feast of All Saints;
Funerals; Souls
Death rates. *See* Population, and
mortality
Deeds of sale, 100
Demography. *See* Migration of
Indians; Population
Dependence, economic, 65, 68–69,
71–73, 76, table 1
Descent: and land scarcity, 50,
53, 56–58, fig. 11; Maya ideolo-
gy of, 62, 64; nonunilineal, 50,
fig. 10, 55–57; unilineal, 50, 52,
53, 56–58, fig. 9
Deutsch, Karl W., 191

Development, theories of, 191,
193, 194
Díaz, Porfirio, regime of, 145, 148–
149, 151, 198, table 22
Dispersal of family. *See* Domestic
cycle
Disputes, 79. *See also* Land, disputes over
Distilling. *See* Liquor
Distribution of property. *See*
Land, inheritance of
Division of parcels, 90
Divorce, 95–96, 98, table 6
Domestic activities, 43, 46, 64. *See
also* Women, work of
Domestic cycle: in Amatenango
del Valle, 72; in *Apas*, 69, 87–
91; in Chamula, 70–71; in Chan
Kom, 72, 73; in Chichicastenango, 62, 64–65; in Chimaltenango, 68–69; and clustering of
households, 65, 68–69, 71–73,
table 2; and colonization, 201–
202; and house construction, 64,
68–69, 71–72; land and, 205;
methods for study of, 222; and
settlement-pattern shifts, 154–
155. *See also* Domestic groups;
Households; Local-descent
group
Domestic groups: dispersal of, in
Apas, 87, 89–90; organization
of, in *Apas*, 80, 81, table 4. *See
also* Domestic cycle; Households
Dominical mechanism, 184, 185,
187, 190
Doubling of corn, 34
Drought, 120. *See also* Ritual, for
agriculture
Duby, Gertrude, 213

Ecological explanation, xiii, xiv,
3, 107, 207–212; and analysis of
subsystems, 9; of ethnicity, 16–
17. *See also* Conditioning fac-

tors; Environment; Habitat; Locale; Niche

Education: and federal policy toward Indians, 195, 197–198, 202, in refuge region, 185, 187, 207, plate 29; in townships, 79

Eggan, F., 60

Eidheim, Harald, 210

Ejido lands: in *Apas*, 28, 35, 46, 88–89, 96–97, maps 5, 12; inheritance of, 89, 97; in *Muk*ta hok*, 37

Ejido program: in *Apas*, 103; archives of, 223; bureaucracy of, in Tuxtla Gutiérrez, 199–200, 202; as conditioning land use, 6; expropriation under, 139, 150; and Indian leadership, 146; and integration of Indians nationally, 202; and Ladino ranches, 150; in *Muk*ta hok*, 37; as national Indianism, 6, 197–198; in Zinacantán, 139, 145–146, 150, 199, map 12, table 22

Elders, 79, 142, 144. *See also* Leadership

Elections, Indian participation in, 202

Elites, 185, 187, 194–195, 202, 207, 212

Environment: concept of, 6, 207, 209–211; as conditioning factors, 3, 47. *See also* Ecological explanation

Equilibrium. *See* Stability

Erosion. *See* Soil erosion

Estate building, 100–101, 103–105

Ethnic boundaries: as barriers, 15, 205; crossing of, 135, 138, 154–161, 181; flexibility of, 183; as interactional, 183, 186. *See also* Caste; Ethnicity; Indian-Ladino differences; Indian-Ladino relations; Indians as bloc

Ethnic groups as blocs, 192–194, 196. *See also* Indians as bloc

Ethnicity: change in, 183; and class, 194; as distinction between Indians and Ladinos, 120–121; as dominical mechanism, 185; dynamic character of, 138; emergence of, 191, 194, 202; explanation of, 183; food-chain analogy for, 136; gradients of, 187; and leadership, 138, 151, 154; and marginality, 5, 16–17, 125, 136, 137, 207, 212; and national integration, 191–193, 194, 195, 202; niche of, 201–203, 207, 212; outside Chiapas, 187, 190; in refuge region, 6, 125, 136, 183–190 passim, 191, 195; regional analysis of, 107; as reinforced by Indian nationalism, 198; and specialized occupations, 8, 16, 135, 138, 161, 167–181, 183, fig. 17, plates 24–28; as system, 138, 157, 183, 186, 206

——, persistence of, 137, 181, 183, 186–187, 190, 195, 207; and colonization, 202; and migration of Indians, 15, 157, 160–161

Ethnohistory, 223

Evangelization. *See* Church

Extractive economy. *See* Raw materials

Factions, 81, 138, 145. *See also* Leadership

Fallowing: in *Apas*, 36–43; in Chamula, 110; quantitative analysis of, 19, 39–43, 219–221, figs. 4–5, tables 25–27; and regrowth, 19; system for, in *Muk*ta hok*, 37, 39; and vegetation succession, 28

Family and land, 205–206; in *Apas*, 79–107; comparative

analysis of, 49, 59; in Maya area, 60–78

Farming. *See* Highland farming; Lowland farming; Lowland rental farming; Reuse of fields

—, swidden: in Chamula, 109, 111, plate 12; cycle of, fig. 1; land reform important for, 209; in lowlands, 126; in Maya culture area, 60, 61; perpetuated by colonization, 201; shifting and nonshifting stages, 111; stability of, 28; and vegetational succession, 28; wage labor important for, 209. *See also* Agricultural cycle; Farming, techniques of; Resettlement

—, techniques of: in *Apas*, 19, 28–34; highland compared to lowland, 19, 34. *See also* Burning of fields; Doubling of corn; Fallowing; Felling of forest; Harvesting; Reuse of fields; Seeding; Weeding

—, yields. *See* Highland farming, yields of; Lowland farming, yields of

Fathers and sons, 62, 64–65, 68–73, 76, 205, tables 1–3. *See also* Ideology, of family and land

Favoritism in land inheritance, 68–69

Feast of All Saints, 91, plate 11

Felling of forest, 30

Fences, 111, 126

Fertility. *See* Population, and fertility; Population, growth of

Fertility of soil, 30, 38–39, 110

Fields. *See* Ecological explanation; Land

Fire, 39. *See* Burning of fields

Firewood, 32, 43, map 6

Fireworks, 149, 186

Forest, 25, 35, 110

Fortes, Meyer, 50, 53

Foster, George M., 52, 58

Fragmentation of land, 71

Fuel. *See* Firewood

Functional alignments. *See* Industrialization

Funerals, 69, 87, 88, 90–91, 100

Furniture. *See* Carpentry

Game, hunting of. *See* Hunting

Gamio, Manuel, 198

Geertz, Clifford, 192–194, 202, 210

Gemeinschaft, 193

Genealogical distance in nicknaming, measurement of, 93, 95–96, 98, fig. 14

Genealogy, 52, figs. 9–10. *See also* Kinprogram

Geography. *See* Physiography

Gesellschaft, 192–193

Goffman, Irving, 200

Goldschmidt, Walter, 208

Goodenough, Ward H., 50, 53, 56, 58–59

Goodman, L. A., 219

Gossen, Gary, 118–119, 222

Government, Indian. *See* Township, Indian, administration of

Grass, 38, 46, 111

Grijalva River valley: and cattle ranching, 21, 207; and physiography of Chiapas, 20; in relation to *Apas* farmland, 28; road construction in, 130, map 11; Zinacantecos in, 28, 126, 144–145, 198–201, 205. *See also* Lowland rental farming

Guatemala. *See* Chichicastenango; Chimaltenango

Haaland, Gunnar, 210

Habitat, 209. *See also* Ecological explanation

Hamlet, 7–8, 155, map 8. *See also* Local-descent group; Local organization

Harvard Chiapas Project, 213–214

Harvesting, 33–34, 126, 128

Hechter, Michael, 194
Heirs, 87, 88. *See also* House parcels, inheritance of; Land, inheritance of; Women, inheritance by
Herding. *See* Sheep
Heronimo, Romin, 46, 103–105, 222, map 10
Hierarchy. *See* Rank
Highland farming, 19–47 passim, 125–130 passim; combined with lowland farming, 34; conditioned by lowland farming, 137; continuous, 38–39; costs of, 125–126, 128, 130, fig. 15, table 13; decline of, in *Apas*, 36, 40–43; intensity of, 35, figs. 2–3, 40–43; returns of, compared to lowland returns, 43; for subsistence, 6, 11–12; techniques of, 19, 28–34; trends in, 19, 34–43, 219–221; yields of, 35–36, 126. *See also* Agricultural cycle
Hinterland, 183, 190. *See also* Periphery
Hired labor. *See* Wage labor
History: of agrarian policy, 196; of colonization, 196; of commerce, 147; of communal lands, 34, 139, 142, 144, 147, map 12, plate 19, table 22; of ejido in *Apas*, 35, 103; of ejido in Zinacantán, 139, 145–146, 150, map 12, table 22; of farming in *Apas*, 28, 36–43; of indentured labor, 35, 121, 144–145, 147–150, table 20; of land tenure in Zinacantán, 139–146, 151, 160–161, map 12, table 22; of land use in Chamula, 115; of population, 155–161, table 22; sources for, 226; summary of, table 22. *See also* Indianism, in colonial period
Horticulture, 61, 111
House construction: and the domestic cycle, 64, 68–69, 71–72; timber for, 46, 110
Household industry. *See* Specialized occupations
Households, 65, 68–69, 72–73, 81, 87, 89, tables 2, 4. *See also* Domestic cycle; Domestic groups
House parcels: inheritance of, 64, 68–69, 71, 88–89; purchase of, 99; sex bias in distribution of, 101–103, table 12
Hunting, 46, 110

Ideology: agrarian, 5, 196, 199. *See also* Ejido program
—, of family and land: and ancestors, 62; in *Apas*, 87–91, 98, 106; and authority, 65, 69–73, 76, tables 1, 3; and Maya land ownership, 62, 64, 68–73
—, Maya, of contemporary Indians, 12
—, nationalist, 5, 6, 191, 195. *See also* National Indianism
—, of nature and man, 109, 116, 118–121
Illness, 79, 120, 156
Indentured labor, 35, 121, 144–145, 147–150, 198, table 22
Indian Affairs Department, 175, table 22
Indian identity, 15, 16–17, 137, 151, 160–161, 181, 183. *See also* Ethnicity; Leadership; Specialized occupations; Township, Indian
Indianism, in colonial period, 139, 142, 146–147, 155–157, 176, 181, 195–196, table 22. *See also* National Indianism
Indian-Ladino differences, 9–12, 14, 116, 120–121, 167, 202, 206
Indian-Ladino relations, 6, 137–138, 206; and Indian role playing, 200–201; materials for study of, 225; in refuge region,

184–187; regional analysis of, 107; as a social field, 16. *See also* Caste; Dominical mechanism; Indians as bloc; Land, encroachment on

Indian nationalism, 195, 198–203

Indians as bloc: in colonial period, 146–148, 156, 195–196, table 22; in post-colonial society, 148, 150, 151, 195, 197–198, 202–203, 207; in refuge region, 185

Indigenismo. *See* National Indianism

Industrialization, 193–194, 202

Inheritance of land. *See* Land, inheritance of

INI. *See* National Indian Institute

Instituto Nacional Indigenista. *See* National Indian Institute

Integration, 192–193. *See also* National integration

Integrative revolution, 192–193

Interethnic relations. *See* Indian-Ladino relations

Isolation, 17, 211

Itek Corporation, 215

Ixtapa, 174, 180

Juárez, Benito, regime of, 144, 148, 197, table 22

Key informant, use of in this study, 216–218

Kinprogram, 216

Kinship: and colonization, 201–202; comparative analysis of, 49; and land scarcity, 49, 50, 57, 58, 59; localization of, 80; Maya, 49, 60–78 passim; as primordial tie, 191–192; principles of, and rights to land, 49–50; ritual, 147. *See also* Bilateral kinship; Conflict model; Curvilinear model; Descent; Domestic cycle; Family and land;

Matrilineal kinship; Patrilineal kinship; Social organization; Solidarity model

Labor: contracting for, 121; and cooperation in burning fields, 32; and cooperation among kin, 64, 69, table 1; exploitation of, in refuge region, 184–185, 212; for gathering of firewood, 43; and inputs for farming, 30, 32, 34; wages for, 223. *See also* Highland farming, costs of; Indentured labor; Lowland farming, costs of; Wage labor

Labor reform, 149, 150, table 22

Ladinos: as caste, 181; domination of refuge region by, 6; national orientation of, 4, 12; settlement pattern of, 7, 11, 206. *See also* Commerce, Ladino domination of; Elites; Indian-Ladino differences; Indian-Ladino relations

Land: attitudes toward, 62, 109, 116, 118–121; availability of, 73, 76–77, table 3; disputes over, 64, 68, 90, 199; encroachment on, 144, 199; holdings per capita of, 96, 97, 98, table 9; national, 145; ownership of, 8, 35, 50, 57, 62; private, 97, 144–145, 185, table 8; purchase of, 72, 99, 100–101, 150–151; reform, 209; rental of, 59; rights to, 14, 49–50, 72; sale of, 59, 79, 99–101, 145, 205, table 10; scarcity of, 49, 50, 53, 57–58, 59, 72, 73, 76, 79, 109–111, 205, table 3; and solidarity of lineages, 91–101, 103–107; tenure in Zinacantán, 139–146, 151, 160–161, map 12, table 22; titles to, 142, 144, 199–200, table 22; unused, 72; value of, 79, 205. *See also* Communal lands; Conflict model; Curvilinear model; Ejido lands; Ejido

program; Lowland rental farming; Resources, declining; Solidarity model
—, inheritance of: and actual distribution, 88–90; bilateral, 71, 72; counterbalanced by land sale, 79; and the family, 5, 88; and favoritism, 68, 69; and fragmentation of parcels, 71; ideology of, in *Apas*, 87–91, 98, 106; and local-descent group, 7; in Maya areas, 62, 64–65, 68–73, 76–77; and methods for study, 212; and Mexican law, 88; and patrilineal kinship, 5; and trends in privately owned land, 97, table 8; and unilineal descent, 50, 52; witnesses to, 64, 88–89; by women, 71, 79, 88–89, 97, 99, 101–105, tables 11–12. *See also* House parcels, inheritance of
—, use of: in *Apas*, 19–47, 219–221; in Chamula, 109–116, 119–123, plates 12–16; as conditioned by wage labor, 109, 121–123; domestic cycle and, 205; external conditioning of, 6; other than for farming of corn, 43–46. *See also* Highland farming
Language: distribution of, map 3; Indian, 9, 14, 60, 217–218, map 3; Spanish, 9, 137–138, 200–201
Larraínzar, 119, table 23
Las Casas, Fray Bartolomé de, 196
Law: customary, 100; Mexican, 88, 138, 161, 199. *See also* Ejido program; Ley de Obreros; Leyes de Reforma
Lawyers, 200. *See also* Leadership, of native lawyers
Leach, Edmund R., 209–210, 212
Leadership: in *Apas*, 46, 81, 105; as bossism, 146, 149–150; and castes, 187; as colonization by Indians, 199, 200; and coopera-

tive stores, 150; as cultural brokerage, 138–139, 146, 149–151, 201; and ejido program, 146; by elders, 79; and ethnicity, 138, 151, 154; federal programs and, 213; by Indians in colonial period, 196; and labor reforms, 149; in lowland rental farming, 126, 138; and National Indian Institute, 201; of native lawyers, 138, 199; in 19th century, 142, 151; sources for study of, 226; and struggle for land, 181; use of Spanish language in, 137–138. *See also* Heronimo, Romin; Indian identity
Ley de Obreros, 149, table 22
Leyes de Reforma, 144, 145, 150, 197, table 22
Liberalism, of 19th century, 144, 148, 196. *See also* Juárez, Benito, regime of
Lime for cooking corn, 46
Lineages, 81, 95–96, 97, 98, 145, tables 6, 9. *See also* Patrilineal kinship
Lineage segments, 86, 91, 93–96, 98, fig. 13
Lineage solidarity, 91–107, tables 7, 11–12
Lipset, Seymour, 193–194
Liquor: distilling of, 174–176, 180, 205, table 22; Indian reputation for alcoholism and, 206; for ritual, 89–90, 99, 149, 174, 176, 186, 206, plate 25
Local-descent group, 7–8, 80, 87, 100–101, 106–107, 202, 205. *See also* Lineage segments; Nicknames
Locale, 4, 47, 58, 107, 209–210. *See also* Ecological explanation
Localization of family. *See* Clustering of households
Local organization: in *Apas*, 79, 80, 105–106, 137; dynamics of,

105, 106, 205; variation in, 8, 205
Lowland farming: costs of, 125–126, 128, 130, 132–134, fig. 15, tables 13, 15, 16–21; returns of, compared to highland returns, 43; as supplement to highland farming, 201; yields of, 126
Lowland rental farming: as alternative to highland farming, 19, 34, 106–107, 205; compared to highland farming, 34, 125–136; expansion of, 126, 130, map 11; and hired labor, 126, 132, table 16; as stabilizing highland farming, 4, 6, 19, 137; as supplementing highland farming, 35–36, 43, 47, 125–126; transport to and from, 126, 128, 133, map 11, tables 18–19, 21; variation of scale in, 126, 128, 130, 134, tables 14–21; zones of, 130, map 11, tables 15–21. See also Lowland farming

McQuown, Norman, 213, 215
Mae-Enga kinship, 53, 56, 58
Malayo-Polynesian kinship, 50, 53, 56
Man-in-Nature project, 213
Manufacturing, 167, 186. See also Specialized occupations
Mapping, 215–216. See also Aerial photography
Marginality, 5, 125–136, 137, 183–185. See also Refuge region
Markets, 62, 81, 174, 177, 185, fig. 17, plate 28
Markov model for fallowing, 219
Marriage: and domestic group membership, 80, 81; early, and fertility, 121, 158–160, table 24; among Maya, 62, 64, 68–69, 71–72, tables 1–2; and surname exogamy, 86; in Zinacantán, 87.

See also Bride price; Courtship; Divorce; Residence after marriage
Matrilineal kinship, 56–57
Maya: culture area of, 60–62, 73, 225; and family and land, 49, 60–78 passim. See also Ideology, of family and land
Meggitt, M. J., 50, 51, 53, 56–59
Mestizos. See Ladinos
Methodology, 19, 39–40, 59, 213–227. See also Controlled comparison
Metzger, Duane, 214
Mexican Revolution, 145, 149, 197–198, table 22
Microecological approach, 209
Middlemen. See Leadership, as cultural brokerage
Migration of Indians: caused by population growth, 157–158; by colonization, 158, 160–166; and ethnic patterns, 15, 135, 138, 154–161; for wage labor, 68, 70, 121; within Zinacantán, 155, 160. See also Resettlement
Mobility. See Migration of Indians
Monopoly, 175. See also Commerce
Mortality, 157–158
*Muk*ta hok* farming, 37, 39, 217
Mules, for lowland farming, 126
Municipio. See Township, Indian
Murdock, George P., 56
Musical instruments, 176, plate 25

Naming. See Nicknames; Patronymic naming
Nash, June, 72
National Indian Institute, 150, 201, 213, plate 30. See also National Indianism
National Indianism, 136, 191, 195–198, 201, 202, 203. See also National Indian Institute

National integration, 191–195, 202, 211

Nationalism, development of, 191–192, 194. *See also* Ideology, nationalist

Nationalist policies, 16–17, 186. *See also* Ejido program; Ideology, nationalist; National Indianism

Nature. *See* Ideology, of nature and man

Navencauk, plate 2

New Guinea, 50, 53, 56, 58

Niche: concept of, 177–181, 209; of ethnicity, 201–203, 207, 212; of ethnic populations, 125, 135; townships as, 206. *See also* Ecological explanation

Nicknames: and factions, 145; and lineage segments, 86, 91, fig. 13, table 5; methods for study of, 222; and solidarity of lineages, 86, 91, 93–96, 98, fig. 14, table 6

Obedience in Maya family, 65, 69–73, 76, tables 1, 3. *See also* Ideology, of family and land; Maya, and family and land

Open system, 186

Pan American Highway, 174, plate 4

Paniagua, Flavio, 223

Patrilineal kinship: influenced by land inheritance, 5, 7, 79; in Maya culture area, 60, 61, 73, 76; in Polynesia, 57; in Zinacantán, 69, 81. *See also* Descent, unilineal; Lineages

Patrilocal residence. *See* Residence after marriage, patrilocal

Patronymic naming, 61, 68, 72, 86

Peonage. *See* Indentured labor; Ley de Obreros

Periphery, 191, 194–195, 202, 203, 207, 212. *See also* Core and periphery

Photo interpretation, 215–217. *See also* Aerial photography

Physiography: affecting whole townships, 121–123, 205; of *Apas* farmlands, 28; of Chamula, 109–110; of Chiapas, 19, 20, map 4; materials for study of, 225; of refuge region, 183, 184. *See also* Altitude; Chiapas, climate of; Vegetation, natural

Plantations, 20, 207

Planting. *See* Seeding

Plants, wild, 46. *See also* Vegetation, natural

Pluralism, 9, 13, 14, 185

Political leadership. *See* Leadership

Politics, local-level. *See* Factions; Leadership

Polynesia, 50, 53, 56

Population: of *Apas*, 81; decline of, in colonial period, 155–157, table 22; density, 61, 70; distribution of, 142, table 22; and fertility, 157–158, table 24; and mortality, 157–158; studies of trends of, 226; of various Indian townships, table 23. *See also* Land, scarcity of; Migration of Indians; Resettlement

—, growth of, 157–161, table 23; as cause of colonization, 201; as cause of migration, 157–158; in Chamula, 109–111, 121–122; and declining resources, 19; effect of, on local organization, 106; and farming intensity in *Apas*, 35; and land capacity, 6; as threat to stability of family, 78; and wage labor, 5, 109, 121, 137

Porfiriato. *See* Díaz, Porfirio, regime of

Pottery, 72, 167, 173, plate 26

Pozas, Ricardo, 70–71
Prestige. *See* Leadership; Rank
Price, Richard S., 37, 217
Primogeniture, 64
Primordial ties, 191–194, 196, 202
Private lands. *See* Land, private
Probability model for fallowing, 39–43
Prokosch, Eric, 149
Property. *See* Land, ownership of
Public health facilities, 185, 187
Purchasing of land. *See* Land, purchase of

Quarrels, 79. *See also* Land, disputes over
Quiché. *See* Chichicastenango

Race, concept of, 184–185, 192
Rain, 21, 30, 32, 126, fig. 1
Ranches, 21, 150, 207. *See also* Indentured Labor
Rank, 52, 53, 199
Rappaport, Roy A., 210
Raw materials, 184, 186, 207
Rebellion: of Chamulas, in 1869, 148, 175, 187, 223, 226, table 22; and national integration, 191; Tzeltal, of 1712, 147, 187, 223, 226, table 22
Redfield, Robert, 72
Reducción, 196
Refuge region, 5, 6, 7–8, 107, 136, 183–192, 195. *See also* Marginality
Regional analysis, 107, 182; of Chamula's situation, 109, 121–123; of ethnicity, 183; of marginality, 125, 135. *See also* Refuge region
Regrowth: in Chamula, 109–111, plate 12; factors affecting, 19, 37, 38, 39, 110; statistical analysis of, 219–221, tables 25–27
Rental of land. *See* Land, rental

of; Lowland rental farming
Rent for lowland fields, 126, 128, 133, tables 20, 21. *See also* Land, rental of; Lowland rental farming
Repartimiento, 176–177
Reseeding, 32
Resettlement, 72, 110–111, 154–155, 196, 205
Residence after marriage: in *Apas*, 81, 87, 95–96, 98, table 7; in Maya area, 64–65, 68–73, tables 1–2; patrilocal, 64, 68–69, 71–73, 81, 95–96, 98, tables 1–2, 7
Residential land. *See* House parcels
Resources, declining: in Chamula, 109–111, 115–116, 120–123; and colonization, 201; of firewood, 43; in highlands, 19; and overuse of land, 46; as spur to resettlement, 111. *See also* Soil erosion
Resources, management of, 120
Respect in Maya family, 65, 69–73, 76, tables 1, 3. *See also* Ideology, of family and land; Maya, and family and land
Restitution of land, 146, table 22
Returns of farming, 43. *See also* Highland farming, costs of; Lowland farming, costs of
Reuse of fields, 39–43
Revolution, Mexican. *See* Mexican Revolution
Ritual: for agriculture, 33, 79, 120, 128; of *cargos*, 13, 14, 69, 174, 176, 186, 199, 206, 207; Catholicism in, 12; as dominical mechanism, 185; for health, 79, 120; of inheritance, 89; for land, 64; and liquor, 174, 176, plate 27; among Maya, 60; and paraphernalia, 149, 186; for *sna*, 81; between townships, 157. *See*

also Feast of All Saints; Funerals; Liquor
Rivera, Diego, 197
Roads, 130, 207, maps 2, 11, plate 4. *See also* Pan American Highway; Trails
Rokkan, Stein, 193–194
Romney, A. Kimbal, 214–215
Ruiz, Ramón Eduardo, 198

Sahlins, Marshal, 209
Saints, cult of. *See* Ritual, of cargos
Salt, 174, 180
San Andrés Larraínzar. *See* Larraínzar
San Cristóbal de las Casas: as beneficiary of federal social services, 187; as colonial administrative center, 4, 147; as market center, 167, fig. 17, plate 24; and National Indian Institute regional headquarters, 213; in 19th century, 148–149; physiographic setting of, 20; as seignorial city, 181
San Juan Chamula. *See* Chamula
San Pedro Chenalhó. *See* Chenalhó
Santiago Chimaltenango. *See* Chimaltenango
Scale of farming. *See* Lowland rental farming, variation of scale in
Scarcity of land. *See* Land, scarcity of
Schools. *See* Education
Scribes. *See* Chamula, government in
Seeding, 32
Seignorial city, 179, 183, 190
Settlement pattern, 3–4, 7, 10, 11; in Chamula, 110–111; in Maya culture area, 60; studied by air photos, 216
Sex bias, 102–103, table 12

Shamans, 79, 120
Sheep, 46, 111, 115, 173
Shils, Edward, 192, 202
Siverts, Henning, 177, fig. 17
Slash and burn. *See* Farming, swidden
Sloping of fields, 38, 125
Sna, 8, 80, 81, 105, map 9. *See also* Local-descent group
Social distance. *See* Caste; Indian-Ladino differences; Indian-Ladino relations
Social organization, 49, 52, 58–59. *See also* Descent; Family and land; Kinship
Social services, 185, 187, 207. *See also* Education
Soconusco, 20, 149
Soil erosion: in *Apas*, 43; in Chamula, 6, 70–71, 109–110, 115–116, 155, plates 14–16
Soil fertility. *See* Fertility of soil
Solidarity model, 49, 50, 51, figs. 7–8. *See also* Conflict model; Curvilinear model
Solidarity of lineages, 91–101, 103–107 passim
Souls, 87, 90–91, 119, plate 11
Specialized occupations, 73, 76; as alternative to farming, 205–206; in Chamula, 70, 71, 109, 110, 121–122; in colonial period, 176–177; and ethnicity, 8, 135, 138, 161, 167–181, 183, fig. 17, plates 24–28; and marketing of produce of, 177, fig. 17; resources for, 110; and tribal identity, 14; of Zinacantecos as corn farmers, 125. *See also* Carpentry; Cash crops; Liquor; Pottery; Salt; Sugar; Wool
Stability: of family and external conditions, 77; in hamlet organization, 8; of land use and resettlement, 155; in local organization of *Apas*, 79, 105–

106, 137; of refuge region, 186–187; of swidden farming, 28. See also Ethnicity, persistence of

Stages of land use in Chamula, 110–116, plates 12–16

Stanford University, 214

State, rise of. See Nationalism, development of

Statistical description, 39–43, 219–221

Status, 62. See also Rank

Steward, Julian H., 208–209

Stills. See Liquor

Stoniness, 38, 125

Stores, cooperative, 150

Subsistence agriculture, in highlands, 6, 11–12

Successional sequences. See Vegetation, natural

Succession of rights. See Land, inheritance of

Sugar, 175

Surnames. See Patronymic naming

Swidden farming. See Farming, swidden

System of variables: analysis of, 210–211; core and periphery as, 191, 194; environment as, 209; and refuge-region model, 183–190, 191; theory of, xiv, 9. See also Conditioning factors, of local systems; Ethnicity, as system; Ritual, of cargos; Stability

Technology, 167, 206, 184

Territoriality, 192–194. See also Township, Indian

Thatch, for roofing, 38

Timber, 46, 110, 22

Todos Santos, 91, plate 11

Tools for farming, 30, 32–33

Towns, Ladino settlements as, 11, 206

Township, Indian: administration

of, 7, 79, 138, 146, 149–150; and Indian identity, 7, 14; as niche, 205–206; specialization of occupation by, 167; territorial character of, in refuge region, 185, 187, 206; as unit of analysis, 7, 62, 107, 205. See also Ethnicity; Indian identity

Trade. See Commerce

Trade goods. See Cash crops; Liquor; Markets; Pottery; Salt; Wool

Trade routes, 174. See also Roads

Tradition, Indian, 3, 9; basis of, 15–17, 205–207, 212; and colonization, 202; development of, in periphery, 191, 203; ethnicity as, 107, 181, 206; farming as, 46–47. See also Ethnicity

Trails, 28, 38, 39. See also Roads

Transport, 126, 128, 133, 150, tables 18–19, 21

Travel, 126, 128, map 11. See also Roads; Trails

Trees, 43, map 6. See also Forest

Tribalism, 191, 194

Tribal organization. See Indian identity; Township, Indian

Tribes as ethnic groups. See Ethnicity

Trucks. See Transport

Tulane University, 223

Tuxtla Gutiérrez, 148–149, 199–200, 202, 223, table 22

Tzotzil language, map 3. See also Language, Indian

Unit of analysis, 211–212; hamlet as, 7–8; lineages as, 91; local-descent group as, 7–8, 106–107; Maya culture area as, 61; refuge region as, 7–8, 107; township as, 7–8, 62, 107, 211

Uprising. See Rebellion

Van Den Berghe, Pierre, 161

Vasconcelos, José, 197
Vegetation, natural, 25, 28, 35, 110. *See also* Regrowth
Villa Rojas, Alfonso, 72
Vogt, Evon Z., 80, 84, 213–216

Wage labor: in Chamula, 5, 109, 121–123, 137; as supplementary income, 12, 68–73 passim, 76, 106, 205, 206, 207, 209; and weeding, 33, 126, 132, table 16
Wage rate for agricultural labor, 223
Wagley, Charles, 68
Water-hole groups, 8, 80, 81
Water holes, 84, 115, 155
Web of life, 208–209
Weeding, 33, 126, 132
Weeds, 38
Wheat. *See* Cash crops
Wind, and agricultural ritual, 33
Wolf, Eric R., 58, 150–151
Women: and domestic-group membership, 81; exchange of, in marriage, 62; inheritance by, 71, 79, 88, 89, 97, 99, 101–105, tables 11–12; interviews with, 219; and sharing funeral costs, 90; work of, 32, 43, 46, 64

Wool, 173–174
World view, 118–119, 120, 222–223. *See also* Ideology, of nature and man; Souls

Yields, 35–36, 126
Yucatán, 187. *See also* Chan Kom

Zinacantán: agricultural ritual in, 120; archives pertaining to, 223; and *cargo* ritual, 186; colonization by Indians from, 198–201; and corn farming, 125; family and land in, 69, 79–107; hamlet settlements of, map 8; Harvard Chiapas Project and, 214, 225; history of ejido in, 139, 145–146, 150, 199–200, map 12, table 22; history of land tenure in, 139–146, 151, 160–161, map 12, table 22; local organization of, 79–80; lowland farming by Indians of, 125–136; migration within, 155, 160; population of, table 23; purchase of private land tracts in, 144–145; *sna* in, 81, 105, map 9. *See also Apas*

Milton Keynes UK
Ingram Content Group UK Ltd.
UKHW011814280723
425933UK00014B/192